OXFORD THEOLOGICAL MONOGRAPHS

Editorial Committee

J. BARTON   M. J. EDWARDS
P. S. FIDDES   G. D. FLOOD
D. N. J. MACCULLOCH   C. C. ROWLAND

OXFORD THEOLOGICAL MONOGRAPHS

WHAT IS A LOLLARD?
Dissent and Belief in Late Medieval England
J. Patrick Hornbeck II (2010)

EVANGELICAL FREE WILL
Phillip Melanchthon's Doctrinal Journey on the Origins of Free Will
Gregory Graybill (2010)

ISAIAH AFTER EXILE
The Author of Third Isaiah as Reader and Redactor of the Book
Jacob Stromberg (2010)

CONTRASTING IMAGES OF THE BOOK OF REVELATION
IN LATE MEDIEVAL AND EARLY MODERN ART
A Case Study in Visual Exegesis
Natasha F. H. O'Hear (2010)

KIERKEGAARD'S CRITIQUE OF CHRISTIAN NATIONALISM
Stephen Backhouse (2011)

GENDER ISSUES IN ANCIENT AND REFORMATION
TRANSLATIONS OF GENESIS 1–4
Helen Kraus (2011)

BLAKE'S JERUSALEM AS VISIONARY THEATRE
Entering the Divine Body
Suzanne Sklar (2011)

PAUL TILLICH AND THE POSSIBILITY OF REVELATION
THROUGH FILM
Jonathan Brant (2011)

HINDU THEOLOGY AND BIOLOGY
The Bhāgavata Purāṇa and Contemporary Theory
Jonathan B. Edelmann (2011)

ETHNICITY AND THE MIXED MARRIAGE CRISIS IN EZRA 9–10
An Anthropological Approach
Katherine E. Southwood (2012)

DIVINE PRODUCTION IN LATE MEDIEVAL
TRINITARIAN THEOLOGY
Henry of Ghent, Duns Scotus, and William Ockham
JT Paasch (2012)

The Salvation of Atheists and Catholic Dogmatic Theology

STEPHEN BULLIVANT

This book has been printed digitally and produced in a standard specification in order to ensure its continuing availability

OXFORD
UNIVERSITY PRESS

Great Clarendon Street, Oxford OX2 6DP
United Kingdom

Oxford University Press is a department of the University of Oxford.
It furthers the University's objective of excellence in research, scholarship,
and education by publishing worldwide.
Oxford is a registered trade mark of Oxford University Press in the UK
and in certain other countries

© Stephen Bullivant 2012

The moral rights of the author have been asserted

Reprinted 2013

All rights reserved. No part of this publication may be reproduced, stored in a retrieval system, or transmitted, in any form or by any means, without the prior permission in writing of Oxford University Press, or as expressly permitted by law, by licence or under terms agreed with the appropriate reprographics rights organization. Enquiries concerning reproduction outside the scope of the above should be sent to the Rights Department, Oxford University Press, at the address above

You must not circulate this book in any other binding or cover
And you must impose this same condition on any acquirer

British Library Cataloguing in Publication Data
Data available

Library of Congress Cataloging in Publication Data
Data available

ISBN 978-0-19-965256-3

For Jo and Grace,
and in memory of Peter Clarke (1940–2011)

Table of Contents

Acknowledgements	viii
Note on Translations and References	x
Abbreviations	xi
Introduction	1
1. Who is an Atheist?	13
Defining 'atheist'	14
Credere (in) Deum?	18
Lived atheism	26
Is atheism a religion?	28
Can one *really* be an atheist?	36
Conclusion	41
2. Atheism and Salvation from Pius IX to Vatican II	43
Salvation and 'the others'	44
'From anathema to dialogue'	51
Salvation for atheists?	59
Vatican II	67
Conclusion	76
3. Karl Rahner and the Salvation of Atheists	77
Rahner as representative	80
Pastoral orientation	83
Atheism and anonymity	85
Rahner critiqued	96
Conclusion	112
4. The Salvation of 'Jane' and the Problem of Ignorance	115
Saving Jane	117
The D'Costan paradigm: *pro* and *contra*	126
The problem of ignorance	131
Conclusion	146

5. *Extra minimos nulla salus*	149
'The theology lived by the saints'	154
'Jesus in His distressing disguise'	159
Possible objections	175
Conclusion	178
Conclusion	181
Bibliography	189
Index	211

Acknowledgements

This book would not have happened without a large number of institutions and individuals. The bulk of the research was undertaken as a postgraduate student at Christ Church, University of Oxford. I am extremely grateful to the Arts and Humanities Research Council, without whose financial support the work would not have been possible.

My supervisor, Dr Philip Kennedy OP, agreed to take on the project in its ill-defined early stages, and has ever since been unstinting in his time, support, magisterial comments, and (always constructive) criticisms. Also at Oxford, the late Prof. Peter Clarke read and improved significant portions of the original thesis, in addition to encouraging and advising on the empirical sociological research cited in chapter one. The counsel and example of Susan Clarkson of St Francis House, the Oxford Catholic Worker community, were instrumental in crystallizing the most important ideas in chapter five. Without Prof. Diarmaid MacCulloch, the Oxford Theological Monographs Committee, and all at Oxford University Press – most notably Tom Perridge, Cathryn Steele, Elizabeth Robottom, and Malcolm Todd – this book would have been both much worse, and non-existent.

My two doctoral examiners, Dr Philip Endean SJ and Prof. Gavin D'Costa, deserve special mention for their rigorous and painstaking critique of my original ideas, and their subsequent advice and encouragement as I have modified them (in several cases significantly) for publication. Likewise, the anonymous reader for Oxford University Press offered many judicious and insightful comments. Numerous others have sacrificed considerable amounts of time and effort to read or discuss various aspects of my work over the past six years. Among these are: Prof. Richard Dawkins, Fr David Evans, Prof. Terry Eagleton, Dr Mark Edwards, Prof. Paul Fiddes, Fr John Gaine, Prof. Michael Paul Gallagher SJ, Dr. Karen Kilby, Dr Peter L'Estrange SJ, Lois Lee, Prof. George Pattison, Fr Hugh Somerville-Knapman OSB and Dr Johannes Zachhuber. I am indebted to the staff at the Pontifical Council for Culture, Vatican City – and especially to Richard Rouse – for their help and hospitality

Acknowledgements

in April 2008. Carl Sterkens of the *Stichting Edward Schillebeeckx*, Nijmegen, was instrumental in locating, and moreover lending, an important manuscript. This research has been greatly aided by the librarians of Christ Church, Blackfriars Hall, the Theology Faculty, and the Bodleian in Oxford, of Heythrop College in London, and of St Mary's University College in Twickenham.

St Mary's has, moreover, been my academic home for most of the past two years as I have been, albeit slowly, completing this book. Here, I have been blessed with intelligent, supportive and, frankly, fun colleagues, especially Dr Robin Gibbons, Prof. Michael Hayes, Leonora Paasche, Dr Glenn Richardson, Fr Paul Rowan, Dr Lynne Scholefield, Dr Trevor Stammers, Dr Anthony Towey, Káren Towey, and Dr Peter Tyler. The manuscript was completed while living at Benedict XVI House, and I am especially grateful to our students there for all their company, help, humour, and benevolence: Shaun Bailham, Dennis Jenkins, Daniel McNamara, Jason O'Malley, Emily Pound, and Lucy Wood-Ives.

Parts of this monograph have previously been published in the following venues: 'From *"Main Tendue"* to Vatican II: the Catholic Engagement with Atheism, 1936–65', *New Blackfriars* 90/1026 (March 2009), 178–87; '*Sine culpa*? Vatican II and Inculpable Ignorance', *Theological Studies* 72 (March 2010), 70–86; and 'The Myth of Rahnerian Exceptionalism: Edward Schillebeeckx's "Anonymous Christians"', *Philosophy & Theology* 22/1&2 (2010), 339–51.

Finally, and most importantly, I must record my overwhelming debts of gratitude to my parents, both natural – David and Norma Bullivant, who have always loved, supported, and encouraged me – and in-law – Graham and Sylvia Dunn, who among much else, permitted me to marry their daughter Joanna. It is to her and our daughter Grace, with love and thanks, that this book is dedicated.

Stephen Bullivant
Benedict XVI House
Feast of St Dominic, 2011

Note on Translations and References

All translations from texts originally in Latin are my own. For other languages, I have availed myself of published English translations when available. When unavailable, and unless otherwise stated, the translations are also my own. (These are normally from Italian and German writings, though I occasionally stretch to very short passages of Dutch.) In all cases, I have erred on the side of literality rather than elegance.

Except where quoted from other authors, Bible translations are from the New Revised Standard Version. In a few cases, however, I have made slight changes to give a more literal rendering (e.g. 'one of the least of these my brothers' for 'one of the least of these who are members of my family' at Mt 25.40).

Owing to the large number of works cited, and for the sakes of brevity and ease of reference, I have adopted a variation of the 'author–date system'. Dates given in square brackets – e.g. Rahner [1964] 1969 – refer to the original date of publication (in its original language, where applicable), as far as this has been ascertainable. However, I depart from this system on a number of occasions – most obviously, when citing from dogmatic sources (see the following 'Abbreviations' section for details). References to archival materials are given in full in the footnotes, as are the URLs of online resources. On a couple of (clearly identified) occasions, when a single text is repeatedly cited in a short space, page numbers will be given in parentheses in the main body of the text itself. Full bibliographical details of all printed sources are, of course, given in the concluding bibliography.

Abbreviations

AAS   *Acta Apostolicae Sedis* (Rome: Typis Vaticanis, 1909–) [Cited by volume, year and page number, in the standard form 'AAS 92 (2000): 743'].
AS   *Acta Synodalia Sacrosancti Concilii Oecumenici Vaticani II* (Rome: Typis Polyglottis Vaticanis, 1970–80) [Cited by volume and pars number, followed by a page reference, in the standard form 'AS IV/i: 23'].
ASS   *Acta Sanctae Sedis* (New York: Johnson Reprint, [1865–1908] 1968–9) [Cited by volume, year, and page number, in the standard form 'ASS 10 (1877): 585'].
CCC   Catechism of the Catholic Church: *Catechismus Catholicae Ecclesiae* (Vatican City: Libreria Editrice Vaticana, 1997) [Cited by item number, in the form 'CCC 1370'].
DH   Heinrich Denzinger and Peter Hünermann (eds.), *Enchiridion symbolorum definitionum et declarationum de rebus fidei et morum*, 37th rev. edn (Freiburg im Breisgau: Herder, 1991) [Cited by item number, in the standard form 'DH 273'. Please note that these numbers differ across the various editions].
GS   *Gaudium et Spes*, Vatican II's Pastoral Constitution on the Church in the Modern World (1965): AS IV/vii: 733–804.
LG   *Lumen Gentium*, Vatican II's Dogmatic Constitution on the Church (1964): AS III/viii: 784–836.
PG/PL J.-P. Migne (ed.), *Patrologia Graeca*, 161 volumes [PG] (Paris: Migne, 1844–64); and *Patrologia Latina*, 221 volumes [PL] (Paris: Migne, 1857–66) [Cited by volume and page/column number, in the form 'PL 20: 281'].

Introduction

On 21 November 1964, the assembled Fathers of Vatican II promulgated *Lumen Gentium*, the 'Dogmatic Constitution on the Church'. At LG 14, in the midst of the document's second chapter *De Populo Dei* ('On the People of God'),[1] the Council reaffirmed the traditional teaching on the necessity of the Church for salvation:

> [The Holy Council] teaches, resting on sacred scripture and tradition, that this pilgrim Church is necessary for salvation. For the one Christ is the mediator and the way of salvation, in whose body, which is the Church, he is made present for us. He himself, by demanding with explicit words the necessity of faith and baptism (cf. Mk 16.16; Jn 3.5), at the same time confirmed the necessity of the Church, into which men enter through baptism as through a door. Therefore those men cannot be saved, who not being ignorant [of the fact that] the Catholic Church has been founded as necessary by God through Jesus Christ, are nevertheless unwilling either to enter it, or to persevere in it. (AS III/viii: 795)

This indispensability of the Catholic Church does not, however, entail that only those who are formally members of it have the possibility of salvation. While it does not mention salvation explicitly, LG 15's positive appraisal of 'the baptized who are honoured by the name Christian, but who neither profess the whole faith nor preserve the unity of communion under Peter's successor' (ibid.: 796) certainly implies optimism for non-Catholic Christians on this matter. This reading is supported by LG 8's admission that, while Christ's Church 'subsists (*subsistit*) in the Catholic Church, [. . .] many elements of

---

[1] The biblical concept of the *Populus Dei* is central to LG's ecclesiology (Congar 1965; McNamara 1968; Ratzinger 2000: 68–9). Note especially that: 'The "people of God" does not mean here the mass of the faithful in contrast to the hierarchy, but the Church as a whole, with every group of its members' (Grillmeier 1967: 153).

sanctification and truth are discovered outside of its structure' (ibid.: 789). Furthermore, in article 16, attention is given to 'those who have not yet accepted the Gospel [but] are related to the People of God in diverse ways.' Following assurances regarding the possibility of salvation for Jews, Muslims, and 'those who in shadows and images seek the unknown God', the Council declares:

> Those indeed who are, without fault, ignorant of the Gospel of Christ and his Church, yet who seek God with a sincere heart, and who knowing his will through the command of conscience, strive under the influence of grace to accomplish works, are able to obtain eternal salvation. Nor does divine Providence deny the assistances necessary for salvation to those who, without fault, have not yet arrived at an express recognition of God and who, not without divine grace, endeavour to attain to an upright life. (Ibid.: 796-7)

The primary purpose of this study is to explore and explicate these two sentences. Specifically it asks, and (eventually) will answer, the question: *how, within the parameters of Catholic theology, is it possible for an atheist to be saved?*

This is by no means a straightforward task. For approaching half a century now, Catholic theologians have devoted a great deal of attention to LG 16's optimism for members of the world religions. Their various hypotheses both draw upon and presuppose a huge (and growing) corpus of theological literature on 'the religions'. This, in turn, is informed by ongoing work in the disciplines of history, philosophy, sociology, psychology, and anthropology, as well as in other areas of theology. Ideally, something similar would be true for the theologian approaching LG 16's optimism for unbelievers. This too must be understood in light of a wider theological understanding of atheism, illumined by research in other fields. But despite early signs of vibrancy, and a handful of notable exceptions (Gallagher 1980; Kasper [1982] 1984), atheism has yet to fulfil its conciliar promise of becoming a major field for theological exploration. Its similar neglect by other disciplines, except perhaps the philosophy of religion, is also well-documented (Pasquale 2007; Bainbridge 2008; Zuckerman 2010). Happily, for reasons which are themselves sociologically interesting, these lacunae have begun to attract attention, especially within the social sciences. The slow process of filling them has recently begun, not least by my friends and colleagues in the international and interdisciplinary *Nonreligion and Secularity*

Research Network, founded by researchers at Cambridge and Oxford in late 2008.

Dogmatic theology may seem to some readers to be – for better or (more likely) worse – remote from exciting, original research in other, largely secular disciplines. To many, no doubt, it seems remote from excitement and originality full stop. But regardless of how the word seems, *this* exercise in dogmatics, at least, will be wide-ranging – and necessarily so. This is most obvious in chapter one, which begins with the deceptively simple question: 'Who is an atheist?' Drawing principally on history, philosophy, and sociology, in addition to theology, the brief studies there are in a certain sense prolegomenal: modest attempts to *comprehend* atheism before either theologizing about it myself, or commenting on others' theologizing about it. While this is important in itself, they are not merely of 'background' significance. A number of insights and ideas will prove crucial to solving the *problemata* of this study, both negatively in critiquing previous understandings of how atheists may be saved (chapter three), and positively in developing and arguing for my own (chapters four and five).

Chapter two centres around Vatican II's treatment of atheism and salvation, how it developed, and how it has been understood; both LG 16 and *Gaudium et Spes* 19–21, the Council's dedicated statement on atheism, are situated within their historico-theological contexts, with particular attention given to the specific issue of the salvation of atheists in theological writings in the decades immediately preceding the Council. The understanding of how atheists may be saved in the thought of a particular theologian, Karl Rahner, is expounded and then critiqued in chapter three. As I shall argue throughout chapters two and three, Rahner's views on this subject, in many important respects, are broadly representative of the Catholic mainstream. In casting doubt on the plausibility of certain aspects of Rahner's approach, I am thereby casting doubt on the dominant account of the salvation of atheists within Catholic theology. Yet this does not mean that I am rejecting Rahner's theology *in toto*. While I find much to criticize in certain, technical elements of Rahner's famous theologoumenon of 'anonymous Christians', I am well aware that my own theorizing owes much to wider aspects of his thought, especially concerning the relationship of nature and grace.

The ground thus prepared, chapters four and five propose a new account of how, in light of LG 16 and the Catholic tradition, an unbeliever may attain eternal life. This is the *telos* of the whole book: the goal to which all preceding chapters, in their diverse ways, are ultimately striving. My account draws substantially on a framework recently advanced by Gavin D'Costa from within the Catholic theology of religions. His theory is propounded and interrogated at length, with several issues requiring further attention duly identified (chapter four). These difficulties are addressed in the course of both a renewed understanding of 'invincible/inculpable ignorance' (also chapter four), and a close reading of a specific interpretation of Mt 25.31–46 that is firmly embedded, albeit not dominantly so, in the Catholic tradition (chapter five).

As already mentioned, this study is – or rather hopes to be – a work of (Roman) Catholic dogmatic theology. Furthermore, it is undertaken in the general spirit of the Congregation for the Doctrine of the Faith's 1990 'instruction on the ecclesial vocation of the theologian', *Donum Veritatis*:

> Freedom, which is proper to theological investigations, is exercised within the ambit of the Church's faith. Daring, therefore, which is often imposed by the feelings of the theologian, cannot bear fruit or 'edify', unless accompanied by that patience which permits those same fruits to mature. New opinions, proffered from the understanding of the faith, 'are but offerings made to the whole Church. Many corrections and broadening of perspectives within the context of fraternal dialogue may be needed before the time comes when the Church is able to accept them'. From this it follows, that 'this service, very generously offered to the community of the faithful', which theology is, 'essentially entails careful discussion, fraternal dialogue, an openness and willingness to modify one's own opinions'. (Art. 11; AAS 82 [1990]: 1554–5, quoting John Paul II, 'Allocution to the Theologians of Altötting', 18 November 1980 [AAS 73 (1981): 104])

This vision of theology is not, I readily concede, one that will be accepted by all my readers, whether Catholic or not. In explicitly theologizing from within the confines of a specific tradition – and indeed, within a particular construal of those confines – I trust that I will not alienate those who share neither this position, nor the 'controlling beliefs' (D'Costa 2009: 4) which I understand it to imply. The noble causes of ecumenism and academic scholarship are not, I submit, best served by theologians pretending that they themselves do not belong to an ecclesial tradition, if in fact they do. St Josemaría Escrivá once pointedly asked, 'Have you ever stopped to think how absurd it is to leave one's Catholicism aside on entering a university, a professional association, a cultural society, or Parliament, like a man leaving his hat at the door?' ([1939] 1985: 92). How much more absurd it would be for a Catholic dogmatic theologian, fortunate enough to be working within a Catholic university college, to do the same!

It is better, therefore, simply to be transparent about these things. Personal theological prejudices and parochialities, rather than (inevitably) creeping in unannounced, may thus be recognized and taken into account. Should a reader happen to share all or most of my Catholic perspective, then all well and good. But if not, this ought not to hinder his or her following and entering into the thread of my argument. Indeed, this monograph may perfectly adequately be read as an elaborate thought-experiment: '*supposing* that LG 14 and 16 are both correct, and *supposing* also the rectitude of certain other Catholic dogmatic principles (to be discussed), *how* is it possible for an atheist to be saved?' Framed in these terms, the project becomes one of examining the *coherence* and *consistency* of a set of premises. One no more needs *actually* to affirm these premises, in order to engage with the ideas herein, than one needs to believe that *actual* bishops may only move diagonally, in order to play chess. Hence this study's acceptance of certain dogmatic axioms may be viewed as a species of 'methodological Catholicism' – that is, a set of presuppositions, the hypothetical acceptance of which, *in itself*, neither affirms nor denies the truth of Catholicism.[2] One remains, of course, at liberty to dispute (i) whether my arguments, showing how the axioms of this thought-experiment are logically consistent, are themselves cogent ('internal validity'); and (ii) whether, stepping outside the thought-experiment, these axioms and arguments have any genuine bearing on the salvation of atheists, or whether there is such a thing as salvation at all ('external validity').[3] With respect to the *inner logic* of this enquiry, however, only objections of the former type are applicable.

In any case, it is this methodology that motivates, and justifies, the various appeals to authority used throughout this book, and most

---

[2] In precisely the same way, the sociologist of religion's 'methodological atheism', properly understood, neither affirms nor denies the existence of God (see Berger [1967] 1990: 179–80).

[3] On the ideas of 'internal' and 'external validity', which I have borrowed from social-scientific methodology, see Ruane 2005: 38–42.

especially in chapters four and five. These authorities may be divided into three categories, together providing the primary sources for this enquiry: 'sacred scripture, sacred tradition, and the teaching authority (*magisterium*) of the Church' (*Dei Verbum* 10; AS IV/vi: 601). The first of these is self-explanatory, except to say that I include within 'sacred scripture' the deuterocanonical books. Appeals to the second, 'sacred tradition', will chiefly include early Christian credal statements, the writings of the Church Fathers, the *sensus fidelium*, and the teachings and example of those whom the Church recognizes to be saints or blesseds (these will be referred to as 'St' or 'Bl.' only when such ecclesiastical status is relevant to the argument being made, as for example in chapter five, and only then when first mentioned). The 'teaching office' of the (hierarchy of the) Church is expressed, with greatly varying degrees of dogmatic weight (see Sullivan 1996: 12–27), in conciliar documents, papal pronouncements, and formal statements of the Curia, most notably from the Holy Office or (post-1965) the Congregation for the Doctrine of the Faith.[4] For brevity's sake, these will be collectively referred to as 'magisterial' documents: a term that, in its present sense, like its cognate *magisterium*, is a relatively recent addition to the Church's technical vocabulary (Congar [1976] 1982a; Sullivan 1983: 25–6; Hill 1988: 75).

According to Vatican II, all three categories – scripture and tradition as forming the 'one sacred deposit of the Word of God', and the Church's teaching authority as entrusted with their authentic interpretation – are 'so linked and united among themselves that one cannot stand without the others, and all together, and each in its own way, under the action of the one Holy Spirit contribute effectively to the salvation of souls' (*Dei Verbum* 10; AS IV/vi: 601). As such, they are the pre-eminent sources for Catholic dogmatic theology. Given the centrality of magisterial documents in particular, along with certain other Latin writings (e.g. the works of Sts Augustine and Thomas, and medieval hagiography), to this exploration, all Latin sources will be given according to my own translations. This will permit certain theological nuances, obscured in the standard English translations, to be brought to the fore. On occasion, these will be commented upon in the footnotes.

---

[4] These too, of course, also form part of the tradition. Hence I will occasionally refer to the Church's magisterial authority as 'the dogmatic tradition'.

Accepting the normativity of 'sacred scripture, sacred tradition, and the teaching authority of the Church', crucial to the brand of 'methodological Catholicism' adopted herein, need not reduce Catholic theology to a slavish and ahistorical exegesis of oracular pronouncements – 'Denzinger-theology' in the most negative sense of the term (Congar [1976] 1982b: 327). Certainly, texts collected in Hünermann's 37th edition of Denzinger's *Enchiridion* (1991) will be cited frequently in this monograph, albeit usually from other sources.[5] Rightly or wrongly, this follows from the conviction, enunciated by Rahner, that:

> If we wish to proceed as true theologians [...] then we will have to take the doctrinal pronouncements of the Church as our starting-point (for these are the beginning and end of all theology) [...] But the 'end' must be understood here in the sense that the doctrinal pronouncements of the Church are not only the starting-point, but also the abiding norm of all dogmatic theology. Whenever theology, sustained by faith and the desire for salvation, does moreover not forget its existential source and aim, then it will also continually serve the teaching authority itself, and it will then ultimately be possible to include it, with its newly gained insights, in the very teaching of that authority. ([1947] 1963: 2, 3 n. 2)

Rahner – who significantly, in addition to being a leading critic of 'Denzinger-theology', edited three volumes of the *Enchiridion* between 1952 and 1957 – also, of course, recognized the fact that:

---

[5] Monumentally useful though the *Enchiridion* (DH) is, it is still only (to translate its Latin title) a 'handbook of creeds, definitions and declarations'. These are all, of course, of varying dogmatic weights – a fact which may be obscured by simply citing, without comment, the relevant Denzinger numbers (cf. Hill 1988: 79). There are also problems regarding its selectiveness (see Rahner [1954] 1961: 3 n. 3), although these have been partially addressed in the expanded, recent editions. Decisively, in the vast majority of cases more comprehensive, critical editions of the texts are available elsewhere. For this reason, documents from Vatican II (including draft schemas and interventions by the Council Fathers) will be cited according to the authoritative, multi-volume Latin *Acta Synodalia Sacrosancti Concilii Oecumenici Vaticani II* (AS). Documents from ecumenical councils prior to Vatican II will be cited from the Latin of Norman Tanner's bilingual, two-volume *Decrees of the Ecumenical Councils* (1990a; 1990b). Papal and other magisterial documents from 1909 to the present will normally be cited from the official *Acta Apostolicae Sedis* (AAS); and from 1865 to 1908, from its predecessor, *Acta Sanctae Sedis* (ASS). Pronouncements from the pontificate of Pius IX (1846–1878), however, will be cited from the *Pii IX Pontificis Maximi Acta*. These aside, DH will be used either (i) where the text may be found in none of the above (e.g. papal pronouncements prior to 1846); or (ii) to briefly substantiate a cursory reference to an item in the dogmatic tradition. Please see the 'Abbreviations' section for notes on citation formats.

> In the transmission and expression of dogmas properly speaking there may be inseparably mingled ideas, interpretations, etc., which are not part of the binding content of the article of faith concerned but which have not been explicitly separated from this article at a particular epoch in history by traditional theology or even by the Church's magisterium, and for historical reasons cannot be separated up to a certain point in time. There may be such amalgams (if we may use this admittedly problematic expression) even with dogmas properly so called. ([1977] 1983: 11)

This monograph, therefore, aspires to what Francis Sullivan has deemed 'creative fidelity':

> Fidelity describes the theologian's effort to grasp the authentic meaning of a dogma, and to preserve that same meaning in any reconceptualization and reformulation of it. 'Fidelity,' then, has to do primarily with the meaning of a dogma, rather than with its verbal expression. However, there is a sense in which the theologian's 'fidelity' also includes a certain respect for the traditional language in which the faith has been expressed and is professed. (Sullivan 1996: 116–17)

This, at least, is my intention.

In more practical terms, my approach is evidenced in the very nature of my *quaestio*. My concern is with the question of *how* an atheist may be saved. The logically anterior question of *if* one can be saved has, I am assuming, been settled in the affirmative by LG 16. This assumption is based on the dogmatic weight proper to a 'dogmatic constitution' promulgated by the pope and assembled bishops at a general council of the Catholic Church – a document which, while defining no new dogmas, nevertheless participates in the Church's 'authoritative magisterium' (see Sullivan 1996: 19, 162–7). Importantly, however, this also means that LG 16 can neither be affirmed, nor properly interpreted, in a dogmatic vacuum. Needless to say, for example, whatever intrinsic authority LG 16 possesses, it is equally held by the rest of the document, including LG 14.[6] In fact,

---

[6] On the necessity of interpreting the Council's texts as a whole, and in continuity with the wider tradition of the Church, see Kasper [1987] 1989: 172–3. This is the same approach to the conciliar documents advocated by Pope Benedict XVI, described both as a 'hermeneutic of reform' in his 'Address to the Roman Curia' in December 2005 (AAS 98 [2006]: 44–5) and as a 'hermeneutic of continuity' in a footnote to the 2007 apostolic exhortation *Sacramentum Caritatis* (AAS 99 [2007]: 107).

since LG 14 reiterates a number of previously defined doctrines (albeit without citing them), it possesses a higher degree of (extrinsic) dogmatic weight. This places considerable constraints on how the salvation of atheists can be here conceived. Thus in explicating LG 16, none of the following principles may be denied: that the Church is necessary for salvation (cf. DH 870, 1351, 2867); that Christ, whose body is the Church, is the unique mediator of salvation; that both faith and baptism are necessary for salvation (cf. DH 1524, 1532, 1618); and that a person who is cognizant of the Church's necessity, but who fails to enter and/or persevere in it, cannot be saved (cf. DH 2866). *Fidelity* to these principles, whether implicitly (throughout) or explicitly (principally in chapters four and five), will shape this entire enquiry. (For reasons already given, this 'fidelity' can, if one so chooses, be understood simply as an adherence to the constraints of the thought-experiment.) *Creativity*, on the other hand, should arise naturally in comprehending them in light of both LG 16 and the realities of contemporary unbelief.

This book's title raises two obvious points requiring clarification: what exactly is an 'atheist'; and in what does 'salvation' consist? The former will be considered, at some length, in the following chapter. The latter, however, may briefly be answered here. According to Christian teaching, the consequences of the Fall include the corruption of human nature, and the onset of death: 'sin came into the world through one man, and death came through sin, and so death spread to all because all have sinned' (Rom 5.12). The Council of Trent speaks here of original sin as the *mors animae*, or 'death of the soul', by which it means the deprivation of sanctifying grace (*Decree on Original Sin* 2; Tanner 1990b: 666; see Ott [1957] 1963: 110–11). Free will, though weakened and debased, remains, but such is the dominion of sin and death that (again according to Trent) 'not only the gentiles by the force of nature, nor even the Jews by the very letter of the law of Moses were able to be liberated or rise up therefrom' (*Decree on Justification* 1; Tanner 1990b: 671). Yet all was not, of course, lost: 'when the fullness of time had come, God sent his Son' (Gal 4.4); 'the Father has sent his Son as the Saviour of the whole world' (1 Jn 4.14). Thus in the words of St Gregory of Nyssa:

> Labouring in sickness, our nature needed medicine. Having fallen, we needed to be raised. Having died, we needed to be enlivened. Having fallen away from goodness, we needed it restoring to us. Closed off in

shadows, we wanted for the presence of light. Captive, we sought a saviour; conquered, a helper; slaves, a liberator. Are these things small or insignificant, which moved God to descend and visit human nature, since humanity was so miserably and unhappily affected? (*Orat. Catech.* 15, 3, quoted from CCC 457)

As is well known, the New Testament employs a range of terms and images in describing the Christian hope for eternal life: salvation, freedom, liberation, justification, redemption (see Edwards 1986: 6–13; O'Collins 2007: 1–18). Furthermore, it regards salvation as having past, present, and future aspects. Catholic teaching affirms that the primary purpose of Christ's incarnation, death, and resurrection was 'to redeem us from sins and from eternal death, and to reunite us with the Father unto eternal life' (Paul IV, *Cum quorumdam*, 1555; DH 1880). This redemption and reuniting cannot, however, be viewed simply as two 'events', one past and one future. It requires also a present and ongoing process of human transformation and growth, which is begun in this life (ordinarily with the removal of original sin, and the restoration of sanctifying grace, effected by sacramental baptism).[7] This is both made possible by the Cross (past), and comes to maturation and completion – i.e. *final* salvation – in the post-mortem entry into heaven (future). This idea will become important in chapters four and five.

Unsurprisingly, I follow the Catholic trifold schema of heaven, hell, and purgatory. Souls in the latter, understood as a place and/or state of purification (cf. Ratzinger [1977] 1988: 228–33), may rightly be said to be on the way to heaven – and thus ultimately, albeit not-quite-yet, *saved*. Purgatory may thus be viewed as a post-mortem continuation of the 'ongoing process of human transformation and growth' mentioned above (see Salkeld 2011: 11–32). This is the usual path to heaven, for Christians and non-Christians alike. As such, I take the ultimate salvation of atheists to imply a period in purgatory. That said, the hypothetical possibility of a non-Christian saint (i.e. one who enters directly into heaven upon death) will be touched upon briefly in chapter four. Heaven itself, of course, is also a rich and contested concept, both in scripture and the subsequent Christian traditions. Here I take it to be 'a place and condition of perfect supernatural bliss' (Ott [1957] 1963: 476) primarily, but by no

---

[7] For a non-Catholic statement of this idea, see Fiddes 1989: 14–34.

means exhaustively, constituted by the beatific vision, i.e. the unmediated knowledge of God: 'For now we see in a mirror, dimly, but then we will see face to face. Now I know only in part; then I will know fully, even as I have been fully known' (1 Cor 13.12). Benedict XII's constitution *Benedictus Deus* (1332) remains the classic doctrinal statement of the *visio beatifica*. Those who either have no need of purgatory, or have already undergone it:

> have been, are, and will be in heaven, in the kingdom of heaven and the celestial paradise with Christ [...] and see the divine essence by intuitive vision, and even face to face, without a mediating creature [...] but the divine essence immediately revealing itself uncovered, clearly, and openly, to them. And seeing this, they fully enjoy the same divine essence, from which such vision and enjoyment their souls, which have now departed, are truly blessed and have eternal life and rest. [...] After such intuitive and face-to-face vision and enjoyment in these has or will be begun, the same vision and enjoyment will exist continually, without any intermission or departure, and will continue all the way to the last judgement, and from then even into eternity. (DH 1000–1; cf. Saward 2005: 198)

These essential points aside, no more need be said about the specifics of Christian eschatology until chapter four.

Finally, I began work on this project in 2005–6 with research for a master's dissertation on Rahner's theology of atheism. This then led to a doctoral thesis, which eventually (after substantial revision) became the book you are now reading. Since the start of that long process, the unprecedented successes of books by, among others, Sam Harris, Richard Dawkins, and Daniel Dennett have thrust atheism firmly into the popular and media spotlight. This 'New Atheism' has made conducting this research even more interesting and enjoyable than it would otherwise have been, and I have gained much from engaging – in thought, conversation, and print – with this remarkable social and intellectual phenomenon. Nevertheless, this research is in no way intended as a *response* to the New Atheism. This is a contribution to an important but technical point of Catholic dogmatics, not a work of Christian apologetics. While, I hope, atheists may find things to interest them in these pages – no doubt in amongst a great many 'grotesque piece[s] of reasoning, so damningly typical of the theological mind' (Dawkins 2006: 65) – this book is written neither to nor for them. That said, it will indeed challenge one item in the New

Atheists' arsenal. Sam Harris gives the following example of 'religious information':

> The pope says that Jesus was born of a virgin and resurrected bodily after death. He is the Son of God, who created the universe in six days. *If you believe this, you will go to heaven after death; if you don't you will go to hell, where you will suffer for eternity.* ([2004] 2006: 74; my emphasis)

Commenting on heaven elsewhere, Harris writes: 'Of course, overly rational people and other rabble' – pre-eminent among whom, of course, are atheists – 'will be kept out of this happy place' (ibid.: 36). Worse, inattentive readers of Daniel Dennett's *Breaking the Spell* might get the impression that the following, quoted from the actor Mel Gibson, accurately represents the Catholic doctrine of salvation:

> 'There is no salvation for those outside the Church,' Gibson replied. 'I believe it.' He explained: 'Put it this way. My wife is a saint. She's a much better person than I am. Honestly. She's, like, Episcopalian, Church of England. She prays, she believes in God, she knows Jesus, she believes in that stuff. And it's just not fair if she doesn't make it, she's better than I am. But that is a pronouncement from the chair. I go with it.' (Quoted in Dennett 2006: 289)

That these do not accurately represent the Catholic understanding of salvation will, I believe, be abundantly clear from what follows.

1

Who is an Atheist?

The global number of atheists is difficult to discern. A lack of reliable data, the ambiguity of key terms, and the prevalence in many countries of social or political coercion (whether for or against) all conspire against precision. Yet tentative, informed estimates may usefully be made. The *World Christian Encyclopedia*'s figures for mid-2000, for example, counted 150 million 'atheists', and a further 750 million 'nonreligious' (Barrett et al. 2001: 4). This terminological distinction, on the dubious criterion of presumed 'militancy', need not detain us here; on my definition, discussed below, both groupings may be deemed atheistic. Thus corrected, the encyclopedia, which is based on a vast bricolage of polls, surveys, and censuses, gives a grand total of 900 million. The 1999–2004 findings of the World Values Survey, collating data from sixty-six countries, revealed that 12.8 per cent of people *do not* 'believe in God'. This proportion, if extrapolated to the world population, would equate to around 870 million individuals.[1] Lastly, Phil Zuckerman's synthesis of numerous recent studies (including the *World Christian Encyclopedia*) offers a 'conservative' estimate of between 500 and 750 million 'atheists, agnostics, and non-believers in God'. Rightly cautious though his figures may be, he points out:

> Given the above estimates, we can deduce that there are approximately 58 times as many atheists as there are Mormons, 41 times as many atheists as there are Sikhs, and twice as many atheists as there are Buddhists. Finally, nonbelievers in God as a group come in fourth

---

[1] Statistics taken from: <http://www.worldvaluessurvey.org.>. Accessed on 11 June 2010. This extrapolation is intended only illustratively. It is not a scientific estimate. Unfortunately, the question 'do you believe in God?' appears not to have been asked in the WVS's most recent, fifth wave (2005–2008).

place after Christianity (2 billion), Islam (1.2 billion), and Hinduism (900 million) in terms of global ranking of commonly held belief systems. (2007: 55)

Even allowing generously for the above estimates' shortcomings, and indeed the general dubiety of religious statistics (Bruce 1996: 32; Davie 1994: 45), contemporary atheism is demonstrably a vast, worldwide phenomenon. Given that there have also been many atheists in the past, and are likely to be a great many more in the future, the question of their possible salvation is by no means a trifling matter.

DEFINING 'ATHEIST'

Before proceeding further, it is necessary to clarify what is meant by the term *atheist*. Given the range of definitions, applications, and connotations that this word has historically possessed, this is an important preliminary. In classical Greek, *atheos* sometimes signifies (i) one who *denies* the gods (as with Socrates in Plato's *Apology*), but is also used of (ii) one *abandoned* by the gods or 'godforsaken', as well as in the negative moral sense of (iii) 'godless' or 'ungodly' (Liddell and Scott 1869: 27). It is in the second sense, although possibly with overtones of the third, that the word makes its only appearance in the New Testament. The gentile converts of Ephesus are reminded of when they were 'without Christ, being aliens from the commonwealth of Israel, and strangers to the covenant of promise, having no hope and without God (*atheoi*) in the world' (Eph 2.12). In modern English, it is the first sense which has most securely attached itself to the word. In common speech, an atheist is often understood to be one who actively (and perhaps stridently) *dis*believes in the existence of God. This is similar to Alister McGrath's recent usage in *The Twilight of Atheism*: 'By "atheist," I mean precisely [...] a principled and informed decision to *reject* belief in God' (2004: 175).

Yet although widespread, such a definition is not at all ubiquitous. One illustration of this is provided by a survey of over 700 students at Oxford University in 2007 (Bullivant 2008a). Only slightly over half (51.8%) opted for 'A person who believes that there is no God or gods'. For a further 29.1%, however, the term also implied a level of *conviction* beyond simple (dis)believing: 'A person who is convinced that there is no God or gods'. In addition, 13.6% chose the broader 'A person who lacks a belief in a God or gods', 0.6% went for 'Don't know', and thirty-five respondents (including eight who had already specified one of the suggested meanings) availed themselves of the option to provide their own definition. It is worth noting also that, depending on where one lives, 'atheist' can carry certain negative connotations – some, though not all, relating to the second and (especially) third classical meanings given above. In the USA, for example, the term is heavily stigmatized in public opinion, and can conjure up images of anything from communism to drug abuse (Wolf-Meyer 2005). According to a much-discussed 2006 study by the University of Minnesota, 'atheists' are America's least trusted social grouping (Edgell et al. 2006). Even in secularized Britain – where unbelief *itself* carries few of its erstwhile negative connotations, and where suspicion is instead reserved for the seemingly too religious (Levitt 1996; Bullivant 2010; Bagg and Voas 2010) – relatively few people would choose to apply the term 'atheist' to themselves. Steve Bruce, commenting on the inclusion, and relative unpopularity, of a 'convinced atheist' option on the 2000 Soul of Britain survey, has remarked: 'It may be different in other cultures, but there is a danger that to British ears "convinced atheist" will suggest cranks in sandals' (2002: 193). Even those happy to apply the term to themselves may still be apprehensive about how the descriptor is perceived by others. To quote from a recent interview conducted by Lois Lee, as part of her groundbreaking qualitative research into 'nonreligion' in London:

> Yeah, I am [happy to call myself an 'atheist']. The only, my only concern with it is it often comes across as being quite aggressive. Calling yourself an 'atheist' in *company*, can occasionally seem like holding up a big sign saying, 'if any of you are anything other than atheists, I think you're all ****ing morons'. Um, which... [pause] is disrespectful in the extreme. Obviously. (2011)

Defining atheism is, then, a fraught field. One cannot simply appeal to any established, universally-agreed definition. Nor can one assume that the sense in which the word 'atheist' is intended is the sense in which it is, or will be, understood (and vice versa). This is especially so if one chooses to champion a definition that departs from the popular, common-speech, 'McGrathian' meaning – which is precisely what I am about to do.

For the purposes of this study, then, the word 'atheist' will signify the following: *a person who is without a belief in God (or gods)*. This encompasses both those who believe that God does not exist, and those who, while not necessarily disbelieving, do not possess a belief in God's existence either. Among others who follow this broad, neutral definition of 'atheist', these two categories are often designated 'positive atheism' (believing-not) and 'negative atheism' (not-believing) respectively (e.g. Robertson 1970: 238; Flew 1976: 14; Martin 2007a: 1). (On this schema, agnosticism is a species of negative atheism. Agnostics are, therefore, in this sense 'atheists', and for the purposes of this study need not be dealt with separately. Also included under 'negative atheism' are those, like the logical positivist A. J. Ayer, who deny any meaning to the word 'God', and thus to all positions regarding his existence or lack of it: 'if the assertion that there is a God is nonsensical, then the atheist's assertion that there is no God is equally nonsensical' [(1936) 1990: 121].)

This deviation from the common meaning requires justification. In the first place, this usage both has a strong tradition within atheist literature, and has gained a wide acceptance among atheist scholars. Beginning at least with Charles Bradlaugh, who in 1866 founded the National Secular Society, many prominent atheists have argued for the accuracy of this definition (e.g. Flew 1976: 14; Smith [1979] 1989: 8; Hiorth 2003: 9). Frequently, appeal is made to the etymology of *atheos/atheist* on comparison with similarly constructed words such as 'amoral' and 'asexual'. Given that its *alpha privativum* prefix strictly means 'without', *a-theist* ought literally to mean '*without* (a belief in) God'. Admittedly, bearing in mind that historically the word has only rarely meant this (and even did not, as we have seen, in classical Greece), there is danger here of falling prey to the etymological fallacy. Nevertheless, the great utility of this definition, and its pervasive – although not universal (see Baggini 2003: 3; Cliteur 2009) – deployment in recent scholarship on contemporary atheism, more than support its usage herein. Not insignificantly, this sense is advocated in the recent *Cambridge Companion to Atheism*. On the first page, Michael Martin writes:

> If you look up 'atheism' in a dictionary, you will find it defined as the belief that there is no God. Certainly, many people understand 'atheism' in this way. Yet this is not what the term means if one considers it from the point of view of its Greek roots. In Greek 'a' means 'without' or 'not,'

and 'theos' means 'god.' From this standpoint, an atheist is someone without a belief in God; he or she need not be someone who believes that God does not exist. (2007a: 1; see also Martin 1990: 463)

There are also theological motives for my adopting this definition. Historically, the question of the salvation of atheists has been framed in terms of Hebrews 11.6: 'And without faith it is impossible to please God, for whoever would approach him must believe that he exists and that he rewards those who seek him' (see Rahner [1954] 1967a: 364; Congar 1957: 291). *Prima facie*, then, 'believing that God exists' is one of the criteria for Christian salvation. It is, therefore, all who are *without* this belief, rather than just those who have an opposing belief that God does *not* exist, who are (as it were) salvifically problematic. It is for this reason also that both agnostics and anti-theists may be included in the same broad category. (This is not to imply, of course, that there are no salvifically relevant differences between the two groups. Nevertheless, both groups share in lacking belief in the existence of God, and it is this which is the *primary* issue. The relative culpabilities of agnosticism and anti-theism will be touched upon in chapter four.) Were this enquiry only to concern itself with 'atheists' in the common-language, McGrathian sense, the great majority of this Hebrews-defined category would be ignored. Further, LG 16 speaks not of those who disbelieve in God, but rather of 'those who, without fault, have not yet arrived at an express recognition of God (*expressam agnitionem Dei*)'.[2] One may note also that the broad usage of 'atheist', encompassing both positive and negative varieties, is also well attested in writings by Catholic theologians (e.g. Lombardi [1942] 1956: 147–65). Importantly, given the normativity of magisterial teaching to this enquiry, *Gaudium et Spes* 19 concurs in advocating a broad definition:

> The word 'atheism' designates phenomena that differ very greatly among themselves. For whilst God is expressly denied by some, others believe that man is able to assert nothing at all about him. Still others bring such a method of examination to the question of God that it would seem to lack all meaning. Many, unduly transgressing the limits

---

[2] Agreeing with Tanner (1990b: 861), I diverge here from the common English translation of these words as 'explicit knowledge of God' (e.g. Flannery 1975: 368). 'Express recognition of God' is both more literal, and preserves the ambiguity of the Latin original. The atheist's eventual *recognition* of God will be developed in chapters four and five.

of the positive sciences, either contend that all things can be explained by scientific reasoning, or, on the contrary, avow that there is no such thing as absolute truth. Certain people exalt man so greatly that faith in God becomes weakened; they are more inclined, it would appear, to affirm man than to deny God. Yet others portray God to themselves in such a way, that this figment, which they deny, is in no way the God of the Gospels. There are others who never raise questions concerning God; who seem not to experience religious disquiet, nor see why they should concern themselves with religion. (AS IV/vii: 743)

Throughout this work, therefore, 'atheist' (except, in some cases, where quoted from other authors) will be used in the generic, above-described sense: that is, at the risk of tedious repetition, *a person who is without a belief in God (or gods)*. To avoid monotony, though, this will sometimes be replaced by the words 'unbeliever' and 'non-believer' (along with their cognates). These terms, it is true, also carry their own shades of meaning. But here they are synonymous with 'atheist'.

I am, of course, well aware that this definition is open to objection from a number of different quarters. I wish to dwell upon two of these: (i) that it assumes an overly propositional – and un-Catholic – understanding of *belief*; and (ii) that it is overly reductive in defining atheists solely by a belief they do not possess. My countering of these objections is only partly for reasons of self-defence. Far more importantly, each of these possible objections opens up an interesting perspective on atheism itself. In exploring and countering these objections, therefore, we stand to gain a better comprehension of the nature and significance of atheism. This rationale likewise motivates the other remaining sections of this chapter, which will ask, in turn, 'Is atheism a religion?', and 'Can one really be an atheist?'. These are interesting questions in themselves, but will likewise stand us in good stead in the forthcoming, more explicitly dogmatic, chapters. But before we turn to these longer discussions, the two objections must first be considered.

CREDERE (IN) DEUM?

Firstly, it may be objected that, in a contribution to the Catholic theology of salvation, my definition is too narrowly propositional. It could be argued, for example, that by identifying lack of belief in the *existence* of God as the atheist's defining, salvifically problematic feature, there is a danger of misrepresenting the Christian conception of faith and belief. For on this understanding, *believing in God* is not simply a matter of *having a belief in the existence of God*. And (it may be argued) it is the atheist's lack of the former, rather than of the latter, that is *really* salvifically problematic. Although seemingly obscure, this difference may easily be grasped. Following Augustine, three types of believing may be distinguished: *credere Deo* (to believe God), *credere Deum* (to believe *that* God exists), and *credere in Deum* (to believe *in* God) (e.g. Augustine, *Sermones ad populum* 144, 2; PL 38: 788; see also *Summa theologiae*, IIa IIae, q. 2, a. 2; Thomas Aquinas [1265–74] 1974: 64–8). Believing in the second, *credere Deum* sense, means assenting to the proposition 'God exists' or 'there is a God'. In the third, *credere in Deum* sense, however, 'believing' connotes something very different: having faith, or trusting, in God. (Hence, of course, our Latin-derived words '*confide*', '*confidence*', '*fiduciary*', all of which cluster around meanings of trust.) It is for this reason that the Nicene and Apostles' creeds are not mere lists of assented-to propositions, but rather professions of *faith*, beginning as they do: '*Credo in*...'. Evidently, it is possible to believe that God exists (*credere Deum*) without believing in God (*credere in Deum*). Thus according to Jas 2.19, even the demons believe *that* God is one. Believing *in* the God who is one, i.e. having faith, is something else entirely.

Yet in English and other languages, as Nicholas Lash has observed, the question 'do you believe in God?' can be understood in either of these two, distinct senses ([1992] 2002: 18–21). This ambiguity (which is partly to blame for some of those misconstruals of the Catholic position mentioned in the introduction) allows for a special category of so-called 'atheism', which not too long ago was keenly discussed by Catholic theologians: *practical* or *lived* atheism. According to Rahner, for instance, practical atheism consists of: 'a lifestyle in which no (discernible) conclusions are drawn from the (theoretical) recognition of the existence of God' (1957: 983; see also [1960] 1966a: 475; [1978] 1979: 14; Endean 2001: 117). Compare also Henri de Lubac's seemingly paradoxical remark: 'One can be an atheist and profess belief in God' ([1956] 1960: 116–17). Nor have such ideas been confined only to Catholics. For Karl Barth:

The atheism that is the real enemy is the 'Christianity' that professes faith in God very much as a matter of course, perhaps with great emphasis, and perhaps with righteous indignation at atheism wild or mild, while in its practical thinking and behaviour it carries on exactly as if there were no God. It professes belief in him, lauds and praises him, while in practice he is the last of the things it thinks about, takes seriously, fears or loves. ([1963] 1971a: 46–7)

As such, it may be argued, it is not 'not believing that God exists' (*non credere Deum*) that is primarily salvifically problematic, but rather 'not believing in God' (*non credere in Deum*). And furthermore, by setting so much store by the former, the post-mortem fate of a great many atheists (albeit 'practical' ones) will go unexplored.

Practical atheism?

The question of practical atheism is one that is worth pursuing – especially since, as noted above, these objections are intended as a springboard for further (and hopefully interesting) examination. To the best of my knowledge, the phrase first entered theological currency following a 1947 essay by the lay French philosopher Jacques Maritain. (Although as we shall see in chapter two, the basic idea appears earlier in the writings of Maurice Blondel.) According to Maritain, practical atheists are those 'who believe that they believe in God (and who perhaps believe in Him in their brains) but who in reality deny His existence by each one of their deeds' ([1947] 1953: 97; see also 1949: 268). Later on in the same work, he describes them as 'Christians who keep in their minds the settings of religion, for the sake of appearances or outward show, [...] but who deny the gospel and despise the poor' ([1947] 1953: 99). Maritain's basic point is that believing (say) the articles of the creed ought to have practical, concrete ramifications. Again, the distinction is between 'mere' believing (*credere Deum*) and 'believing in' (*credere in Deum*): believing in 'God, the Father almighty, maker of heaven and earth...' should make a positive difference to one's life. For Maritain, those who only assent to such propositions 'in their brains' might as well, for all the difference it makes to their practical lives, not have those beliefs at all.

As alluded to above, the Letter of James contains a lengthy discussion of precisely this point, playing on the Greek word *pistis*. This carries the same ambiguity as 'belief', and may refer either to propositional assent, or to genuine faith. Since the latter is the word's usual meaning in the New Testament, English translations typically render it as 'faith' (although its cognate verb, *pisteuō*, is translated as 'to believe'). This is unfortunate, since it makes the author of James seem to be a proto-Pelagian, which he is not. Most famously, he asks:

> What good is it, my brothers, if you say you have belief (*pistis*) but do not have works? Can belief (*pistis*) save you? If a brother is naked and lacks daily food, and one of you says to him, 'Go in peace; keep warm and eat your fill', and yet you do not supply their bodily needs, what is the good of that? So belief (*pistis*) by itself, if it has no works, is dead. (Jas 2.14–17)

This passage is traditionally, and notoriously, cast as an opposition between 'faith' and 'works' – hence Luther's judgement that 'in direct opposition to St Paul and all the rest of the Bible, it ascribes justification to works' ([1522] 1961: 35). A more nuanced reading suggests, however, that James' real distinction is, like Maritain's, between 'belief' and 'faith': or rather, between mere 'belief', and a belief that expresses itself in works. This much is clear later on in the passage: 'Show me your belief (*pistis*) without works, and I by my works will show you my belief (*pistis*).' The contrast here is between two, qualitatively different kinds of *pistis*: 'belief' and 'faith', *credere Deum* and *credere in Deum*. The latter presupposes the former (one must believe that there is a God, in order to believe *in* him), but goes far beyond it. Like Maritain, James also thinks that those who only possess *pistis* in the former sense, insofar as it has no practical ramifications, might as well not have it at all: 'So belief (*pistis*) by itself, if it has no works, is dead.'

A practical atheist is not, therefore, a real atheist at all, but is rather a defective form of *believer*. As in James, the distinction is between 'belief' and 'faith', and not 'belief' and 'unbelief'. As noted above, it is motivated by the conviction that Christian belief ought to make a discernible difference to the way that believers conduct their lives. The phrase is thus *intended* to pass comment not on atheists, but on Christians. Yet that said, in Maritain's usage at least, the phrase does indeed, implicitly, pass comment on atheists themselves. By saying that, in terms of their practical life, Christians who 'despise the poor' *may as well be* atheists, Maritain is using 'atheist' in an obviously morally pejorative manner. It is not surprising, then, that atheists themselves have objected to this. According to George H. Smith, for example:

[T]he idea of a hypocritical Christian offends Maritain's sensibilities. The belief in god is morally good, and the theist who does not measure up to certain moral standards then somehow does not *really* believe in god. As to how one can become an atheist through one's actions, Maritain provides a simple answer: if one is sufficiently immoral or hypocritical, one deserves to be called an atheist. Under the cloak of classifying, Maritain purifies theism by pushing its undesirables into the atheistic camp, where he has no difficulty accepting their deviant behavior. After all, what more can one expect from a godless man? ([1979] 1989: 19–20)

Now, the offence or distaste of non-Catholics is not, in itself, normative for Catholic theology. But on this occasion, Smith certainly has a point. The idea that atheists are, or ought to be, dissolute, and indeed despair-ridden, has a long history in Western thought and culture (Beit-Hallahmi 2010). But this caricature is not, and probably never was, borne out by the facts. Sociological studies of this question (themselves plagued by considerable methodological difficulties) report no huge, or unambiguous, differences between believers or unbelievers across a range of morality-related scales (see, variously, Davenport [1980] 1991; Farias and Lalljee 2008; Beit-Hallahmi 2010). That said, there is some evidence that committed, practising religious believers are disproportionately more likely to give to charity, or to do voluntary work, than either non-believers or other, less committed or non-practising believers (e.g. Gill 1992: 16–20; Brooks 2006). This indeed supports Maritain's and James' contention that genuine faith (which commitment and participation might imply) does have positive, practical ramifications. Yet it does not follow that those *without* such faith, whether these be nominal Christians or unbelievers, are fairly characterized as 'those who despise the poor'.

Furthermore, we are talking here at the level of statistical *trends*, rather than individuals. Maritain's pejorative use of 'practical atheists' seems to imply that all atheists are, at best, only as moral as the most indifferent Christians. This is certainly not the case, and there are a great many atheists (not to mention other non-Christians) who lead heroically virtuous lives by any standard. From a Catholic perspective, it must be said that all such lives, whether within or without the Church, are only possible through the grace-full action of the triune God. But that is not, of course, how the unbelievers themselves see it. And it is, moreover, perfectly possible for them to frame a robust, plausible, meta-ethical justification for their doing so, which makes

Who is an Atheist? 23

no reference to either the existence, or will, or activity, of a God or gods. This is neither the time nor place to get into a full discussion of this topic. But since this will become an important point in chapter three, it is worth giving it some cursory attention here. Thus in the words of Kai Nielsen:

> Torturing human beings is wrong, cruelty to human beings and animals is wrong, treating one's promises lightly or being careless about the truth is wrong, exploiting or degrading human beings is vile. If we know anything to be wrong, we know these things to be wrong and to be just as wrong in a godless world as in a world with God. God's not existing has no effect on their moral status or on our moral standing. (2001: 98–9; see also Baggini 2003: 43–4; Norman 2004: 89; and Oppy 2006: 354)

Nielsen's argument is quite plain: some things are simply morally wrong, regardless of the existence or will of any divinity. If God exists, they are wrong. If God does not exist, they are still wrong. And if God did exist, but said that they were right, they would not only still be wrong, but God would be so too (see also Wielenberg 2005: 41–2). Though Nielsen is himself an atheist, one need not be to subscribe to this minimal, meta-ethical position. To give just one example, the Greek Orthodox philosopher Richard Swinburne, in his *Coherence of Theism*, concurs that 'Genocide and torturing children are wrong and would remain so whatever commands any person issued' (1993: 210; see also Mawson 2005: 75–6; and McCabe 2005: 17). Such a moral stance is, furthermore, seemingly sufficient to provide genuine, non-arbitrary meaningfulness to a person's life (see Martin 2002). Albert Camus' novel *The Plague* gives a clear example of just this. Asked why he devotes his life to helping plague victims despite his atheism, Dr Rieux answers, explaining:

> that if he believed in an all-powerful God he would cease curing the sick and leave that to Him. But no one in the world believed in a God of that sort [...] Anyhow, in this respect Rieux believed himself to be on the right road – in fighting against creation as he found it. ([1947] 1960: 106–7)

Or as Camus once similarly put it to a group of Dominicans, 'Perhaps we cannot prevent this world from being a world in which children are tortured. But we can reduce the number of tortured children' ([1948] 1964: 52). Importantly, while Nielsen and Camus may be wrong (though I do not think that they are), their arguments – and those of a whole host of other philosophers – are *plausible enough* to justify the moral and meaningful lives lived by a great many unbelievers, without imputing to them any 'anonymous', 'implicit', or 'unconscious' belief in God. What I mean by this, and why it is significant, will become clear later on.

To return to the objection which sparked this lengthy exploration: for the purposes of this study, defining 'atheist' in terms of *non credere in Deum* rather than of *non credere Deum* – that is, in terms of *faith* rather than of propositional *beliefs* – is infeasible. In the first place, it would be very confusing. 'Atheist', as we have seen, in both its strong and weak senses, is near-universally understood as a position relating to God's *existence*. As we have seen, the phrase 'practical atheist' is intended to highlight the difference between different modes of Christian believing, rather than the difference between belief/faith and unbelief per se. As such, the word atheist is being used there in a largely figurative and rhetorical sense. Smith's justified criticism of Maritain's pejorative labelling of Christians who 'despise the poor' as *atheists*, implying such behaviour to be typical of them, must also be heeded. The precedents set by GS 19 in defining 'who is an atheist' were invoked in the previous section. Note also that although this text refers explicitly to Christians who 'in their own religious, moral or social lives, conceal [...] the true countenance of God and religion', these are not designated 'atheists', practical or otherwise. Finally, even when united by their mutual not believing *in* God, an essential distinction must be drawn between Christians who do, and atheists who do not, believe *that* God exists. So essential, in fact, that in the context of the Catholic theology of salvation, these two groups cannot in any useful sense be treated together. The primary reason for this, the crucial principle of *invincible* or *inculpable ignorance*, will become clear as this enquiry progresses, especially in the final two chapters. To again cite the Letter of James: 'You believe that God is one; you do well. Even the demons believe – and shudder' (Jas 2.17). The demons are right to shudder, but precisely because they are *not* atheists.

As an appendix to this section, it is worth briefly commenting on one further issue raised by practical atheism. Despite not featuring in GS 19's very broad and wide-ranging typology, the phrase has in recent years been revived in the Church's magisterial pronouncements. For example, John Paul II's 2003 post-synodal exhortation *Ecclesia in Europa* describes how: 'All the great certainties of faith have yielded in many people to a vague and undemanding religious sentiment; various forms of agnosticism and practical atheism (*ateismo pratico*) spread themselves, which contribute to aggravating the divide between faith and life' (art. 47; AAS 95 [2003]: 678). More recently still, quoting Benedict XVI's 2009 social encyclical *Caritas in Veritate*: 'the deliberate promotion of religious indifference or practical atheism on the part of many countries obstructs the requirements for the development of peoples, depriving them of spiritual and human resources' (art. 29; AAS 101 [2009]: 664). Neither of these quotations has any direct bearing on the theology of salvation, so the above arguments are unaffected regarding the definition of atheism used herein. Nevertheless, two points are worth remarking upon. The first is that, in the quotation from John Paul II, 'practical atheism' appears to refer to religious indifference and a pervasive disjunction between theoretical belief and practice. As a comment on much of Europe, with Britain very much included, John Paul is quite correct (Bruce 2002; Voas and Crockett 2005; Bagg and Voas 2010). This usage of 'practical atheism' is, it will be noted, very similar to Maritain's – although, significantly, without the morally pejorative overtones to which Smith took exception.

In the quotation from Pope Benedict, however, the meaning is somewhat different. Unlike Maritain or John Paul, he appears to be speaking of 'practical atheism' (*atheismus practicus*) in a collective, societal sense, and the most obvious interpretation is that it is being used as a synonym for a certain mode of political secularism: the maintenance of a secular (and thus allegedly 'neutral') public square, demanding a relegation of religious beliefs and convictions to the private sphere (see Taylor 1998; Williams 2008). This is by no means unrelated to the classic meaning of the phrase (and indeed, one could certainly argue that these two varieties of practical atheism are likely to be mutually reinforcing), but gives it a more specific sense – and one very well-suited to the pope's concerns at the advance of secularism in Western societies.[3] Both

---

[3] It is worth noting that the pope is not alone in this usage among members of the Catholic hierarchy. To give just one example, from an interview with Archbishop José Gómez of Los Angeles in June 2010: '"Practical atheism" has become the *de facto* state religion in America. The price of participation in our economic, political, and social life is that we essentially have to agree to conduct ourselves as if God does not exist. Religion in the U.S. is something we do on Sundays or in our families, but is not allowed to have any influence on what we do the rest of the week.' Available online at: <http://www.catholic.org/national/national_story.php?id = 36844>. Accessed on 18 May 2010.

quotations raise important questions regarding the Church's engagement with contemporary Western culture and society. These topics, however, will have to wait for future books.

LIVED ATHEISM

A different kind of criticism might also be made: identifying atheists exclusively in terms of a specific belief that they do not possess gives an overly abstract, reductive impression of what concrete, lived atheism actually is. The philosopher Charles Taylor, for example, has expressed dissatisfaction with the way that 'in our societies, the big issue about religion is usually defined in terms of belief' (2007: 4). On this understanding, believers and unbelievers, or (for the purposes of this book) Christians and atheists, are cast merely as subscribers to 'rival *theories*' (ibid.). Taylor seeks instead to 'focus attention on the different kinds of lived experience involved in understanding your life in one way or the other, on what it's like to live as a believer or an unbeliever' (ibid.: 5). And in this vein, he argues that the reason why atheism has become so convincing in the modern West is not primarily due to Science's inexorable obsolescence of Religion (as on the standard 'death of God' narrative), but:

> has rather to be explained in terms of the power of a certain packaging uniting materialism with a moral outlook, the package we could call 'atheist humanism', or exclusive humanism [...] This presents materialism as the view of courageous adults, who are ready to resist the comforting illusions of earlier metaphysical and religious beliefs, in order to grasp the reality of an indifferent universe. (2007: 569, 574; see also Buckley 2004: 70–98)

Against this backdrop, it could be argued that the proposition-driven definition adopted here fails to capture most of what is interesting and distinctive about contemporary atheists. These people are not, primarily, non-subscribers to a certain theoretical understanding of the universe. They are instead real, concrete individuals, who lead their lives more or less in accordance with a particular worldview, only one minor component of which is the absence of belief in the existence of God. Somewhat similar considerations underlie many such people's dislike of labels such as 'a-theist' and 'un-believer', which (as they see it) define them *negatively* – in terms of one specific belief that they do not possess. Hence, to quote Paul Kurtz:

> [W]e are surely *nontheists*, but that does not mean that we should *simply* be defined as atheists. We do not believe in the Tooth Fairy, or Santa Claus either, but that does not define us. [...] I concede, of course, that we are atheists – but the point is that *we are more than that*. (2007: 4, 5)

This point is undoubtedly valid. It is, of course, no part of my argument that, considered in themselves, the most noteworthy characteristic of atheistic individuals is their lack of belief in the existence of God. But in the ambit of the Catholic theology of salvation, as explained above, this is certainly one of their most relevant features. (In the same way, the fact that a person does not vote in local elections is unlikely to be the single, defining feature of their life. For a political scientist researching voting behaviour, though, this may indeed be their most interesting and pertinent trait.) That said, the frequent appeals to sociological research in this chapter and others are intended, in part, to concretize contemporary atheism. Furthermore, throughout this work, references are made to works by contemporary atheist writers, the majority of whom could be placed, and would place themselves, in the humanist tradition – a tradition that is, it should be said, very broad. This is primarily because (secular) humanism is, at least in the West, currently the dominant atheistic worldview. (For the same reason, examples given by earlier theologians, quoted in later chapters, are typically taken from Marxist writers.) It should be stressed, however, that these illustrations are taken from only one possible atheistic stance. In itself, atheism neither entails nor implies humanism; the two are by no means co-extensive (Norman 2004). Indeed, John Gray, arguably humanism's most strident critic – e.g. 'Humanism is a secular religion thrown together from the decaying scraps of Christianity' ([2002] 2003: 31); 'Humanism is not an alternative to religious belief, but rather a degenerate and unwitting version of it' ([2002] 2004: 48) – is himself, by my definition if not necessarily his own, an atheist.

On the subject of lived atheism, a final difficulty is raised by the awkward case of members of non-theistic religions, such as Theravada Buddhism and (more controversially) Jainism and Confucianism (see Martin 2007b: 221–9). Since they are 'without a belief in God (or gods)', these too are atheists in the sense adopted here. It would seem, therefore, that what is said in this study will apply to them also. This may well be the case. However, with regard to salvation, the situation of these 'religious' atheists is arguably very different to that of the 'non-religious' atheists upon whom I am focusing. The reasons for this, and the two groups' salvifically relevant similarities and differences, will be very fruitfully explored in chapter four. Until then, without denying this enquiry's (possible) relevance to understanding the salvation of Buddhists, Jains, or Confucians, no explicit mention will be made of these groups. This is again in accordance with GS 19's definition of atheism, which, although broad, does not extend to the members of non-theistic religions.

IS ATHEISM A RELIGION?

Gray's comments, and the mention of atheistic religions, raise a further issue needing clarification. The suggestion that atheism, or rather a given (Western) atheistic system, is itself a *religion* is frequently encountered. Gray aside, Lash has recently described 'evolutionism' as 'a new religion', with Dawkins as its 'high priest' (2007: 521). And Michael Ruse, himself an atheist and Darwinian philosopher, has described the dispute between evolutionism and creationism as a 'clash [...] between two religions' (2005: 287). More consideredly perhaps, some religious studies scholars have argued that secular humanism and Marxism-Leninism qualify as religions. These claims are worth considering, especially since, if atheism itself, or a certain atheistic worldview, is indeed a religion, then the question of the salvation of atheists might well be subsumed under a general Catholic theology of religions, rather than necessitating a specific theology of atheism.

First of all, it can be stated categorically that atheism itself cannot be a religion. Atheism is, after all, simply the absence of belief in the existence of God. For precisely the same reason, theism is not a religion either. Certainly, theism – belief in the existence of God (or gods) – is a component of many of the world's religions. Likewise, as we have seen, atheism too can be part of a religion. To think that atheism or theism is itself a religion, however, would be to commit a category mistake. On the other hand, if Theravada Buddhism and Jainism may well be genuine atheistic religions, then what about humanism or Marxism-Leninism? Such suggestions are not, it is worth stressing, the preserve of *tu-quoque*-ing theologians. Gray's appraisal of humanism was noted above. And Sam Harris is eager to attribute communist atrocities to the supposedly religious natures of Stalinism and Maoism, despite the atheism of both *Weltanschauungen* ([2004] 2006: 78; [2006] 2007: 41). It is worth noting, however, that for both writers, 'religion' is used as a term of abuse. As such, their appraisals of what does, or does not, count as a religion must be treated with caution. This is particularly clear in Harris' case. According to him, for example, Buddhism – of which, unlike communism, he approves – is 'not a religion of faith, or a religion at all, in the Western sense', apparently *because* of its atheism. This leads him to berate 'millions of Buddhists' (along with, implicitly, hundreds of religious studies scholars) for ignorantly supposing otherwise ([2004] 2006: 283 n. 12).

Much rests, of course, on how 'religion' is defined. This is, of course, a controversial issue. According to Peter Clarke and Peter Byrne, for instance:

> There are three initial sources of doubt about the possibility of producing a satisfactory operational definition of 'religion'. They relate to conflicts and unclarities in the ordinary use of 'religion'; the confused meaning left to the word from its history; and the obvious divergence in scholarly purposes and approaches to the definition of 'religion'. (1993: 4–5)

As they further point out, even 'ordinary use tolerates conflicts in the meaning of "religion" quite happily: it would be correct in ordinary English to say both that China of the 1970s had no religion and, in another context, that Maoism had become the religion of the Chinese Republic in that period' (ibid.: 5). Scholarly usage is no more sharply defined. At its broadest, as on some sociologists' functional definitions (that is, loosely speaking, those defining religions by what they *do* in a society, rather than what they substantively *are*), religion may be found in several surprising places – not least, to quote from a recent German article, in the 'secular liturgies' enacted at football stadia, and in the modern-day 'cult of brand-names [which is] a form of icon veneration' (Gräb 2007: 86). Others go further, presuming all questions of an existential or ethical nature to be *de facto* religious ones. In this vein, Edward Bailey gives as a criterion for his own notion of *implicit religion*: 'the presence of commitment, *of any kind*'

(1998: 18). This is not necessarily illegitimate, provided it is clear that one intends 'religion' in a specifically sociological, functional sense. But even then, as other sociologists have pointed out, the word can be unhelpful. As Voas and Crockett have it, criticizing Grace Davie's wide application of the word 'religious': 'Such a manoeuvre begs the question; believers may assert that these issues are "surely religious," but no one else is obliged to agree. If we expand the scope of religion by definitional fiat we obscure the phenomenon we should be studying' (Voas and Crockett 2005: 13; see also Bruce 2002: 200–3; and Nielsen 1970: 32–3).

At the other end of the definitional spectrum, however, lies an equal danger: the elevation of a single, substantive criterion to the status of a necessary (or even sufficient) condition for 'religion', thereby excluding a number of, otherwise apparently exemplary, examples of religions. Most famous among such approaches are those defining 'religion' in terms of belief in the existence either of a God or gods, or more generally, supernatural agents or entities of any kind. The nineteenth-century anthropologist E. B. Tylor's famous formulation of 'belief in Spiritual Beings' is a case in point ([1871] 1903: 424; see Pals 2006: 26). Taking Tylor at face value (as he is, rightly or wrongly, typically taken), this lone criterion is both necessary and sufficient for religion. Hence religion is present not only where God is believed in, but wherever any of a panoply of paranormal beings (ghosts, demons, sprites) are too. One need not, of course, go so far as Tylor. But even if one heavily qualifies his definition, Émile Durkheim's criticism nevertheless retains its force: 'there are great religions' – he later cites Jainism and Theravada Buddhism – 'from which the idea of gods and spirits is absent, or at least, where it plays only a secondary and minor rôle' ([1912] 1976: 30).

Even from this cursory discussion, it is clear that defining religion is fraught with difficulties. Yet all is not necessarily lost. In the words of Clarke and Byrne:

> The great variety of competing definitions of 'religion' and the difficulties in proving any one to be correct point in our view not to the futility of the enterprise, but to the need to accept a looser, more informal mode of definition. A family resemblance definition appears to be indicated. (1993: 11)

Hence, although theistic or supernatural beliefs may be a typical feature of religions (e.g. Christianity, Judaism, Hinduism, Islam), a non-theistic system such as Theravada Buddhism is sufficiently analogous to these in other typical respects (it includes an elaborate ritual element, it has a 'professional' priesthood) as also to count. Membership of the genus 'religion' is, however, not hard and fast, and admits of many marginal or borderline cases. Both admitting Durkheim's counter-examples, and avoiding the extremer functional definitions cited above, questions thus arise as to the possibility of a modern, Western, atheistic member of the family of *religions*. And in fact, at least one example, and by no means a marginal or borderline one, leaps immediately to mind: Auguste Comte's 'Religion of Humanity'.

According to the French atheist Comte, one of sociology's founding fathers in the nineteenth century: 'While the Protestants and deists have always attacked religion in the name of God, we must discard God, once and for all, in the name of religion' (quoted in Lubac [1944] 1995: 173–4). In God's place, Comte sought to install Humanity, 'the Great Being', as the object of worship for 'the only real and complete religion' (ibid.: 149). Comte did not intend this in any figurative or poetic sense. This was indeed to be a *religion* of humanity, replete with scriptures and dogmas taken from Comte's own writings; rituals, liturgies, a full nine sacraments, and thrice-daily private devotions; churches and cathedrals (Notre Dame was to become 'the great Temple of the West'); saints and icons; missionaries, priests (Comte's *Catéchisme positive* specified 100,000 worldwide), 'Metropolitans', and even a Paris-based pontificate – the first incumbent of which would, of course, be Comte himself (Wernick 2001: 2–5; Campbell 1971: 63–70). Not surprisingly, the Religion of Humanity was, at least on the magnitude which Comte had envisaged, 'a complete, even preposterous, failure' (Wernick 2001: 5). Even so, Comte was not without followers, and defunct temples and chapels 'to humanity' may still be visited in France. In Brazil, where Comte's religion enjoyed relative success, there remains at least one still-operating 'Positivist Church'.[4]

On Clarke and Byrne's 'family resemblance' schema, *la religion de l'Humanité*, since it self-consciously imitates Catholic Christianity in most respects, may unambiguously be deemed a religion. The possibility of a modern, Western, atheistic religion is thus established. There is no reason, a priori, to assume that it must be the only one.

---

[4] See: <http://www.igrejapositivistabrasil.org.br/english/>. Accessed on 15 October 2008.

What, then, of Marxism-Leninism and secular humanism? The religious studies scholar Ninian Smart, in a standard textbook on religious experience, specifically identified these two as 'rival[ling] religions in certain respects' (1996: ix):

> These two new movements fulfil many roles played by religion. This is especially true of Marxism: it has a set of doctrines to explain the whole of reality, it has a policy for realizing a future 'heaven on earth,' it has grown its own form of public ceremonial, and so on. It would therefore be wrong to describe the religious experience of mankind without trying to understand these new rivals to religions. (Ibid.: 3)

The issue of Marxism-Leninism's parallels to religion has been explored in some depth. For example, in the Soviet Union rites and ceremonies were introduced to supersede those of the Orthodox Church. To replace Christmas, a 'Great Winter Festival' was inaugurated on 6 January, the Orthodox New Year (and the day when 'Grandfather Frost', whom the Soviets retained, brings children presents), complete with red stars atop erstwhile-Christmas trees (Thrower 1992: 61). Also, following earlier, failed attempts at introducing 'Red Baptisms' and 'Red Marriages', Khrushchev had Soviet ceremonies devised for baby namings and marriages, housed in purpose-built 'Palaces' (Bercken 1989: 44–7). The post-mortem apotheosis of Lenin – whose writings, along with Marx's, were accorded canonical status – must also be mentioned. Against his own express wishes, Lenin's corpse was preserved and presented in the manner of an Orthodox saint. Pilgrimages to his tomb, which bore the inscription 'Lenin: The Saviour of the World', were actively encouraged. Schoolchildren learnt songs depicting Lenin as 'the man who did not die', and in some quarters hopes were even expressed that Soviet science might one day resurrect him (see Thrower 1992: 77–92; Bercken 1989: 49–54).

Concerning secular humanism, on the other hand, things are not so straightforward. In its weakest and probably most widespread usage, '(secular) humanism' denotes little more than a vague commitment to doing good, often accompanied by an ill-defined 'not-Godism'. Here, humanist is often a handy euphemism for those who are non-religious, but who shy away from the description 'atheist'. In its more considered expressions, however, humanism is allied to a specific ethical outlook, a promethean stance against (religious) 'unreason' and 'de-humanization', which incorporates both optimism regarding humanity's moral and rational capabilities, and a belief in moral progress (patterned, sometimes explicitly, on modern scientific progress). It is the latter, in particular, which motivates Gray's indictment: 'Humanism is not a science, but religion – the post-Christian faith that humans can make a world better than any in which they have so far lived' ([2002] 2003: xiii). In its more organized manifestations, moreover (manifestations with which, though, the majority of those who identify as 'humanists' have little or no contact), secular humanism can possess both a ministerial and a ritual dimension. Harvard University has had a 'Humanist Chaplain' for over thirty years. The British Humanist Association in the UK, and the Humanist Society in the USA, train and accredit 'humanist celebrants' to preside at a range of humanist ceremonies: baby namings, marriages/civil partnerships, funerals, and memorials. Although flexible, these generally comprise elements recognizable from their religious, and especially Christian, counterparts (see Fowler 1999: 282–309). The BHA's Baby Naming 'liturgy', for example, includes godparents ('supporting adults'), and a humanist *Credo*:

> The centre of our concern is happiness, well-being and self-realisation of the human individuals that make up the world community. But the human community is made up of feeling individuals. On this occasion we are welcoming one special child, [name]. It is she who has just been born. Humanists see her, in common with all individuals, as an end in herself. (Wilson 1995: 21)

Needless to say, most humanists would deny that these are religious ceremonies, and that secular humanism itself is, in any sense, a religion. Jeaneane Fowler, in *Humanism: Beliefs and Practices*, forcibly rejects any such suggestion:

> I cannot see why, in the third millennium, Humanism has to have any connection with religion at all, even if in the past, it was slow to shake off certain religious dimensions. [...] Any principles suggested for Humanism have been formulated with care to avoid over definition of the term, and with similar care to avoid the kind of dogmatism of language so pervasive in religious creeds. [...] Moreover, from what has been said so far, the sheer diversity of expression and beliefs of those who call themselves Humanists militates against any toeing of a specific general party line. (1999: 31)

On the one hand, Fowler's points are well made. It is not surprising that non-religious people should wish to mark life's defining moments with a sense of occasion. (Not forgetting that many people who do define themselves religiously, even if only on their census returns, only venture into their respective places of worship for these events.[5]) The fact that such occasions have hitherto been dominated by religious groups does not prove that, by moving into this territory, secular humanism is thereby a religion. But on the other hand, the simple fact that a group defines itself in opposition to religion(s), does not necessarily mean that it is not itself one (or something very like). After all, Karl Barth's insistence that not only is Christianity not a religion, but is instead the 'happy reversal and elimination of all religion' ([1963] 1971b: 31), has yet to be heeded by religious studies scholars. Note too, in the quotation above, the conception of religion from which Fowler distinguishes humanism. Humanism cannot be a religion, she implies, since it avoids the 'dogmatism of language so pervasive in religious creeds', and exhibits 'diversity of expression and beliefs'. Given that only very few of the major world religions make significant use of credal statements, whether dogmatic or otherwise, and that *all* contain a decuman 'diversity of expression and beliefs', Fowler's point demonstrates nothing. If one defines 'religion' as a caricature of Tridentine Catholicism, then of course humanism is not one. But then neither is very much else, least of all actual Tridentine Catholicism (the diversity of whose expression and beliefs put modern humanism firmly in the shade).

Both Marxism-Leninism and secular humanism, at least in some of their forms, bear certain similarities to actual, historical religions. At the very least, therefore, the question of their *being* religions ought not to be dismissed offhand. But in neither case, however, are they self-evidently or unambiguously so (unlike, arguably, the Comtean Religion of Humanity). Thus James Thrower, from whose research much of the above information on Marxism-Leninism was taken, avers 'it would be difficult, if not impossible, to call Marxism-Leninism a religion' (1992: 111). Regarding secular humanism, a similar conclusion is reached by Ian Markham. While admitting that humanism 'is not a religion', Markham nevertheless accepts that 'curiously it does share certain features with religion' (2000: 6). It is on issues like

---

[5] According to the 2007 British Social Attitudes Survey, among those who claim either to have a religion, or to have been brought up in one, 57.5% *never* attend a place of worship except for weddings, funerals, and baptisms. Data available online at: http://www.britsocat.com/>. Accessed on 29 June 2010.

these that Clarke and Byrne's 'family resemblance' model displays what is both its strength and weakness. Avoiding essentialist definitions, it presents the concept of religion as 'an open-textured one: a concept without fixed, clear-cut boundaries and whose instances are united by overlapping analogies' (1993: 11). However, this subtlety prevents clear-cut judgements as to what is, or is not, a religion (while at the same time presupposing that there are such unambiguous cases, with which to define one's 'family' in the first place). Furthermore, all groups, systems, or organizations surely bear some resemblance, however small, to one religion or another. All presumably, therefore, belong in the 'family', even if only as very distant relations. These considerations do not, however, revoke the model's general utility.

Clearly though, this is not a religious studies monograph, and whether or not Marxism-Leninism or (especially) secular humanism counts as a religion, while relevant, is only indirectly so. The issue has been worth exploring in some depth, both as part of a general desire to understand contemporary atheism before theologizing about it, and more particularly, in connection with Catholic understandings of salvation. The possibility was mooted above that, if certain forms of atheism are indeed religions, then at least the adherents of these might already be accounted for under a general theology of religions. However, even if our excursus *had* yielded a clear positive, it would not in fact have been much help. Once again, LG itself is the arbiter. LG 16 explicitly admits the possibility of salvation for members of non-Christian religions. Note, though, that this possibility is not premised on their being members of a *religion*, but rather, on the relationship with *God* (and thus with Christ) implied by that membership. To give the sentences immediately preceding those already quoted:

> In the first place is that people to whom testaments and promises were given, and out of whom Christ was born according to the flesh (cf. Rom. 9.4–5); according to election, a people most dear on account of their fathers, for without repentance are the gifts and calling of God (cf. Rom. 11.28–9). But the plan of salvation also includes those who recognize the Creator, in first place amongst whom are the Muslims. These profess themselves to hold the faith of Abraham, and together with us they adore the one, merciful God, who is to judge men on the last day. Nor is God himself far from those who in shadows and images seek the unknown God, since he gives to all men life and breath and all things (cf. Acts 17.25–8). (AS III/viii: 796)

Being 'religious', or belonging to 'a religion', is not what counts here.[6] Even if Comte's Religion of Humanity, or Marxism-Leninism, or secular humanism *are* (or can be) religions, this is apparently immaterial to the question of their adherents' salvation.

CAN ONE *REALLY* BE AN ATHEIST?

One final preliminary. The connection between religious (and usually, specifically Christian) belief and positive atheism is frequently commented upon, especially in theological literature. This takes several forms. Modern atheism is seen as a product of Christian thought, whether simply as a reaction to it, or more strongly, as an outworking of its own inner development (Buckley 1987; Buckley 2004; Hyman 2010). Relatedly, some see atheism as 'a fighting creed which, in order to be itself, needs the assertion its denial so violently strikes out' (Borne [1957] 1961: 49), or as 'always parasitic upon a particular theism' (Kennedy 2006: 100). Such views are not restricted to believers. Gray, for example, asseverates: 'Unbelief is a move in a game whose rules are set by believers' ([2002] 2003: 126). And Comte, although assuredly an atheist by the criteria adopted herein, thought that 'confirmed atheists can be regarded as the most inconsistent of theologians, since they occupy themselves with the same questions but reject the only suitable approach to them' (quoted in Lubac [1944] 1995: 165).

Going one step farther, one meets with Denys Turner's suggestion that 'such atheists are but what are called "negative" theologians, but attenuated ones', and 'are, as it were, but theologians in an arrested condition of denial' (2002a: 7, 8; see also 2002b: 15–16). For Turner, these atheists do not deny God, but rather a succession of idols. It is this position, where 'atheism' normally ends, from which proper theology begins. A similar position is evinced by Cardinal Scola, for whom atheism 'liberates the field for the vital arrival of God' (Scola and Flores d'Arcais 2008: 44–5). In an analogous vein, in Dostoevsky's *The Idiot*, Myshkin tells Rogozhin of a train journey he once passed in

---

[6] See also *Dominus Iesus* 21 (AAS 92 [2000]: 762), where it is God's work *in* the world religions that is the central point, rather than their intrinsic 'religiosity'. Note that this may also be the case in non-theistic religions.

the company of 'really a very learned man [...] a true scholar' who was an atheist:

> He doesn't believe in God. Only one thing struck me: it was as if that was not at all what he was talking about all the while, and it struck me precisely because before, too, however many unbelievers I've met, however many books I've read on the subject, it has always seemed to me that they were talking or writing books that were not at all about that, though it looked as if it was about that. ([1868] 2001: 219)

After describing a later encounter he had with a piously joyful peasant woman, Myshkin returns to his erstwhile theme:

> Listen, Parfyon, you asked me earlier, here is my answer: the essence of religious feeling doesn't fit in with any reasoning, with any crimes and trespasses, or with any atheisms; there's something else here that's not that, and it will be eternally not that; there's something in it that atheisms eternally glance off, and they will eternally be talking *not about that*. (Ibid.: 221)

For de Lubac, this is 'a subtle and far-reaching observation' ([1944] 1995: 344). The atheist, it is claimed, either does not or cannot reject the *true* God of Christianity. Instead, he or she rejects only false gods or idols. For Karl Rahner, 'atheism essentially lives on the misconceived ideas of God from which theism in its actual historical forms inevitably suffers' (1975a: 48–9). According to Antonio Pérez-Esclarín, 'atheism may actually be the rejection of false notions of God. It may actually represent a real form of solid faith' (1980: 53; see also Saint-Arnaud 2010). Similarly, Jürgen Moltmann avers that the authentically scandalous nature of the Cross 'is often better recognized by non-Christians and atheists than by religious Christians, because it astonishes and offends them' ([1973] 2001: 28). And later, referring to Karamazovian or Camusian 'protest atheism', he affirms: 'Here atheism demonstrates itself to be the brother of theism' (ibid.: 228). Lastly, Bishop Tikhon, in a section of Dostoevsky's *Demons* that the Russian censors forbade to be published, avouches to Stavrogin that: 'A complete atheist stands on the next-to-last upper step to the most complete faith' ([1872] 2000: 688).

Evidently, these ideas boast a strong pedigree. So ingrained are they in theological discussions of atheism, in fact, that a work of this nature cannot simply pass them by. Let it be said first of all, then, that there is *something* in this kind of approach. Atheists do indeed often reject false images of God (and in this, it must be said, they are indeed on a higher 'step' than many, usually well-meaning, Christians). This is not, furthermore, without a partial patristic precedent. The second-century apologist Justin Martyr, riposting charges of 'atheism' levelled against Christians, confessed in his *First Apology* that 'We do proclaim ourselves atheists as regards those whom you call gods' ([*c.* 150] 1948: 38–9). (He qualifies this, however, by adding 'but not with respect to the Most True God'.) This point was echoed by the twentieth-century Dominican theologian Marie-Dominique Chenu, referring to a group of agnostics who invited him to their meetings:

> One of the group scoffingly quoted the old catechism he had learnt by rote as a child: 'If that is your God', I broke in earnestly, 'you have every right to reject him, and I am an atheist, just like you.' (1975: 141)

Unexpectedly, Richard Dawkins is in general agreement with both Justin and Chenu:

> I have found it an amusing strategy, when asked whether I am an atheist, to point out that the questioner is also an atheist when considering Zeus, Apollo, Amon Ra, Mithras, Baal, Thor, Wotan, the Golden Calf and the Flying Spaghetti Monster. I just go one god further. (2006: 53)[7]

Of course, in the opinion of many critics, Dawkins' 'one god further' is itself another false one: that is to say, the God in whom Dawkins does not believe is not the one in whom Christians do. Assuming that this is true, however, does it necessarily follow that Dawkins and his compatriots are not *really* atheists?

Two responses can be made. Firstly, there is no reason for thinking that atheists *must* 'eternally be talking *not about that*'. A person can certainly understand what it is that Christians mean by the word 'God', and yet not believe that this 'God' exists. Obvious examples include Roberto Ardigo and Anthony Kenny. Both were Catholic priests and eminent philosophers of religion, who came to believe either that God does *not* exist (for Ardigo, who went on to be a distinguished positivist philosopher), or that there are no especially

---

[7] The logic of this strategy should not be pushed too far, however. On the same principle, a creationist could argue that Dawkins too is an 'anti-evolutionist', since he rejects the evolutionary theories of Stephen Jay Gould and others. The creationist, of course, just goes one evolutionary theory further.

compelling reasons for believing that he does (for Kenny, who became and remains an eloquent proponent of agnosticism). Joachim Kahl, a sharp critic of religious belief who was himself once a Lutheran pastor, sums it up well: 'A non-Christian can certainly understand the gospel, take it seriously and reject it' (1971: 22). Frederick Copleston, the Jesuit philosopher, fundamentally agreed:

> [I]t cannot be safely assumed that what an atheist rejects is simply a caricature of the God of Christian faith. There are no doubt cases in which this assumption is verified. [...] But it is by no means all atheists who are ignorant of what Christians believe or, for that matter, of metaphysical ideas of God. If an atheist finds logical difficulties in statements about God, it does not necessarily follow that he is concerned with a caricature. For even a convinced believer can be perfectly well aware of problems arising out of talk about God. It is too easy a way of evading the problem of atheism, it we claim that what atheists reject is a caricature or an idol, but not *God*. The claim may be true in a good many cases; but it seems to me an exaggeration to assert it is always true. (1973: 26)

Only if one, in a crude and philosophically dubious variant of the ontological argument, affirms that the predicate 'existence' is essential to the Christian definition of God, can it rightly be claimed a priori that it is only false gods in which one may genuinely disbelieve.

Secondly, it is further questionable whether one needs completely to understand something in order properly to reject it. It may well be, for example, that the *specific* conception of God that Dawkins attacks is not that of (say) orthodox Catholic theology. But along with this specific rejection, however, goes a wider, general rejection of (as he puts it): 'Gods, all gods, anything and everything supernatural, wherever and whenever they have been or will be invented' (2006: 36). Many atheists have never heard of Numenius of Apamea or Moses Maimonides, let alone be intimately acquainted with their understandings of 'God' (indeed, why should they have?). It is nonetheless true, however, that they *reject* the Numenian and Maimonidean 'Gods', along with every other conception of 'God' – including any *true* one, howsoever that term is understood. In precisely the same way, the Christian need not be an expert on each specific mode of atheism in order to reject 'atheism-in-general'.

As to the thesis that atheism and religion are 'eternal companions' (Jeffner 1988: 53), recently reinforced by Taylor (2007: 591–2), there is again a sense in which this is quite correct. If by atheism one means either the explicit denial of the existence of a God or gods, or a philosophical system arising out of such a denial, then this rejection will naturally be *expressed* in reaction to the prevailing theism(s). Obviously, it is no coincidence that the beliefs of European and American atheists have been typically expressed in anti-Christian terms. Nor is it a coincidence that Islam has recently also begun to feature prominently in their critiques. (Atheists too, in a certain sense, participate in the wider ecumenism!) However, during the period of the Counter-Reformation, Catholicism was frequently expressed in reaction to Protestantism. But it would be absurd to suggest, on this basis, that without Protestantism there could be no Catholicism.

Of course, if there were no theists, then one might expect explicit rejections of theism – i.e. positive atheism – to fall into disuse. (Although this does not follow necessarily. It is a central part of Buckley's argument, for example, that Christian writers vociferously denounced atheism at a time when there were, in fact, no atheists. And in fact, the so-called 'New Atheism' arose when, in Europe at least, standard indicators of both religious believing and belonging were at an all-time low.[8]) But that does not mean, of course, that there will no longer be any atheists – at least, not in the sense in which the word is used herein. If an atheist is a person who is without a belief in God, then if there are no theists, it does not follow that nobody would be an atheist. On the contrary, *everybody* would be one. Moreover, several recent atheist writers have expressed boredom with the primarily *negative* role that atheists have generally assumed. Michel Onfray, echoing Marx, writes:

> If we could get past Christian atheism, we might arrive at a true *atheistic atheism* (no redundancy implied). The term encompasses more than negation of God and of a part of the values derived from him. [...] *Atheistic atheism* would place morality and politics on a new base, one that is not nihilist but post-Christian. Its aim is neither to reconstruct churches nor to destroy them, but to build elsewhere and in a different

---

[8] This is well illustrated by the statistician Peter Brierley's 2006 *Pulling Out of the Nosedive: A Contemporary Picture of Churchgoing* – published the same year as *The God Delusion* – which was tellingly greeted as a sign of hope by church leaders. Brierley's figures neither showed that British church attendance was rising, nor that it was stable. Instead, for the first time in decades, the *rate of decline* was decreasing: 'We are coming out of the nosedive, but no U-turn is yet in sight – we are still dropping' (2006: 18). On this in relation to the rise of the New Atheism, see Bullivant 2010.

way, to build something else for those no longer willing to dwell intellectually in places that have already done long service. ([2005] 2007: 57-8)

Onfray correctly recognizes that while atheism has traditionally occupied itself with theomachy, this is not essential: a genuinely 'atheistic atheism' – that is, one whose expression is not conditioned solely, or at all, by the prevailing theism(s) – is indeed possible.

CONCLUSION

The purpose of this chapter has been twofold. Firstly, it has clarified and justified my specific usage of a word that will be encountered on almost every page: *atheist*. Secondly, it has allowed space for a critical engagement with a number of frequently encountered ideas in the scholarly literature devoted to contemporary atheism. Both enquiries have been shaped, implicitly or explicitly, by this book's central theme: the salvation of atheists, as conceived within Catholic dogmatic constraints. Several of the issues discussed here will prove instrumental to the later, more directly theological chapters. In addition, this chapter is intended to meet Finngeir Hiorth's (partially) justified criticism: 'Christianity is known for many things, but not for its contribution to or analysis of atheism' (2003: 171). According to GS 19, 'atheism may be numbered among the most serious matters of our time and merits more careful investigation'. The brief studies offered above are a modest contribution to that very task.

2

Atheism and Salvation from Pius IX to Vatican II

Although its roots may be found long before, it was not until the 1800s that atheism arose as a mass phenomenon of pressing social, historical, and theological importance.[1] Even then, it took the Catholic Church until 1878 to address atheism directly in a magisterial pronouncement (see Kasper [1982] 1984: 49–50). Leo XIII's encyclical *Inscrutabili Dei Consilio* numbers 'complete forgetfulness of things eternal' among 'the evils by which the human race is afflicted from all sides', and which form 'a deadly kind of plague, which infects the inmost recesses of human society' (ASS 10 [1878]: 585–6; see also *Au Milieu des Solicitudes* [ASS 24 (1891/2): 527]). This document set the tone for eight decades of papal teaching. Indeed, Pius XI might have been speaking for an almost unbroken line of popes, stretching from Leo XIII to his own successor Pius XII, when he wrote in 1937: 'During our pontificate we too have frequently, threateningly and with urgent insistence denounced today's increasing deluge of impiety' (AAS 29 [1937]: 67). Pius XII himself, not to be outdone, accused atheism of 'wretchedly polluting' Christian morality in 1956's *Haurietis Aquas* (AAS 48 [1956]: 313), while denouncing its 'lethal tenets' in 1958's *Meminisse Iuvat* (AAS 50 [1958]: 452). Only six years later, however, Vatican II ratified LG 16's optimism regarding the salvation of atheists. GS 19–21 was promulgated the following year, offering a sympathetic overview of the causes and varieties of modern atheism, admitting that 'believers can have no small part in the rise

---

[1] That is not to say, of course, that there were *no* atheists prior to this time; but rather, that atheism was not yet socially pervasive (Thrower 1971: 97–112; Buckley 2004: 29–43; McGrath 2004: 22–45).

of atheism', and inviting its contemporary adherents to 'a sincere and prudent dialogue'. In GS 22, moreover, the inclusion in the redemptive work of Christ of 'all men of good will in whose hearts grace is active in an invisible manner' (AS IV/vii: 745) was explicitly affirmed.

Evidently, from Pius XII's 'lethal tenets' to the Council's optimism regarding eternal life, profound developments are manifest in the Catholic understanding of atheism; developments which had, in fact, been in progress for at least three decades. These are crucial for properly understanding LG 16 and GS 19–21 – and hence, for this study as a whole. These conciliar texts form both the start and endpoint of this investigation, and a good deal will be said about them, in this chapter and all subsequent ones, both directly and in passing. Here the focus will be on their gestation and context, both at Vatican II itself, and in the decades leading up to it. Before looking at the Council's treatment of atheism and salvation directly, its genealogy in the preconciliar period will be divined along two separate but related trajectories: (i) the debates surrounding the salvation of non-Catholics in general; and (ii) Catholicism's engagement with, and subsequent reappraisal of, atheism and (crucially) atheists. Several hypotheses concerning the salvation of atheists will then be examined, before the conciliar texts themselves are discussed in detail.

SALVATION AND 'THE OTHERS'

According to Pius IX's 1854 allocution *Singulari Quadem*, 'it is certainly to be held by faith that: outside the Apostolic Roman Church, no one is able to be saved; that this is the only ark of salvation; [and] that whoever will not have entered, will perish in the flood'. However, he continues:

> [B]ut equally, it is to be held for certain that they who labour in ignorance of the true religion, if this ignorance is invincible, are not bound by any fault in this matter in the eyes of the Lord. Now truly, who would arrogate so much to himself, as to be able to designate the limits of this kind of ignorance, because of the reason and variety of peoples, regions, natural dispositions, and a great many other things? ([1854] 1864: 626)

These criteria, which Pius repeated in his 1863 encyclical *Quanto Conficiamur Moerore* ([1863] 1867: 613–14), and which also featured in the *Schema de ecclesia* prepared by the First Vatican Council (see Sullivan 1992: 120–2), rapidly became recognized as the *sine quibus non* for Catholic enquiries into the salvation of those (apparently) outside the Church. Naturally, Pius' chief intention was to emphasize the patristic axiom *Extra Ecclesiam nulla salus*, 'no salvation outside the Church'. Nevertheless, both by qualifying his main point with the scholastic principle of *ignorantia invincibilis*, and by refusing to define its parameters, the pope allowed a restricted, but significant, latitude to future theologians – a latitude that was, as has been demonstrated by others, fully mandated by the tradition (see D'Costa 1990; Sullivan 1992). This issue will be further discussed in chapter four.

Writing in the early twentieth century, the French Jesuit Jean Bainvel noted 'a certain uneasiness' felt by contemporary Catholics when contemplating the formula *Extra Ecclesiam*:

> Many there are who wish, though they do not openly avow it, that the Catholic Church would be silent on this point and allow this dogma – since it really is a dogma – peacefully to slumber in the old Latin tomes, unmolested and undisturbed. (1917: iii; see also Lombardi [1942] 1956: xiii; and Congar [1959] 1961: 33)

The roots of such disquiet had arguably been growing, albeit very gradually, since the great geographical discoveries of the late fifteenth and sixteenth centuries. In strange new worlds to the east and west, European missionaries were repeatedly confronted with, to quote Congar, 'hitherto unknown peoples who were civilized *and good*' (Congar [1959] 1961: 97; see also Hill Fletcher 2006: 271–2). Naturally, even medieval Christendom's most isolated denizens were *aware* of the existence of non-Christian peoples. But Jews and Muslims, the subjects of pogroms and Crusades, could psychologically very easily be dismissed as having uniformly, and culpably, rejected the gospel. Yet the same could not plausibly be thought of the vast swathes of humanity who either had never heard of Christ and the Church, or had done so only from the lips of murderous *conquistadores*. Later, the Reformation too brought Catholics, at least in northern Europe, into daily contact with other, equally moral and sincere Christians who were outside the Church. And while these processes began centuries before, the late nineteenth and the early twentieth centuries witnessed their unprecedented acceleration. The beginnings of the media revolution, increased travel and immigration, the lifting of legal restrictions on inter-denominational marriage, and (of course) the rising tide of unbelief, all played their part in confronting Catholics – *existentially*, as it were – with normal, decent people who were not of their faith (Congar [1959] 1961: 27; Magrath 1968; see also *Nostra Aetate* 1; AS IV/v: 616). To put it simply, 'no salvation outside the Church' was all very well in abstraction, but what about when applied to one's colleagues, neighbours, friends, and even relatives?

In light of this new situation, but refusing to forsake the traditional doctrine concerning the Church's necessity for salvation, many theologians began to probe the possibility of a renewed understanding, one which could account for these new, glaring 'facts' about non-Catholics. Karl Adam, then professor of dogmatics in the Catholic Faculty at Tübingen, devoted a chapter of *The Spirit of Catholicism* (1924) to 'The Church Necessary for Salvation'. Naturally, he affirms the infallibility of *Extra Ecclesiam* ([1924] 1969: 83–6). But he cautions that one must understand it 'as the Church would have it understood'; that is, in light of the rest of Catholic doctrine (ibid.: 188). He correctly points out that 'the declaration [...] is not aimed at individual non-Catholics, at any persons as persons, but at non-Catholic churches and communions, in so far as they are non-Catholic communions' (ibid.: 189). Rather, 'Its purpose is to formulate positively the truth that there is but one Body of Christ and therefore but one Church which possesses and imparts the grace of Christ in its fullness' (ibid.). For Adam, non-Catholic Christian denominations, being not merely *extra*, but *contra Ecclesiam*, cannot be ways of salvation. But this does not prevent their members from being among the 'other sheep I have that are not of this fold' (Jn 10.16). In this vein also, he points to Jesus' refusal to condemn the man who was not one of the disciples' followers, but who was exorcizing in his name (Mk 9.38–9; Adam [1924] 1969: 190; see also Küng [1962] 1963: 64–7). Adam stresses the traditional teaching that grace is operative outside of the Catholic Church, and even affirms the possibility of there being saints within Orthodox and Protestant communions. Turning now to non-Christians, and specifically Jews and Muslims, Adam draws on the fact that, since at least the time of St Ambrose, the Church has recognized the validity of a *baptismus flaminis* (baptism of desire) for catechumens who die before being received into the Church. For the invincibly ignorant, of course, an explicit desire to be baptized into the Church is not possible. Instead, Adam suggests the possibility of an *implicit* baptism of desire:

> By that is meant that perfect love, evoked and supported by the redeeming grace of Jesus, has power to sanctify the soul, and that that soul so decisively affirms the will of God that it would at once receive baptism, if it knew of that sacrament or could receive it. ([1924] 1969: 193; see also Bainvel 1917: 56–7)

He also emphasizes the role of conscience: 'Wherever conscience is astir, wherever men are alive to God and His Holy Will, there and at the same time the grace of Christ cooperates and lays in the soul the seeds of supernatural life' ([1924] 1969: 193). Lastly, Adam draws attention to the fact that, historically, it is often Rome – 'Rome that is so violently attacked for her intolerance', as he pointedly remarks – that intervenes to prevent too rigoristic interpretations of the Church's salvific necessity (ibid.: 190). This was as true in the third century, when Pope Stephen I opposed Cyprian over the validity of Novatianist baptisms, as it was in the seventeenth and eighteenth centuries, when Popes Innocent X, Alexander VI, and Clement XI all condemned Jansenism (see Sullivan 1992: 100–1). Crucially here, it was also true in the twentieth century, with the Holy Office's reprimand of Leonard Feeney.

Feeney, a New England Jesuit, was appointed in the early 1940s as the spiritual director of the 'St Benedict Center', a Catholic pastoral and educational institution in Cambridge, Massachusetts, founded in 1940 by three laypeople including the future Jesuit cardinal, Avery Dulles (Carey 2007: 554–7). Under Feeney's increasingly dominant tutelage, the Center became a *locus* for self-professedly 'traditional' Catholics, defining itself in opposition to American Catholicism's perceived compromises with liberal, profane culture. These compromises included, naturally, dialogue and cooperation with non-Catholics, and by 1947 the Center's associates were extolling a literal, exclusivist interpretation of *Extra Ecclesiam*, one which occluded any implicit baptism of desire (O'Dea 1961). By the late 1940s, however, it was not merely theologians who had been endorsing the possibility of an implicit *votum ecclesiae* on the part of non-Catholics. Pius XII's 1943 encyclical *Mystici Corporis*, while stating that only those 'who have received baptism and profess the true faith' are 'really (*reapse*) members of the church', admits of others, that 'by a certain unconscious desire and wish (*inscio quodam voto ac desiderio*) they may be related to the Mystical Body of the Redeemer' (AAS 35 [1943]:

202, 243). As such, in 1949, when Feeney denounced Boston's Archbishop Cushing as a heretic for espousing a similar doctrine, Rome's intervention was inevitable.[2] The resulting letter from the Holy Office to Cushing iterates, as did Adam, that:

> Among those things which the Church has always taught, and will never desist from teaching, is included that infallible principle by which we are informed that 'there is no salvation outside the Church'. However, this dogma is to be understood in the sense in which it is understood by the Church itself. (DH 3866; see Sullivan 1992: 136–7)

Most significantly, elaborating on *Mystici Corporis* (which it quotes extensively), it affirms:

> In order to obtain eternal salvation, it is not always required that someone be incorporated as a member of the Church in reality (*reapse*). But it is required that he at least adheres to it by a desire and wish (*voto et desiderio*). It is not always necessary that this desire is explicit, as is the case with catechumens. But when a man labours in invincible ignorance, God also accepts an implicit desire, so called because it is contained in the good disposition of soul by which a man wants his will to be conformed to God's will. (DH 3869)

Though Rome had spoken, for Feeney the case was not yet closed. Soon expelled from the Jesuits, he was eventually excommunicated in 1953 (AAS 45 [1953]: 100). As Congar wryly remarked: 'Thus a man who held, against the Church, that all those who are in fact outside the Church are debarred from salvation, finished up by being himself excluded from the Church by doing so: an odd situation!' ([1959] 1961: 102).

Vatican II's optimism regarding the possibility of salvation for non-Catholics, and how this gradually developed, should now be becoming clearer. Despite what the Council's detractors might allege, from earlier understandings of *Extra Ecclesiam* to LG 16 there is 'a continuity of essential principles, a development, a new and different expression of principles and their aim in a new and different historical context' (Congar 1979: 101). Before considering Catholicism's *rapprochement* with atheism, and then the conciliar texts themselves, it is worth delineating a further three, general contributions to the debate surrounding the salvation of non-Catholics, offered by French theologians

---

[2] The full and complex history of the 'Boston Heresy Case', which is beyond the scope of this monograph, is related in O'Dea 1961 and Carey 2007.

who were to be of paramount importance at the Council (and indeed, far beyond): Jean Daniélou, Henri de Lubac, and Yves Congar.

Daniélou, a Jesuit professor of Early Christian History at the *Institut Catholique de Paris* (and later, from 1969, a cardinal), broached the subject of salvation for those outside of both the Old and New Covenants in his 1956 study *Holy Pagans of the Old Testament*. Daniélou's work, as was often the case among proponents of the *nouvelle théologie*, while ostensibly a piece of purely historical and exegetical scholarship, was doubtlessly also intended as a contribution to contemporary debates. He appeals to Old Testament figures such as Noah, Abel, Enoch, and the Queen of Sheba, who 'did not belong either to the race or the religion of Israel', but whom scripture and tradition suggest are to be numbered among the saints ([1956] 1957: 1–2). According to Daniélou, therefore: 'Thus we are faced with a curious problem, that namely of people who are presented to us by Holy Writ as saints and yet are neither Jews nor Christians' (ibid.: 2). But if, despite being (concretely) members of 'idolatrous cults', the Queen of Sheba and others are saved, this can only be because they belonged, in some genuine sense, to the *Church*:

> If they were saved, then, it is because they were saved by Christ Who alone saves, Who alone sanctifies. Again, if they were saved, it is because they already belonged to the Church, for there is no salvation outside the Church.

He goes on, his words ringing with contemporary resonance:

> This obliges us therefore to accept the conclusion that the domain of Christ and of the Church extends beyond the limits of the explicit revelation of Christ and of the visible expansion of the Church. In every age and in every land there have been men who have believed in Christ without knowing Him and who have belonged 'invisibly to the Church'. (Ibid.: 9–10)

Daniélou's confrère Henri de Lubac published his first book, *Catholicism*, in 1938. It was profoundly influential, and will be considered in further detail below. Here, however, the chapter tellingly entitled 'Salvation Through the Church' is of specific interest. For de Lubac, 'The human race is one. By our fundamental nature and still more in virtue of our common destiny we are members of the same body' ([1938] 1964: 119). As such, non-Catholics 'In short, [...] can be saved because they are an integral part of that humanity which is to be saved' (ibid.: 123). This is a striking note, and one seemingly very different from the proposals already outlined. De Lubac emphasizes the prevalence of divine grace and mercy, operating at all times and among all peoples. This fact constitutes a genuine *offer* of salvation to all; an offer which is not, however, always accepted. Even prior to *Mystici Corporis* and the Holy Office's intervention in the so-called Boston Heresy Case, he could write:

> In spite of differing explanations of detail and with degrees of optimism or pessimism according to the variations of individual temperament, experience or theological tendencies, it is generally agreed nowadays, following the lead of the Fathers and the principles of St Thomas, that the grace of Christ is of universal application, and that no soul of good will lacks the concrete means of salvation, in the fullest sense of the word. There is no man, no 'unbeliever', whose supernatural conversion to God is not possible from the dawn of reason onwards. (Ibid.: 117)

Needless to say, for de Lubac, this grace, and the concomitant offer of salvation, is mediated exclusively through the Catholic Church: 'Thus this Church, which as the indivisible Body of Christ is identified with final salvation, as a visible and historical institution is the provident means of salvation. "In her alone mankind is re-fashioned and re-created"' (ibid.: 119–20). More will be said about de Lubac's theology of salvation, specifically in relation to atheists, later on. Here, though, it is worth finally quoting his reformulation of *Extra Ecclesiam nulla salus*:

> [I]f it is thought that in spite of all these considerations the formula 'outside the Church, no salvation' has still an ugly sound, there is no reason why it should not be put in a positive form and read, appealing to all men of good will, not 'outside the Church you are damned,' but 'it is by the Church and by the Church alone that you will be saved.' For it is through the Church that salvation will come, that it is already coming to mankind. (Ibid.: 126)

The Dominican Yves Congar advocated a similar approach to *Extra Ecclesiam*. In 1959's *The Wide World My Parish*, he notes that: 'the formula is no longer to be regarded as answering the question "Who will be saved?" but as answering the question "What is it that is commissioned to discharge the ministry of salvation?"' ([1959] 1961: 98; see also Congar 1957: 299–300). This genuine *development* within Catholic theology has, he argues, arisen from the Church's growing knowledge of, and acquaintance with, those (apparently) outside the Church. Expressing an insight of fundamental importance, Congar explains: 'The Church learns through contact with facts. [...] Truth remains unaltered; but it is grasped in a new and undoubtedly more adequate way when men and the world are known *as they are*, in an extent, age and goodness other than what has been believed of them previously' ([1959] 1961: 98). In common with de Lubac, Congar affirms the unity of humankind, and the fact that, in and through Christ and his Church, humanity has itself been redeemed. But also like de Lubac, Congar does not subscribe to universal salvation (ibid.: 70–2). All people can be saved, in that all, Catholics or not, are confronted with a genuine *offer* of salvation – an offer the acceptance of which presupposes faith in the triune God, even if that faith, or its object, are not recognized as such by its possessor (ibid.: 91, 94). The implicit means by which, especially in the case of atheists, this is possible, will be considered below.

Necessarily, the above paragraphs give only a scant overview of a remarkably productive few decades. Even among those agreeing that those formally outside the Catholic Church could indeed be saved, it was debated whether such people would be: 'inside' or 'outside'; 'united', 'ordained', or 'related' to; 'imperfectly', 'tendentially', 'invisibly', or 'potentially' members of; or belong 'invisibly', 'spiritually', or '*in voto*' to the Church (see Eminyan 1960). These distinctions are not, admittedly, unimportant. But their very multiplicity points to a far more significant fact – that, since the decades leading up to the Second Vatican Council, as Ratzinger later put it: 'The primary question is no longer the salvation of the "others," the theoretical possibility of which is assured; the actual guiding question is rather more, *how*, given this undeniable certainty, the absolute requirement of the Church and its faith is still to be understood' (1972: 153).

'FROM ANATHEMA TO DIALOGUE'

Roger Garaudy's phrase 'from anathema to dialogue',[3] while certainly an oversimplification, well captures the transition in Catholic

---

[3] The phrase forms the title of the French philosopher's book on 'the challenge of Marxist-Christian cooperation' (Garaudy 1967), which included an introduction by Rahner. Garaudy was, at that time, a leading light in the French Communist Party. He later became a Catholic (and later still, a Muslim).

theologians' attitudes towards atheism – not to mention (mainly Marxist) atheists' attitudes towards Catholicism – in the decades prior to Vatican II. During this period, for arguably the first time in history, Catholic priests and theologians began seriously to engage, socially and intellectually, with unbelievers. Unsurprisingly, these new perspectives demanded renewed theological understandings; the old caricatures of immoral, irrational atheists became ever harder to sustain. Contemporaneously with the latter two Pope Piuses' denunciations of atheism, a different, *pastoral* approach began gaining ground, primarily in France, Italy, and Germany (see Gallagher 1995: 30). The resulting optimism regarding the salvation of atheists, ratified by the Council, is naturally the primary focus here. Nevertheless, it is but a single facet of a much broader trend, and cannot properly be understood in isolation. The various forms of engagement will therefore be discussed, before broaching this specific issue.

The true beginnings of the dialogue between Catholics and atheists, and Marxists in particular, can be dated with some precision: 1934 to 1938, the era of the French 'Popular Front', a coalition of left-wing parties spearheaded by the French Communist Party (or PCF). This short and turbulent period had a number of notable repercussions. Among these, as David Curtis has argued, 'one facet was a *main tendue* ["outstretched hand"] to Catholics that the Party has never withdrawn' (1997: 1). In 1936 Maurice Thorez, the PCF's general secretary, proposed dialogue with Catholics (Bent 1971: 24). The intention was to reach beyond the Left's traditional, staunchly anti-clerical boundaries, and to cease alienating influential groups, including Catholic intellectuals and members of dynamic, socially committed youth movements like the *Jeunesse Ouvrière Chrétienne* (JOC), who might otherwise be sympathetic to the left-wing parties (Jackson 1988: 259). Irrespective of its political motivations, and whatever its other limitations, there can be no denying that this olive branch to French Catholicism marked a significant watershed. Organized dialogues, involving Christians and atheists actually *talking to* one another, started to be arranged. On the Catholic side, prior to the Council, such encounters were necessarily informal, unofficial affairs, which not infrequently met with great hostility from others within the Church (Arnal 1984b: 533). This did not, however, prevent them from happening.

La main tendue sparked a flurry of responses (see Curtis 1997: 151–62). The Jesuit philosopher Gaston Fessard published *La Main tendue. Le Dialogue catholique-communistique est-il possible?* (*'The outstretched hand': Is the Catholic–Communist dialogue possible?*) in 1937. Fessard's answer, drawing particularly on the 'existential' humanism of the young Marx, was a cautious, qualified 'yes'. The previous year, the lay Thomist philosopher Jacques Maritain had published his own 'remarkable work of "positive" anticommunism' *Humanisme intégrale*, which was itself partly based on Marxist concepts (for which it was, incidentally, criticized by Fessard). The Dominican journal *La Vie intellectuelle*, for which Marie-Dominique Chenu acted as censor, published a series of articles on Marxism in 1937–8. And during the same period, Jean Daniélou (who had previously met Sartre while at the Sorbonne) wrote two articles for *Chronique sociale de France* on the young Marx's humanism.

Catholic intellectuals were hence, again for the first time, engaging sincerely, in a non-polemical way, with some of the key figures of modern atheistic thought.[4] Over the next twenty-five years, a significant number of serious studies on atheistic themes would appear. To name only the more famous figures, de Lubac's magisterial *The Drama of Atheist Humanism* ([1944] 1995) comprises detailed analyses of Feuerbach, Nietzsche, Comte, and, of course, Marx. Hans Küng's licentiate dissertation, written at the Gregorian in the early 1950s, was on Sartre (Kerr 2007: 146). Romano Guardini, also in the early fifties, began (although never completed) a study of Nietzsche (Krieg 1997: 178). In Britain, Frederick Copleston published studies of Nietzsche, Schopenhauer, existentialism, and logical positivism in the forties and fifties. And in Italy, an Institute for Higher Studies on Atheism was opened at the Pontifical Urban University in 1960.

Needless to say, this burgeoning intellectual engagement with atheism engendered new theological understandings. But its implications were felt in other areas also, most notably in ecclesiology. Of particular significance again is de Lubac's *Catholicism*, which was tellingly subtitled: *A Study of Dogma in Relation to the Corporate Destiny of Mankind*. In it, as mentioned above, de Lubac stresses the (ontological) unity of mankind, as affirmed by the Fathers. It is, moreover, clear from his introduction that the impetus for this

---

[4] Contrary to popular belief, these were not typically included on the *Index Prohibitorum Librorum*. Indeed, among the atheist authors mentioned in this paragraph, only Auguste Comte (*Cours de philosophie positive*) and Jean-Paul Sartre (complete works) ever featured on the Index (see Bujanda 2002).

ressourcement lies in criticisms of the Church made by contemporary 'free-thinkers' ([1938] 1964: x). With a litany of quotations, he presents their charges that the Church is 'uninterested in our terrestrial future and in human fellowship', that the Christian cares only for his own soul while ignoring 'the solidarity which unites him with his fellows', and that the pope is 'only the technician of individual salvation' (ibid.: ix–x). De Lubac, of course, disagrees:

> We are accused of being individualists even in spite of ourselves, by the logic of our faith, whereas in reality Catholicism is essentially social. It is social in the deepest sense of the word: not merely in its applications in the field of natural institutions but first and foremost in itself, in the heart of its mystery, in the essence of its dogma. It is social in a sense which should have made the expression 'social Catholicism' pleonastic.

Striking a note that would become, and remains still, fundamental to the Church's understanding of atheism, he continues:

> Nevertheless, if such a misunderstanding has arisen and entrenched itself, if such an accusation is current, is it not our own fault? [...] if so many observers, who are not lacking in acumen or in religious spirit, are so grievously mistaken about the essence of Catholicism, is it not an indication that Catholics should make an effort to understand it better themselves? (Ibid.: xi)

This striking *nostra culpa*, an admission of failure in light of the (erroneous, but nonetheless excusable) criticisms made by sincere unbelievers, motivates the entirety of *Catholicism* – which, as Fergus Kerr recently observed, 'Many, including Congar, Balthasar, Wojtyla and Ratzinger, considered [...] as the key book of twentieth-century Catholic theology, the one indispensable text' (2007: 71).

Slightly earlier even than this, in 1935, Congar published an article in *La Vie intellectuelle* on 'The Reasons for the Unbelief of Our Times'.[5] Commenting on recent sociological studies of the French working classes, revealing 'a generalized state of unbelief', Congar focuses on the *social*, rather than the strictly intellectual, origins of this situation.

> This social character not only of present unbelief, but of its causes and its origins, seems indeed to be one of the dominant data to be retained

---

[5] The English version of the article, published in the Cambridge student journal *Integration*, appeared in two parts.

from the enquiry. If one has not got faith it is because the 'environment' removes it, it is because one has entered into an order of values which, far from demanding it, excludes it, it is because the attitude taken by the Church with regard to modern life has put the very possibility of believing altogether out of the question ([1935] 1938a: 13–14).

Congar identifies two reasons for this. Firstly, the secularizing processes of modern society have forced a separation between faith and life. Secondly, and most importantly, the Church's *reaction* to these processes – 'she fell back upon her positions, put up barricades and assumed an attitude of defence' ([1935] 1938b: 19) – has alienated those who might have otherwise remained. Thus as Gabriel Flynn phrases it, 'The failure or inability of the Church, its members and in particular its leaders, to respond in a positive manner to the problem of the separation of faith and life is an important factor in explaining the phenomenon of continued widespread unbelief in present-day society' (Flynn 2004a: 438; see also Lubac [1953] 1956: 170–2). In later works, Congar identified Christian disunity as a further cause of unbelief: 'Concretely, the division among Christians is a scandal for the world. The world is exonerated, to a degree, from the duty to believe' ([1961] 1962: 148; see Flynn 2004b: 37). In the same piece, referring back to his 1935 article, Congar commented: 'It seemed to me that, *since the belief or unbelief of men depended so much on us*, the effort to be made was a renovation of ecclesiology' ([1961] 1962: 147–8; emphasis in original). Thus Congar's great theological achievement, his hugely influential corpus of ecclesiological writings, was, like de Lubac's *Catholicism*, motivated in large part by the Church's burgeoning engagement with atheism. Indeed, as Flynn has persuasively argued, 'the overarching concern of Congar's whole theology of the Church is precisely to counteract unbelief' (Flynn 2004b: 212).

But the Church's engagement with atheism was not merely theoretical. As briefly mentioned above, already in the 1930s sociological studies of the working classes suggested that French Catholicism was facing a grave new world of mass unbelief (Arnal 1984a: 50–1). In 1943, at the behest of the Archbishop of Paris, Cardinal Suhard, Henri Godin and Yvan Daniel published a curious mix of reportage and manifesto, the seminal tract *La France – Pays de Mission?*. Drawing on social research, their own experiences, and a great deal of anecdotal evidence, the two priests identified certain regions of French society as 'Pagan areas. Missionary areas' ([1943] 1949: 69; see also

Moser 1985: 130–2). Generally speaking, these were the working-class neighbourhoods of large industrial cities such as Paris and Marseille. Godin and Daniel's description of these is significant, and worth quoting at length:

> In this region and in all like it, [... a man] knows nothing of whence he comes, whither he is going, why he is on earth. He has no reason for living, no guiding principles, no scale of values. Nor do you find among such people that basis of Christian values that elsewhere helps you to reach many Christians even though they are unconscious that they are Christians. Even the natural morality is gone, [...] Yes, here we are indeed in missionary country. [...] Here we find nothing, sheer emptiness... with civilization superimposed. ([1943] 1949: 71)

Later on, they support these assessments with lurid (and probably exaggerated, if not outright apocryphal) anecdotes of ubiquitous adultery, abortion, and theft (ibid.: 79–86; see also Anonymous 1954: 191–2). The implication is, of course, that devoid of Christian belief or morality, the working classes inhabit a morass of immorality and meaninglessness (cf. Leprieur 2001: 164). This naturally made the Church's missionary task all the more urgent. To meet this necessity, Godin and Daniel proposed that priests leave behind the bourgeois parish system, and immerse themselves totally in the lives of the proletariat, to bring them the gospel on their *own* terms, and not those dictated by an already (and increasingly) alien culture. Daunting though this project was, *Pays de Mission?* is not without hope for future 'priest-workers':

> Already half Christian are a mother who brings up her children with a great deal of love, a workman who is obliging with his comrades, or, still better, who puts his whole heart into his job. That girl is a Christian who carries out her duties of girlhood in a spirit of charity and joyfulness, Christian that poor man who shares the bread he has begged with one poorer than himself. ([1943] 1949: 185)

Taken together, the above two block quotations are highly instructive. On the one hand, the contemporary proletariat, being *de facto* atheists, are characterized as not possessing even the rudiments of 'natural morality'. But on quite the other, even *here* are sometimes to be found Christians who are ignorant of the fact – *anonymous Christians*, as one might say. This tension should come as no surprise, coming as it does on the threshold of, and moreover helping to usher in, the Catholic reappraisal of unbelievers.

Pays de Mission? had a deep impact. Under Suhard's patronage, a 'Mission de Paris' was founded in 1944 to facilitate the measures advised by Godin and Daniel. Missions in other industrial dioceses, such as Lyons and Marseilles, soon followed, attracting a steady trickle of young priests – including, it seems, a disproportionate number of Jesuits and Dominicans. Henri Perrin, one of the former, was among the first to join this 'priest-worker' experiment.[6] Beginning in 1943, workers in occupied France were conscripted for forced labour in Germany (Moser 1985: 124–7). Since chaplains were forbidden from accompanying them, a number of priests, including Perrin, clandestinely volunteered to go as workers instead (Perrin [1958] 1965: 27–9). Assigned to a munitions factory, he initially avoided detection, but was eventually arrested, imprisoned for several months, and deported back to France. Recovering in Paris, he wrote of his sojourn in a 'foreign land':

> But make no mistake – this foreign land I'm talking about isn't [...] the country in which we lived. No, it's the workers' world, about which we previously knew nothing and which we gradually discovered while we were there. [...] This is the land where Christ is unknown, where the name of God evokes no response; it's the land of men without God [...]. In our new life we were obliged to see and reckon with the mass of ordinary people, non-Christians, those who are not 'one of us,' whom we had never come across except in the silence of the streets, on buses, or in trams. Suddenly, as a result of a conversation or a meeting, [...] we discovered a 'foreign country' – which yesterday was distant and unknown, but is today terribly close and distressing. (Ibid.: 48)

Significantly, Perrin recounts his experiences in terms of *meeting* unbelievers for the very first time. As such, not surprisingly, his initial impressions of fellow-prisoners were not overwhelmingly positive.

> From the first, I resolved not to treat them as Christians; [...] They did not have a Christian's point of view on any of the great problems which must present themselves to a man as soon as he thinks – life, love, money, death, society, the family, justice. [...] They were not Christians, and had no right to claim the title, since they had nothing to do

---

[6] The term 'priest-worker' is preferred here to the now more usual (in English, at least) 'worker-priest'. In addition to being a more literal rendering of the French *prêtre-ouvrier*, 'priest-worker' (or 'priest-workman') is the translation favoured in many of the earliest texts rendered into English.

with Christ. [...] Whether they wanted to or not, they lived in utter paganism. ([1945] 1947: 191)

Before long, however, by living alongside these men and coming to know them better, Perrin's attitudes shifted somewhat: 'actually they were not as ill-disposed as they at first seemed. [...] From Raymond to Hermanus there was a whole crescendo of good will, and even a certain desire [for religious instruction], more obvious in some than in others, more easy to waken in some than in others' (ibid.: 192).

Perrin was not alone in his reappraisal. Jacques Loew, a Dominican priest who went to work as a docker in Marseilles, despite finding the proletariat to be 'a pagan people with Christian superstitions', nevertheless discovered supposedly Christian virtues among them too:

> Take up again the recently published letters of the militants – believers and atheists – shot during the Occupation. We find there much more than 'feelers' for the supernatural; we are breathing its very air: 'There is no greater love than this, that a man lay down his life for his friends...'
>
> Thus, the most authentic aspirations towards the transcendent, towards a *mystique*, find their expression for *non-Christians* in Communism and syndicalism. ([1946] 1950: 93-4; see also Arnal 1984b: 543)

Of course, one may dispute the apparently automatic identification of moral seriousness with (albeit implicit or unconscious) Christianity. But the very recognition that atheists, and especially Marxists, can *possess* such qualities, regardless of how they are 'rationalized' theologically, is itself highly significant. In fact, this followed naturally when priests and Party activists began to socialize and collaborate, forcing *both* sides to revise their erstwhile prejudices. As Oscar Arnal states, the priest-workers 'would encounter Marxists on a daily basis, and these intimate contacts with grass-roots militants would reshape inevitably and profoundly their earlier notions'.

> That is not to suggest that there were not some hostile and suspicious moments, but such discord emerged habitually within an atmosphere of dialogue and leisure. Indeed, informal socializing was the first pattern of Communist-clerical encounters within the context of the neighbourhood and the very nature of this friendly mingling was able to transform conflict into camaraderie. (Arnal 1984b: 538)

Although worlds away from French Catholic intellectual life, the priest-workers' new perceptions were not unknown to some of the academic theologians mentioned earlier. If nothing else, the preponderance of

Jesuits and Dominicans among the priest-workers ensured that their learned confrères – including, among others, de Lubac, Daniélou, Congar, and Chenu – were kept abreast of their experiences. And indeed, when the 'mission' was eventually liquidated by the Holy Office in February 1954, Congar and Chenu's sympathies saw them stripped of their teaching posts at Le Saulchoir and exiled from Paris (Leprieur 2001: 166; Flynn 2004b: 10). This new spirit of dialogue, respect, and collaboration between Catholics and unbelievers did not, however, die with the priest-worker project. And nor was it confined only to France. In Franco's Spain, for example, collaborations between Catholics and communists began happening from the late 1950s, featuring joint ventures between the leftist unions and the Workers' Brotherhoods of Catholic Action. A 1965 article in *World Marxist Review*, carrying the once-unthinkable title 'Towards an Alliance of Communists and Catholics', cited this fact in support of its author's assertion that 'The Catholics are our main allies today in the struggle against Franco. This is a fact. It is perhaps the most characteristic and encouraging feature of the Spanish scene today' (Alvares 1965: 27–8). Elsewhere in Europe also, Catholics were increasingly confronted with the presence of unbelievers within their own families, requiring a very different form of 'collaboration'. As Karl Rahner suggests in his 1954 essay 'The Christian among Unbelieving Relations', for many this brought the Church's (hitherto 'abstract') denunciations of atheists into painful relief, and showed up their inaccuracies and inadequacies ([1954] 1967a; see also Ratzinger 1958).

SALVATION FOR ATHEISTS?

The two trajectories traced above (the development of the Catholic doctrine of salvation, and the renewed understandings of atheism and atheists) naturally converge on the question that forms the subject of this book: the possibility of salvation for atheists. Rahner's celebrated contributions to this topic will be discussed and critiqued in the following chapter. But he was not the only major theologian to occupy himself with these issues in the preconciliar period and beyond. Furthermore, Rahner's main ideas are by no means as peculiar to him as they are often assumed to be. Here, therefore, the contributions made by several other key thinkers will be surveyed.

Different though these indeed are, it will nonetheless become clear that they hold much in common, both with each other, and with the more famous work of Rahner.

Although composed slightly before the period in question, the writings of the French lay philosopher Maurice Blondel laid the groundwork for much that was to follow. In *L'Action*, his 1893 doctoral dissertation submitted to the Sorbonne, Blondel proposes a philosophy of 'action', characterized by Gerald McCool as: 'a dialectic of the "willing will," the spiritual dynamism whose built-in yearning would be satisfied by nothing short of the concrete God of Revelation' (1994: 48). Since, according to Blondel, every action both is grounded in, and points towards, God, the question of God's existence is rendered ineluctable: 'To pronounce oneself for or against is equally to let oneself get caught in the gears and be crushed in them completely. [...] To avoid taking a stand, believing one can succeed in doing so, is another shortsighted illusion' ([1893] 1984: 16). Blondel's reasoning here is, admittedly, obscure. However, in his 1934 work *La Pensée* he spells out more clearly the applications of his philosophy for the understanding of atheism. 'Pure atheism', he states, 'is an impossibility and a nonsense.' Blondel affirms that *everybody*, at some level of his or her being, recognizes 'prior to all reflection and to all explanation, a congenital and indestructible assertion, the affirmation of a "beyond"; it appears, this affirmation, from the first traces of prehistory, and it outlines all the scholarly negations.' He continues:

> One can be profoundly mistaken on the sense and contents of this fact. But suppose that, by a sudden and total revelation, this mysterious *beyond* manifests itself, we could assuredly find ourselves forced to confess our illusions and our errors. *Therefore we were wrong.* But we should not pretend that we have been entirely unaware: *we are not ignorant.* And it's in this sense that at the depth of conscience there is a 'language known by all' and an interior principle of judgement. (1934: 390–1)[7]

The suggestion here is, it seems, that there exists – albeit perhaps at some sub-linguistic, preconceptual level – an encounter with God, to which all human beings are privy.[8] While the precise nature of this 'mysterious *beyond*' may well be misinterpreted or misunderstood,

---

[7] I am indebted to Pauline Westwood and Matthew Harris for their invaluable translation of this text from the French.

[8] This is an idea which the Belgian Joseph Maréchal, a key influence on Rahner, would later make his own (see Matteo 1992: 7, 109).

were it to manifest itself completely, nobody could deny having been already cognizant of it. According to Blondel, therefore, simply by acting, thinking, *living*, one necessarily admits a 'tacit affirmation of the secret and active presence of the transcendent that I call *God*' (ibid.: 392). And although, as in the case of the (apparent) atheist, 'one can *believe that one does not believe in God*' (ibid.; emphasis in original), it naturally follows that this belief must be false.

Surprisingly, however, Blondel immediately affirms: 'And there are some who *really* do not believe in God.' But how is this possible? For Blondel, there are *two* forms of atheism. One is propositional and intellectual; i.e. a lack of belief in the existence of God. It is this which, as we have seen, Blondel considers to be 'impossible and a nonsense' – at most, one can only believe that one does not believe. The other form, and by far the more serious, is what one might term *existential*. This is the human's refusal of God, a failure to allow oneself to be enveloped by the mystery; this is the practical, lived atheism discussed in the previous chapter. Once one understands this distinction, then Blondel's most striking, seemingly paradoxical, statement becomes comprehensible: 'If then one can say that *there is no atheist* one can also truly say that *it is difficult and costly not to be an atheist*' (ibid.: 393; emphasis in original). It also follows that, even if one considers oneself to be an atheist in the first sense, one may not be one in the second, more fundamental sense (and vice versa). Lastly and significantly, especially in light of the question of salvation (which Blondel does not, admittedly, address directly), he delineates the various ways in which an apparent 'atheist' might not be one at all.

> There is the atheism of those who do not know how to perceive and name the interior host, the inevitable light 'which shines on all men coming into this world'. But insofar as they do not 'sin against this light' they serve 'the unknown God'; and the label of atheist is only a label.
>
> There is the atheism of those who, in the presence of defective ideas of God which are presented to them, or faced with the sometimes monstrous abuses which are made of the false conceptions of God, reject idols and superstitions. And their atheism is an unconscious homage to a higher ideal, an aspiration which can be pious beneath the shades of impiety. (Ibid.)

According to Blondel, therefore, one can think oneself to be an atheist, and yet unwittingly give honour to the true God. Equally, one can think oneself to be an atheist, and yet reject only idols, that is, *false* conceptions of the authentic God whom one thereby also unknowingly honours.

Jacques Maritain, who was of course at the vanguard of the French Catholic dialogue with Marxism, offered his own version of this manner of engaging atheism. In 1953's *Approaches to God*, Maritain identifies a 'primordial way of approach through which men become aware of the existence of God' ([1953] 1955: 2). In common with Blondel and Maréchal (both of whom he quotes), he argues for the inescapability of knowledge of God:

> Once a man has been awakened to the reality of his existence and of his own existence, when he has really perceived that formidable, sometimes elating, sometimes sickening or maddening fact *I exist*, he is henceforth possessed by the intuition of being and the implications it bears with it. (Ibid.: 3)

From this existential realization, he thinks, the human mind is forced irrevocably to the thought of God. This approach to God is, moreover, not a new one. Rather, 'it is human reason's eternal way of approaching God'. Philosophical arguments for the existence of God, such as Aquinas' Five Ways, are but secondary attempts to rationalize this basic, 'prephilosophical' intuition (ibid.: 9).[9]

Later in the same book, Maritain offers another significant 'approach' to God, that via morality or conscience:

> It is not possible rationally to justify fundamental moral notions such as the notion of unconditional moral obligation, or inalienable right, or the intrinsic dignity of the human person, without rising to the uncreated Reason from which man and the world proceed and from which is the subsistent Good itself. Philosophical reflection on moral life and experience has thus its own proofs of the existence of God. (Ibid.: 74–5)

Maritain gives the example of a child who, for the first time, refrains from telling a lie 'not because he risks being punished if the lie is discovered or because this was forbidden him, but simply because *it is bad*' (ibid.: 75; emphasis in original). Now the child is not aware of any cognition about God; God does not, so far as he is concerned, come into the question at all. According to Maritain, however, 'he knows God, without being aware of it':

---

[9] On this point in Maritain's philosophy, see O'Callaghan (1986: 23–30). A similar idea can also be found, just over a decade before Maritain, in the work of Étienne Gilson (e.g. [1941] 2002: 115–17).

Atheism and Salvation from Pius IX to Vatican II 63

He knows God because, by virtue of the internal dynamism of his choice of the good, he wills and loves the Separate Good as the ultimate end of his existence. Thus, his intellect has of God a vital and nonconceptual knowledge [...]. The intellect may already have the idea of God and it may not have it. The nonconceptual knowledge which I am describing takes place independently of any use possibly made or not made of the idea of God, and independently of the actualization of any explicit and conscious knowledge of man's true last End. (Ibid.: 78)

Genuine morality is, for Maritain, impossible without knowledge and recognition of God. This holds true, he thinks, even if such knowledge resides only at a 'nonconceptual' level of the person's mind. This idea was not, of course, unique to Maritain. As we have seen, Blondel (followed by Maréchal) also appealed to 'implicit' belief in God, although without making any direct appeal to morality.[10] Maritain's explication of this common theme is, however, far more detailed. In a very important passage, he spells out precisely the ramifications this has with regard to atheists:

> It follows from this that, given all the cleavages and the discords, schisms, divisions and contradictions, unknown by the subject to himself, which can be produced between the conscious and the unconscious, it is possible that a man in whom the knowledge of which we speak exists in an unconscious way, may not only be ignorant of God in his conscious reason but may even take sides in his conscious reason against the existence of God (because of some conceptual mistake and error of reasoning) and professes atheism. He believes that he is an atheist. He cannot be one in reality if he has chosen, and as long as he has chosen, the way of the good for the sake of the good, in his basic moral choice. He is a pseudo-atheist. (Ibid.: 81)

This category of *pseudo-atheists* is a central one for Maritain. They first feature in a typology of atheists which he developed in the late 1940s alongside our previously encountered *practical atheists* and '*absolute atheists*, who actually deny the existence of the very God in Whom the believers believe and who are bound to change entirely their own scale of values and to destroy in themselves everything that connotes his name'. Absolute atheism, he explains, 'is in no way a mere absence of belief in God' (which, like Blondel and Maréchal, he

---

[10] For similar ideas see also Lombardi ([1942] 1956: 171–2) on Claeys-Bouuaert; and Eminyan (1960: 48–51) on de Letter.

regards as formally impossible): 'It is rather a refusal of God, a fight against God, a challenge to God' ([1947] 1953: 97–8). Like de Lubac, he blames this phenomenon on those so-called 'Christians' who are nothing more than practical atheists. Pseudo-atheists, on the other hand, are those 'who believe that they do not believe in God and who in reality unconsciously believe in Him' (ibid.: 97; also Maritain 1949: 268). And these, in virtue of this fact, may presumably – although, like Blondel, Maritain never quite says so – attain salvation.

Pseudo-atheists, although not named as such, appear also in de Lubac's *The Drama of Atheist Humanism*. There, commenting on Dostoevsky's Christian anthropology, he observes that for the novelist: 'Man is a "theotropic" being. Violently attacked on all sides, faith is indestructible in his heart' ([1944] 1995: 344). Dostoevsky's nihilist character Kirillov (*Demons*), moreover, de Lubac describes as being one in whom 'extreme atheism joins hands with sainthood' (ibid.: 316), and suggests that, Kirillov's conscious atheism aside: 'If he could read what is at the bottom of his own heart, the chances are he would find something quite different from what he thinks are his convictions' (ibid.: 319). This is a point to which we shall return in chapter three. Elsewhere, in de Lubac's 1956 book *The Discovery of God*, which is itself a revised third edition of his controversial 1944 *De la Connaissance de Dieu*, he quotes Thomas Aquinas' maxim: 'All knowers know God implicitly in all they know' ([1956] 1960: 39; quoting *De veritate*, q. 22, a. 2, ad 1; Thomas Aquinas [*c*. 1259] 1925, 529). According to de Lubac (and here again a debt to Blondel is evident):

> Every human act, whether it is an act of knowledge or an act of the will, rests secretly upon God, by attributing meaning and solidity to the real upon which it is exercised. For God is the Absolute; and nothing can be thought without positing the Absolute in relating it to that Absolute; nothing can be willed without tending towards the Absolute, nor valued unless weighed in terms of the Absolute.

He continues:

> The supreme contradiction is to use God in order to control the flux of existence, to organise chaos, to make statements, to judge, to choose – in a word to act spiritually and not to fall into contradiction at each step, and then, simultaneously, refuse to recognize him; to think him away without whom thought would only be a physical manifestation: the

supreme contradiction is to lean upon God in the very act of denying him. (Ibid.: 40)

It follows that those who believe themselves to be atheists cannot really be so, since their very denial of God's existence relies on an implicit, unconscious, or 'secret' recognition of that existence. Later in the same work, de Lubac makes the Maritainian move of arguing for the necessity of God from the recognition of moral duty. Furthermore, he suggests, 'If God is already known in some way in our knowledge of duty, (even by those who think themselves unable to see him and call themselves atheists), it may be said that God is found and possessed in some way in the fulfilment of duty' (ibid.: 103).

This notion has analogues in the writings of other major theologians around this time. Edward Schillebeeckx, in a 1953 lecture to young Dominicans, asserted it was difficult to believe 'that a sincere militant communist atheist possesses not one shred of authentically theistic faith.' He added,

> Wherever there is some sense of justice, truth and above all genuine brotherhood, there is God too. Anonymous religion can take hidden forms. Wherever, despite complete rejection of the church and even moral degradation, sincerely objective values are accepted, to the point where people are prepared to fight for them, there is a latent but genuinely religious life. ([1953] 1971: 32)

Strikingly, especially in light of Rahner's later advocacy of anonymous Christianity, he speaks also of 'anonymous devotion to God' (*anonieme godsdienstigheid*), the pagan's 'smouldering, anonymously-theistic heart' (*smeulende anoniem-theïstische kern*), 'anonymously-supernatural faith in the "God of salvation"' (*anoniem-bovennatuurlijke geloof in de 'God van het heil'*), 'anonymous faith in God' (*anonieme Godsgeloof*), and 'anonymously-religious brotherliness' (*anoniem-religieuze broederlijkheid*).[11]

For Daniélou too, 'there is a fundamental religious attitude wherever there is recognition of an absolute' (1949: 19). He suggests, further, that the 'religious hunger' supposedly common to all humans might, in somewhere like communist Russia, find appeasement in secular substitutes:

---

[11] *Stichting Edward Schillebeeckx*, Nijmegen. MS 53/6: 'Herbronning van het priesterlijk apostolaat en activering van het laïcaat', 43 pp. ['159-202'], 159-60.

For instance, they will accept the ideal of Soviet Russia as a kind of absolute for which they will be willing to give their lives. Will a complete absence of religion ensue? I do not think so. There will be a distorted, deformed religion, but the religious hunger, transposed toward another object, will none the less exist. The day true religion is revealed to these children, many of them will recognize that they have been groping for it in various ersatz forms. (Ibid.)

In a very similar vein, Congar mooted the possibility that, in the case of 'the mass of men who know nothing of God, or whose knowledge is as good as nothing':

> Their meeting with God could take place under the form of one of those master-words that stand for a transcendent absolute to which they may have given their love, words that are often written with a capital letter: Duty, Peace, Justice, Brotherhood, yes, and Humanity, Progress, Welfare, and yet others. People often give themselves to these ideals at the cost of their own personal interests and comfort, at the cost of themselves, and even sometimes of life. ([1959] 1961: 124; see also Congar 1957: 292–3)

For Congar, de Lubac, Daniélou, and Schillebeeckx (and numerous other theologians in this period), these possibilities, taken in conjunction with the new salvific optimism for those traditionally considered to be *extra Ecclesiam*, more than permit Catholic theologians to speak hopefully of the salvation of atheists (or rather, of those who consider themselves to be such).

This was, therefore, the position which mainstream Catholic theology had reached on the subject of atheism by the eve of Vatican II. To sum up very briefly: the old view, still manifest in papal pronouncements of the late 1950s, that 'speculative atheism is an impossibility for any man who has the use of reason and is in good faith' (Garrigou-Lagrange [1914] 1939: 28), had proven to be untenable. That many unbelievers did, as an obvious matter of fact, lead moral and meaningful lives, was widely understood by theologians as demonstrating an 'implicit', 'anonymous', 'secret', or 'unconscious' belief in the Christian God on the part of (apparent) atheists. Furthermore, although such people were obviously not explicit members of the one Church outside of which no one can be saved, this might plausibly be for non-culpable reasons – most notably, those arising from Catholics' own inadequate witness. As such, as had recently become clear from the Church's renewed understandings of its own doctrine of salvation, atheists need not be debarred from the possibility of salvation. To once again quote Congar's crucial dictum:

> The Church learns through contact with facts. [...] Truth remains unaltered; but it is grasped in a new and undoubtedly more adequate way when men and the world are known *as they are*, in an extent, age and goodness other than what has been believed of them previously. ([1959] 1961: 98)

The account of these developments has, admittedly, been a long one. Such aetiological detail is, however, necessary for a full and proper understanding of Vatican II's landmark teachings on the subject of atheism and salvation – and hence for all subsequent Catholic theology which broaches these topics. It is these to which we may now turn.

VATICAN II

Following the death of Pius XII, Cardinal Angelo Giuseppe Roncalli, the Patriarch of Venice, was elected to replace him in October 1958. Within three months, on 25 January 1959, this new Pope John XXIII announced his resolution to convene 'a general Council for the universal Church', with the express purpose of 'fostering the good of souls and bringing the new pontificate into clear and definite correspondence with the spiritual needs of the present day' (quoted in Alberigo 2006: 1). In retrospect, then, it does not seem surprising that atheism became a significant theme for the resulting Second Vatican Council (1962–5). Indeed in the opinion of Johann Baptist Metz, 'The problem of unbelief is no doubt one of the most pressing and difficult questions raised in Vatican Council II by Schema XIII [i.e. GS]' (1965: 32). And for Ratzinger, GS 19–21 'may be counted among the most important pronouncements of Vatican II' (1969: 145).

Given these assessments, however, and the great upsurge of theological interest in atheism in the decades preceding the Council, it is sobering to think that Vatican II might have very easily ignored the subject altogether. Despite evident and wide-ranging interest in the subject, expressed in the *vota* collected in 1959 by the 'ante-preparatory commission', atheism received very little attention in the

Council's preparatory *schemata* (MacNeil 1997: 16–24).[12] Indeed, even a relatively late proto-version of Schema XIII, distributed in advance of the Council's Third Session in Autumn 1964, merely mentions, in passing and without comment, 'errors which spring from materialism, especially from dialectical materialism or communism' (Hebblethwaite 1967: 25).[13] This draft fared badly in the ensuing debates, and among the various complaints levelled against it, the phenomenon of atheism was frequently cited (MacNeil 1997: 41–127). To give just one example, on 20 October, the first day of debate, Cardinal Silva Henríquez of Santiago, Chile, spoke 'on the need for dialogue with contemporary humanism [...] The Church must try to comprehend atheism, to examine the truths which nourish this error, and to be able to correspond its life and doctrine to these aspirations' (AS III/v: 236). The draft of Schema XIII, its unsatisfactory treatment of atheism included, was duly rejected and sent for rewriting.

The draft Schema's approach to atheism was not merely out of step with current theological opinion. Since 6 August 1964, when Paul VI (who had ascended to the papacy following John's death the preceding June) promulgated his debut encyclical *Ecclesiam Suam*, it was behind the Church's magisterial teaching too. Addressing what he himself described as 'surely the most serious matter of our times' (art. 100; AAS 56 [1964]: 651), the pope urged dialogue with the 'very many people who [...] profess no religion' (art. 99; ibid.: 650–1). While by no means uncritical in his comments on atheism, he nonetheless expressed sympathy for many non-believers. Many atheists, Paul admits, 'demand a higher and purer presentation of divine matters than that prevailing in certain imperfect forms of language and worship'. Moreover, 'We observe them, driven by a demanding and often a noble concern, [...] dreaming of justice, progress and a social order which appears to them to be an ultimate, and all but divine, goal'. And yet further:

---

[12] The *vota* were suggestions elicited from bishops, curial offices, Catholic universities, and papal nuncios. On this process, see Fouilloux 1995.

[13] This text was, in fact, the Council's third attempt at composing something suitable *De Ecclesia in mundo huius temporis*. The impetus for such a document had emerged during the First Session of the Council itself, chiefly inspired by the Brazilian bishop Hélder Câmara (see Krier Mich 1998: 120–1).

They are sometimes endowed with great breadth of mind, impatient with the mediocrity and self-seeking which infects so many aspects of human society in our times. We see that they expertly employ sentiments and expressions brought forth from our gospel, referring to the necessity of human brotherhood, aid and compassion. Surely some day we shall be able to lead the cries of today, by which good morals are signified, back to their obviously Christian sources? (Art. 104; ibid.: 652–3)

Needless to say, in light of these new papal emphases, Schema XIII's 'errors which spring from materialism' was greatly lacking. This fact did not go unremarked upon in the bishops' interventions (e.g. AS III/v: 236). As such, when the Dogmatic Subcommission set about revising the Schema, a group led by the *periti* Giulio Girardi and Gabriel-Marie Garrone was entrusted with preparing a new section on atheism (Moeller 1969: 50). The resulting chapters of the 'Ariccia text' (named after the town near Rome where the Subcommission was based), distributed among the Council Fathers in June 1965, generated much debate (AS IV/i: 446–8; MacNeil 1997: 129–205). Ultimately, however, it too was rejected, and the task for writing its replacement, which would eventually form part of the promulgated GS, was entrusted to Cardinal Franz König of Vienna, and his newly formed Secretariat for Non-believers (AS IV/ii: 456).

The foundation of the Secretariat, announced without fanfare in the 9 April 1965 issue of *L'Osservatore Romano*,[14] marks the beginning of what is in many ways the most important chapter of the Catholic engagement with atheism *so far* – a chapter which falls mainly, however, outside the scope of this study. The pope's remit for the Secretariat was reportedly very broad: to König's requests for clarification, he answered only '*Usus docebit*', you will learn by doing (Hebblethwaite 1967: 41; König 1986: 39). Yet the next month Paul, addressing the Society of Jesus' 31st General Congregation (convened to appoint Jean-Baptiste Janssens' successor as Superior General),

---

[14] The Secretariat's archives are housed at the Pontifical Council for Culture, Vatican City. On the Secretariat's foundation and early formation see, in addition to König 1968: *Archivio Segretariato per i Non-Credenti* [Hereafter '*Arch. SNC*']. Box 1. [Loose] Elisabeth Peter, 'Breve Storia del Segretariato per i Non Credenti' (undated, 1972?), 15 pp.; and *Arch. SNC*. Box 1/000. File 'Relazioni', fol. 6: 'Relazioni della Riunione di alcuni esperti del Segretariato per i Non Credenti', 14 April 1966, 3 pp. On the Secretariat in general, see also Miano 1967; Secretariat for Non-believers 1968; Hebblethwaite 1975: 135–63; König 1968; König 1986: 59–66; and König 2005: 104–16.

charged 'the companions of Ignatius' with making 'a stout, united stand against atheism'. To help them in this, Paul counselled them (among much else) 'to conduct research, to collect information of all kinds, to publish material, to discuss among themselves, to prepare specialists in the field' (AAS 57 [1965]: 514). Now, unlike the task entrusted to the Jesuits, the Secretariat's purpose was emphatically not one of *fighting* atheism. Indeed, as König once had occasion to point out, the Secretariat was named 'for', rather than 'against', non-believers (Moeller 1966: 416). Nevertheless, in some respects at least, the projects were similar. As its newly appointed secretary, the Salesian philosopher Vincenzo Miano, explained to Vatican Radio, the Secretariat's purpose was:

> to collect, sort out, and synthesize all the bibliographical, statistical, and other information having to do with the rejection of faith in the divinity; to fine-tune a method for grasping the atheistic mentality; to organize groups of priests and lay people who will be well prepared to enter into a dialogue with atheists, should the occasion arise. (Quoted in Burigana and Turbanti 2003: 611)

To facilitate this, branches were formed in major European countries with a mandate to recruit specialists in sociology, philosophy, and theology. Among the first to be co-opted were Rahner (König's *peritus*), Metz, Loew, Congar, Chenu, Miano, de Lubac, and Girardi (Secretariat for Non-believers 1966).[15] The latter three, in addition to Daniélou, were chosen to work on the new text for Schema XIII. In addition to König, the Council's bishops Šeper (Zagreb), Auferdeck (Erfurt), Hnilica (a Czech Jesuit based in Rome), and Kominek (Wroclaw) were also appointed to the group (Hünermann 2006: 398). Together they formulated what would become a landmark contribution to the Christian *rapprochement* with modern unbelief.[16]

---

[15] Consultors were not *formally* appointed to the Secretariat until after the Council, beginning in January 1966. This would, perhaps, explain the eighty-year-old Chenu's suggestion that the Secretariat was created after the Council (1975: 141). However, given that the Secretariat was clearly active during the Council, drafting parts of Schema XIII and releasing a series of informative reports for the Fathers – e.g. *Arch. SNC*. Box 6/000. File 'Documentazione varia', fol. 6: 'Contemporary Atheism', *DO-C [Documentatie Centrum Concilie/Documentazione Olandese Concilio]*, no. 201 (undated), 5 pp.; and fol. 7: 'Marx-Leninist Atheism', *DO-C*, no. 202 (undated), 12 pp. – it is clear that its consultors were already at work; if not yet, in Vatican terms, 'officially'.

[16] Confusingly, it is sometimes said that the Secretariat worked on GS 18 and 19 (e.g. König 1986: 60). In the Ariccia text, articles 18 and 19 were indeed devoted to

Key aspects of the resulting statement are discussed in detail elsewhere in this monograph, notably in chapters one and five. The paragraphs will, therefore, be synopsized here only briefly (AS IV/vii: 743–5; see also Gallagher 1995: 13–21; Kasper 2006; and Routhier 2006: 148–53). Given the nature of the preceding decades' theological engagement with atheism, not to mention Daniélou's and de Lubac's influence on the definitive statement, their emphatically *pastoral* orientation comes as little surprise. Notable in this regard is the fact that, despite pressure and petitions from a vocal minority of Fathers, no condemnation of communism was issued (Hebblethwaite 1967: 50–1; König 1986: 43). Instead, the text begins by observing that while man was created and dignified by God, to whose communion he is called, and without whom he 'cannot live fully according to truth':

> Yet many of our contemporaries either fail to perceive, or explicitly refuse, this intimate and vital relationship with God. Hence atheism may be numbered among the most serious matters of our time and merits more careful investigation.

This is followed by the delineation of the numerous forms of modern atheism, quoted in chapter one. While blame is apportioned to 'those who wilfully try to drive God from their heart and to avoid religious questions, not following the dictate of their conscience', this is swiftly mitigated by the admission that:

> believers can have no small part in the rise of atheism, since by neglecting education in the faith, teaching false doctrine, or through defects in their own religious, moral or social lives, they may be said rather more to conceal than reveal the true countenance of God and of religion.

This was, of course, a familiar theme in the preconciliar discussion – as evidenced above, for example, in the quotations from Maritain, Congar, and de Lubac – and will be further discussed in chapter four. Article 20 provides more detailed outlines of two 'systematic' atheisms: *existential* and *communistic* (although neither term is used in the text itself). As Ratzinger suggests, these were presumably intended to represent both western and eastern forms of atheism, and to

---

atheism (AS IV/i: 446–8). During the Secretariat's redrafting, however, these were expanded into three articles. Additions and reorganizations earlier in the document then shifted the position of the paragraphs on atheism to 19–21 (AS IV/vi: 437–40).

underline the fact that atheism is not only pervasive *behind* the Iron Curtain (cf. Ratzinger 1969: 147).

Article 21, the climax to the statement, reminds the world that the Church 'cannot desist from painfully but with all firmness reproving, as it has done in the past, those pernicious teachings and actions, which contradict reason and the shared experience of humanity, and rob it of its innate excellence.' Nevertheless, it seeks to discern 'the secret motives for the negation of God in the minds of atheists [...] and led by its love for all men, it believes that these motives deserve a serious and more profound investigation.' Dismissing claims that exalting God equals debasing man, and that hope for a future life entails neglecting the present one, it forwards the counter-claim that *without God*: 'The enigmas of life and death, of guilt and of suffering, remain without solution, so that men are not rarely cast into despair.' Furthermore, remarking that 'every man remains an unsolved question to himself', it is averred that 'To this question, God alone can fully and with complete certainty offer a response.'

Addressing itself now to believers themselves, the constitution warns:

> The remedy for atheism is to be sought in presenting doctrine in a fitting manner, and through the complete life of the Church and its members. [...] This faith should manifest its fruitfulness by penetrating the whole life, including the worldly activities, of believers, and by moving them to justice and love, especially towards those in need.

It proceeds to affirm that 'all human beings, believing or unbelieving, are obliged to contribute to the just construction of this world, in which all live together', something possible only on the basis of 'a sincere and prudent dialogue'. Thinly veiled criticism of Soviet religious persecution follows, accompanied by a concluding invitation to atheists 'to consider Christ's Gospel with an open heart':

> For truly the Church knows that its message is in harmony with the most secret desires of the human heart, since it champions the dignity of the human calling, restoring hope to those who now despair of their higher destiny. [...] Apart from this message nothing can satisfy the human heart: 'You have made us for yourself', Lord, 'and our heart is restless until it rests in you.'

On the subject of salvation, GS 19–21 is silent. This is, of course, because the possibility of salvation for atheists is authoritatively dealt with elsewhere. LG 16 had been approved during the Third Session on 21 November 1964. It too emerged out of a series of revisions and redrafts. The constitution's original version, which was heavily criticized in the first week of conciliar debate, had affirmed only the abstract possibility of being related to the Church 'through an implicit and unconscious desire':

> This is the case whether with a sincere wish they want what Christ himself wants, or being ignorant of Christ, they sincerely desire to accomplish the will of God and of their Creator. For the gifts of heavenly grace are by no means lacking to those who, by divine light and with a sincere soul, wish and seek to be renewed. (AS I/iv: 18)

The final text, of course, goes much farther – in tone and emphasis, if not (so much) in terms of pure theology. Significantly, this was among the several portions of LG which Congar worked on (Flynn 2004b: 53; Melloni 2000: 110 n. 437). For a start, actual groups are identified to whom the Council's 'salvific optimism' applies. These include not only members of the major world religions, but also – it would appear – 'all men of good will', whether they yet possess 'an express recognition of God' or not. The mention of '*express* recognition' (or 'knowledge') here, along with the appeal to 'conscience' slightly earlier in the paragraph, is an unmistakable allusion to recent developments in the theological understanding of atheism. This reading is supported also by *Ad Gentes* 7, where, despite stressing the unceasing importance of *mission*, it is nonetheless admitted that 'in ways known to himself God is able to lead men who are, without fault of their own, ignorant of the Gospel to that faith without which it is impossible to please him (Heb 11.6)' (AS IV/vii: 677). But that said, unlike in the original draft where an unambiguous appeal *is* made to an 'implicit and unconscious desire' as the (apparent) unbeliever's means of salvation, LG 16 refuses to be pinned down on any particular hypothesis (cf. Grillmeier 1967: 184).

Also different in LG 16, as compared both to its earlier drafts and (especially) to the magisterium's previous statements on the same subject since Pius IX, is what Francis Sullivan has termed Vatican II's 'presumption of innocence' (1992: 150–1). This will be further explored in chapter four. Here, though, it is worth recalling Pius IX's affirmation that while there is indeed 'no salvation outside the Church', it is *also* true that 'they who labour in ignorance of the true religion, if this ignorance is invincible, are not bound by any fault in this matter in the eyes of the Lord' ([1854] 1864: 626). Fundamentally, this is the same doctrine as espoused in LG 14 and 16. But while Pius seems to doubt that there are very many who might fulfil this requirement, LG seems almost to assume the opposite. As seen throughout this chapter, numerous theologians in the early twentieth century (with Congar chief among them) had begun to realize that there are a great many, inculpable reasons why a person might fail to recognize the truth of Catholicism, and the salvific necessity of belonging to the Church. Thus, to quote Sullivan:

> The profound difference between the medieval view and the doctrine of Vatican II on the salvation of non-Catholics is that instead of a presumption of guilt, the attitude expressed by the council involves a presumption of innocence. [...] But if we presume that those outside are inculpable, then we must conclude that they can be saved. And this applies to the majority of the world's people who have neither Christian faith nor baptism. The question now is not whether, but how they can be spared. (1992: 151)

As noted above, this was already the theological consensus regarding *Extra Ecclesiam nulla salus* by the eve of the Council. However, this does not imply – *contra* Hans Küng – that, by promulgating LG 16, the Church abandoned its traditional claim to be the exclusive means through which a person might attain salvation, thereby rendering obsolete the 'infallible, ancient dogma' of no salvation outside the Church (Küng [1974] 1978: 97; see also 1967: 317; 1991: 232–3). On the contrary, as Suso Brechter stated in his commentary on *Ad Gentes*:

> [T]he old axiom *Extra Ecclesiam nulla salus*, though not very happily expressed, retains its validity even today, if correctly interpreted. It means that anyone who is saved finds salvation through Christ and the Church. [...] The old, frequently misunderstood and misapplied axiom must therefore be explained and modified: *Sine Ecclesia nulla salus*, or: *Extra Christum nulla salus*. This does not in any way state who, when and how many are saved, but how, in what way and by what means men attain salvation. (Brechter 1969: 123; cf. Landucci 1976: 97)

This is, as also noted above, the same conclusion reached by (among others) Congar, de Lubac, and Ratzinger.

LG 16, although undoubtedly the *locus classicus* of Vatican II's declarations on the salvation of atheists, is not the only relevant text. GS 22, which immediately follows the section on atheism, stresses the fact that 'by his incarnation, the Son of God has in a certain way (*quodammodo*) united himself with every human being.' From this it follows, both that each Christian has 'been made a partner in the paschal mystery, and configured by the death of Christ, will go forward to the resurrection, strengthened by hope', and that furthermore:

> This holds true not for only for the Christian faithful, but also for all men of good will in whose hearts grace is active in an invisible manner. For since Christ died for all, and since all men are in fact called to the one destiny, which is divine, we are obliged to hold that the Holy Spirit offers to all the possibility of being made partners, in a way known to God, in the paschal mystery. (AS IV/vii: 745–6)

Atheists are not mentioned specifically here. Nevertheless, the position of these words in GS, and the fact that LG 16 had already spoken of grace being operative in unbelievers' moral strivings, implies that they are certainly to be included. In the opinion of Ratzinger, for one, GS 22 represents a definite 'advance over *Lumen Gentium*'. According to his 1969 commentary, whereas LG 16 lays too much stress on man's 'work' in gaining salvation, GS 22 gives proper weight to the inscrutable action of *God*: 'its essential content is not determined by the categories of good will (a very questionable formula which can very easily border on Pelagianism), but by the paschal mystery, that is, by the very centre of Christology'. As such, he affirms:

> In this way, at the last moment, as it were, the Council gave a re-reading of its own statements and replaced the extremely unsatisfactory expressions of *Lumen Gentium*, art. 16, by better ones. If one is dealing with the views of Vatican II on the question of the salvation of the many, it would be better in future to start from this passage of *Gaudium et Spes* rather than from the Constitution on the Church, whose less fortunate approach has been considerably improved. (1969: 163)

It might be argued that Ratzinger's preference was later evidenced in *Dominus Iesus*' declaration 'on the unicity and salvific universality of Jesus Christ and the Church', issued under his prefecture by the Congregation for the Doctrine of the Faith. There GS 22 is cited once; LG 16 not at all (art. 10; AAS 92 [2000]: 751). (That said, art. 3 is clear regarding the limited scope of the document, and the fact that it is not intending to offer a systematic doctrinal statement [ibid.: 745–6].) Ratzinger may perhaps be correct in preferring the former's phrasing, although he does not, of course, reject LG 16. Nevertheless, if there *is* a difference between the two, then it is one of tone and emphasis; the latter does not contradict the former. Thus while GS 22 stresses the divine initiative as providing the possibility of salvation in the first place – 'since Christ died for all [...] the Holy Spirit offers to all the possibility of being made partners [...] in the paschal mystery' – LG 16 focuses more on how it is that human beings may, freely, *co-operate* with grace in realizing this potential. For its part, LG 16 is quite clear about the primacy of God's grace-full action in the salvation of non-Christians. That said, however, the danger of a Pelagian misreading of it (and attempts at explicating it) is indeed a real one – and one that will be addressed in later chapters.

CONCLUSION

This chapter has covered a great deal of ground. The purpose has been, throughout, to gain a fuller understanding of Vatican II's pivotal statements on the subjects of atheism and salvation. These are, as stated in the introduction, the foundational texts for this book as a whole. As such, it was necessary to narrate (albeit in a summary fashion) the crucial developments which occurred in several spheres of Catholic theology, beginning in the early decades of the twentieth century, and which underlie many of the Council's declarations. And although, in a sense, primarily *historical* in nature, these studies will be of vital importance in the forthcoming, constructively *theological* chapters. In particular, we have seen the theories proposed by several eminent philosophers and theologians – specifically Blondel, Maréchal, Maritain, de Lubac, Schillebeeckx, Daniélou, and Congar – on this study's central issue: *the salvation of atheists*. Without exception, these appeal to an 'implicit', 'anonymous', or 'unconscious' belief and/or faith. In the following two chapters, the contribution of one further theologian, Karl Rahner, will be considered and critiqued in depth.

3

Karl Rahner and the Salvation of Atheists

The German Jesuit theologian Karl Rahner's engagement with atheism spanned almost forty years, from his 1946 sermons published as *On Prayer*, to a number of interviews on Marxist–Christian dialogue given in Budapest in March 1984, the same month as his death. Within this period, and true to his own dictum that 'the "struggle" against the mass-phenomenon of atheism must begin by taking it seriously' (1968: 121–2), Rahner produced a large number of occasional pieces (articles, lectures, encyclopaedia entries) dealing with the many questions it posed. These approach atheism from a wide range of perspectives: historical, sociological, psychological, dogmatic, missiological, and – above all – pastoral. In addition, Rahner was among the first consultors appointed to the Secretariat for Non-believers, and was a leading figure in the dialogue with atheists, even founding and editing (with Herbert Vorgrimler) a journal devoted to the subject, *Internationale Dialog Zeitschrift*.[1] Most significantly, of

---

[1] One should not, however, overestimate the extent of Rahner's involvement in these ventures. True, he attended and spoke at a number of the Munich-based *Paulusgesellschaft*'s meetings on Christian–Marxist dialogue (e.g. [1966] 1972a; [1966] 1972b; cf. Hebblethwaite 1977: 18–30). He also delivered at least one lecture under the Secretariat's auspices ([1968] 1974). Compared with several other of the consultors, however, Rahner's file in the Secretariat's archives – which should, in theory, detail all his correspondence and activity with them – is notably empty: see Arch. SNC. Box 6. File 'R. Padre KARL RAHNER S.J.'. His actual work on the *Internationale Dialog Zeitschrift* was probably also fairly minimal. At the very least, all of the editorial 'spade work' appears to have been done by Vorgrimler. Again, see: Arch. SNC. Box 1/000. File 'Rivista del dialogo'; also Arch. SNC. Box 13/20. File 'VORGRIMLER'. Finally, Rahner seems to have had little part in the Jesuits' own activities in this area. For example, he was not a recipient/correspondent of the intra-Jesuit *Letters on the Service of Faith and New Cultures*, which began in the mid-1970s, and which was, as its founding editor Jean-Yves Calvez stated, 'essentially an instrument for exchange and communication of experience and information among Jesuits

course, Rahner is famous for the theologoumenon of 'anonymous' (or 'implicit') Christians (or Christianity), his much-discussed explication of how non-Christians, and particularly atheists (Rahner's favoured example), might attain salvation.

To put it very briefly, he argues that if (i) membership of the Church is absolutely necessary for salvation, and (ii) God wills the salvation of all people (cf. 1 Tim 2.4), then: 'somehow all men must be capable of being members of the Church; and this capacity must not be understood merely in the sense of an abstract and purely logical possibility, but as a real and historically concrete one' ([1964] 1969: 391). According to Rahner, therefore:

> [T]here must be degrees of membership of the Church [...] in descending order from the explicitness of baptism into a non-official and anonymous Christianity which can and should yet be called Christianity in a meaningful sense, even though it itself cannot and would not describe itself as such. (Ibid.)

Even so brief a statement as this raises a host of questions – for example, is it true that Catholic doctrine demands that *membership* (as opposed to simply mediation) of the Church is necessary for salvation?[2] – and it will come as no surprise to learn that Rahner's

---

more directly concerned with the Service of the Faith in New Cultures (unbelief, secularism, religious indifference, atheism, as well as new expressions of faith in the context of new cultural environments)' (1980: 1). For evidence of Rahner's non-involvement, see Calvez (1976; 1981).

[2] This is an interesting ecclesiological issue, to which no detailed answers either can, or need, be offered here. It certainly seems possible to read key statements of the magisterium as implying that saved non-Catholics are saved despite their *not* being members of the Church, even though it is only through and because of the Church's mediation that they are so. As we saw in chapter two, Pius XII's *Mystici Corporis Christi* states that only baptized Catholics are 'really' (*reapse*) members of the mystical body of Christ (i.e. the Church), though he admits the possibility that others may nevertheless be saved. Likewise, LG 16 speaks only of those who are 'related (*ordinantur*) to the People of God'. These texts do not, however, necessarily foreclose Rahner's subtler position, a version of which he was advocating as early as his important commentary of *Mystici Corporis Christi*: 'besides the simple straightforward membership of the Church, there are other lesser and looser ways of belonging to Christ and to the Mystical Body of Our Lord which reaches concrete form in the Church' ([1947] 1963: 55).

As detailed in the previous chapter, both Congar and de Lubac before Vatican II, and Ratzinger after it, advanced interpretations of *Extra Ecclesiam* in terms of mediation, rather than of membership (e.g. Lubac [1938] 1964: 123; Congar [1959] 1961: 98; and Ratzinger 1972: 152–3). A similar sense must be given to the assertion of the current *Catechism of the Catholic Church* (a project over which Ratzinger presided) that:

Karl Rahner and the Salvation of Atheists 79

proposals have generated a huge, and ever growing, secondary literature. As we have seen, Rahner is by no means the only major Catholic theologian to have turned his mind to the 'salvation of the others'. Yet it is his theory of anonymous Christians which is by far the best known, the most discussed, and thus, inevitably, the most frequently criticized.

It was, therefore, also inevitable that a monograph such as this should devote a significant amount of attention to Rahner. Importantly, he is as up front as I am about the dogmatic constraints on his theologizing. He too accepts the trifold necessity of faith, baptism, and the Church for salvation, and, from the mid-1960s onwards, is explicit in relating his own ideas to the teaching of Vatican II, and especially, of course, LG 14 and 16 and (on the subject of atheists) GS 19–21. Against the background of his more general theology of atheism, which he developed and refined over a period of several decades, and which is arguably the most complete and nuanced yet offered by any Catholic theologian, Rahner's account of the salvation of atheists constitutes a significant achievement of 'creatively faithful' dogmatic theology. It is important to stress this right from the start, since much that will follow in this chapter (especially in its latter sections) is rather critical of Rahner, and this will prepare the way for the rather different account of the salvation of atheists developed in chapters four and five. However, my critique here focuses on a single, albeit crucial, aspect of Rahner's theory: *the question of faith, and specifically, how it is that a saved atheist is able to fulfil the criterion of possessing it*. This is, as Rahner quite rightly states, a necessity of means, rather than simply of precept:

> The Christian is convinced that in order to achieve salvation man must believe in God, and not merely in God but in Christ; that this faith is not merely a positive commandment from which one could be dispensed under certain conditions [. . .]. On the contrary, this faith is in itself necessary and therefore demanded absolutely, not merely as a commandment but as the only possible means, not as a condition alone but as an unavoidable way of access, for man's salvation is nothing less than the fulfilment and definitive coming to maturity of precisely this beginning, for which therefore nothing else can substitute. ([1964] 1969: 390–1)

'Formulated in a positive manner, it signifies that all salvation proceeds from Christ the Head through the Church, which is his body' (CCC 846: '*Modo positivo formulata, significat omnem salutem a Christo-Capite per Ecclesiam procedere quae corpus est Eius*'). It proceeds to quote LG 14.

To pre-empt myself slightly, Rahner argues (not unreasonably, it must be said) that it must be possible for an atheist to have – unbeknownst to herself or indeed any other living person, and in some necessarily 'anonymous' or 'implicit' manner – a saving faith in the here and now. For example, in a characteristically Rahnerian turn of phrase, he speaks of 'the possibility of coexistence of a conceptually objectified atheism and a non-propositional and existentially realised theism' ([1967] 1972: 148).

Rahner's idea has much merit; this will be clear from the following elucidation. There are, however, a series of notable difficulties with it, some of the most important of which will be detailed towards the end of this chapter. Considered cumulatively, I will argue that these difficulties cast considerable doubt on Rahner's account of the salvation of atheists. These objections will not, it must be said, rule out appeals to an 'implicit' or 'anonymous' faith *tout court*. And indeed, I will be offering one example (albeit a fictional one) where such an appeal seems not only permissible, but perhaps mandatory. But nevertheless, the general thrust of my critique will be strongly against such a solution to the problem of the salvation of atheists – at least, on the magnitude envisioned by Rahner – pointing towards my own, tentative solution (itself, of course, not devoid of difficulties!) advanced in chapters four and five. Yet note well that this counter solution will not only be, in many other respects, not anti-Rahnerian, but will betray the great Jesuit's influence at several important junctures.

RAHNER AS REPRESENTATIVE

Rahner is not, of course, the only theologian to have appealed to 'implicit', 'anonymous', 'secret', 'hidden', or 'unconscious' faith in explicating the salvation of atheists. Indeed, as shown throughout chapter two, this kind of move was endemic among Catholic theologians in the decades preceding Vatican II. In critiquing Rahner's theory of anonymous Christians on this point, I am thereby also critiquing the expressed views of, among others, Bainvel, Blondel, Adam, de Lubac, Daniélou, Schillebeeckx, Küng, and Congar, insofar as they all also proposed, at one time or another, this solution to the problem (although some of them would later change their minds).

Hence I am taking Rahner to be *representative* of a much wider trend in twentieth-century Catholic theology. This is very important to note, since it is all too easy to get the impression that Rahner's thinking was substantially *outré*: it was not. Of course, it is true that 'anonymous Christianity' was strongly criticized by Congar, de Lubac, Schillebeeckx, Balthasar, Küng, Kasper, and Ratzinger – that is, by a veritable 'Who's Who' of post-conciliar theology. However, every single one of these theologians agreed, at least at one time, with Rahner on certain essential points: that the Catholic Church is absolutely necessary for salvation; that those who are not formally members of the Church are not thereby necessarily excluded from the possibility of salvation; and that, in the case of a conscious atheist, a purely implicit or anonymous faith in the Christian God could be sufficient for salvation. Naturally, there were other differences between them and Rahner, as there also were among themselves, but these do not eclipse the basic agreements shared by them all. Even the genuinely divisive issue between Rahner and the others, and the root of most of the criticisms that have been levelled against him – that is, his terminology of anonymous *Christians* or *Christianity* – should not be overstated.

The case of Schillebeeckx illustrates this point very well. In his 1971 book *The Understanding of Faith*, Schillebeeckx argues that:

> It is [...] not really possible to speak of 'anonymous Christians', even though it is certainly necessary to express in one way or another the fact that non-Christians are not, because of their orthopraxis, deprived of salvation. On the contrary, Christians call themselves such in an explicit, conscious and justified way. ([1971] 1981: 101)

That same year, Rahner published an article entitled 'Observations on the Problem of the "Anonymous Christian"', citing Schillebeeckx's book as part of a brief survey of the theory's critical reception ([1971] 1976: 281). As noted in the previous chapter, however, Schillebeeckx was comfortable speaking of 'anonymous religion', the pagan's 'smouldering, anonymously-theistic heart', and even 'anonymously-supernatural faith in the "God of salvation"' in a 1953 lecture. Furthermore, when editing this text for publication in 1966's collection of his articles *Wereld en Kerk*, Schillebeeckx's own pen added the words *Anoniem Christendom*, 'Anonymous Christianity', as the subtitle to this section.³ Prior to this, in 1957's *Christ the Sacrament*, he had referred to 'unconscious Christianity' (*onbewust christendom*; [1957] 1966: 19), and in a 1961 lecture – and hence, as we shall see, only the year after Rahner had premiered the phrase – he used the specific term 'anonymous Christian' ([1961] 1979: 77). His 1965 article 'The Church and Mankind', published in the very first issue of *Concilium*, is largely devoted to what he repeatedly calls 'implicit' or 'anonymous' Christianity, the existence of which (he affirms) 'must be taken as a fact' (1965: 43). What is more, in theological articles of the mid-1960s it is common to find 'anonymous Christianity' ascribed to both Rahner and Schillebeeckx – and sometimes even to Schillebeeckx alone (e.g. Bortnowska 1965: 3; Hillman 1966: 362; and Nys [1966] 1968: 267; see also Preston 1966: 10–11, where 'German and Dutch theologians' presumably refers to Rahner and the Belgian-born but Dutch-based Schillebeeckx).

Obviously, by 1971 he had changed his mind regarding the phrase's accuracy – under the influence, perhaps, of Balthasar's (in)famously searing critique in 1966's *Cordula oder der Ernstfall* ([1966] 1994). But it nevertheless shows that, even on this point, Rahner was by no means so exceptional as is commonly thought. And indeed, among Rahner's other much-cited critics, de Lubac, although he rejected the notion of an anonymous 'Christianity' in 1967's *The Church: Paradox and Mystery*, conceded in the selfsame work: 'That "anonymous Christians" will be found in diverse milieux where, one way or another, the light of the gospel has penetrated, no Christian could possibly still deny' ([1967] 1969: 87–9).⁴ And even Ratzinger, who in 1985 criticized the 'extreme form' that some accounts of the salvation of non-Catholics have taken 'on the basis of theories like that of "anonymous Christians"' (1985: 197), could write in a 1965 article, without passing any negative comment, that 'the fundamental Christian dispositions' which inhere in a person's conscience 'distinguish the "anonymous Christians" from pagans (Rahner)' ([1965] 1970: 51).

Ultimately, all three theologians would – in my view, absolutely correctly⁵ – follow Balthasar in denying the applicability of the name

---

³ *Stichting Edward Schillebeeckx*, Nijmegen. MS 53/6: 'Herbronning van het priesterlijk apostolaat en activering van het laïcaat', 43 pp. ['159–202'], 159.

⁴ De Lubac had, moreover, mooted the possibility of *un christianisme implicite* as early as the 1930s, and thus long before Rahner (Conway 2004: 111).

⁵ For a rather different appraisal of Balthasar's rectitude, see Endean 1998.

'Christian' or 'Christianity' to those to whom LG 16 refers (Schillebeeckx [1971] 1981: 101; Ratzinger 1985: 197; and Lubac [1967] 1969: 87–9), the basic point being that: 'To use the term "Christian" is to imply knowledge of Jesus Christ leading to baptism, and therefore the term "anonymous Christian" is contradictory' (Congar 1974: 7; from a Lutheran perspective, see also Jüngel 1975). Yet even Balthasar, writing in a footnote to *Cordula*, could admit: 'Of course, this is not to deny Karl Rahner's notion that there is a *fides implicita* [implicit faith] and a corresponding supernatural love outside the sphere of Christianity (see Lk 21.1–4) and of the Bible (see Mt 15.21–28), as well as with those who are theoretically atheists (Rom 2.14–16)' ([1966] 1994: 114 n. 42). Contrary to Rahner's own frequent claims (e.g. [1964] 1969: 396; [1967] 1972: 145; [1971] 1976: 281; [1982] 1990: 166), I do not believe that the disputes surrounding his terminology are purely semantic. But this is far from the only, or even the most, important issue at stake here. Most importantly, on the question of *implicit faith*, the focus of this chapter, Rahner's position was far from contentious. So much so in fact, that on this point, as on rather more than is sometimes supposed, Rahner was not merely 'the typical inclusivist' (Kilby 2004: 121), but the typical Catholic theologian.

PASTORAL ORIENTATION

One need not look far for what prompted Rahner's interest in atheism. Looking back on his career in 1979 he confessed: 'I wasn't really interested in scholarship for the sake of scholarship. My needs and outlook were completely, immediately, and genuinely pastoral.' Supporting this, he adds: 'the fact that I wrote an article many years ago about Christians and their unbelieving relatives [...] shows very clearly that pastoral motivations were behind my work' ([1979] 1985: 21–2). This is, in itself, highly significant. Unlike many of his theological contemporaries, whose first forays into the study of atheism were scholarly treatises on Nietzsche or Marx, the attraction for Rahner was, from the outset, an avowedly pastoral one. Indeed his subsequent, academic writings on the subject – and on this topic, as on most others, Rahner's writings can be very 'academic' indeed – can be traced back to this primary motivation.

Rahner's 1954 article, 'The Christian among Unbelieving Relations', thus begins with the observation:

> Anyone who has a knowledge of life and does not live in a milieu which one might call medieval will already be aware from the mere title of this essay what dark, confused and bitter questions it summons up. The Christian of today lives in a Diaspora which penetrates deep into the circle of his relatives. ([1954] 1967a: 355)

Needless to say, this casts the phenomenon of unbelief in an entirely different light than if it were simply an abstract, theoretical issue for contemporary Catholics. In his words:

> If these were people towards whom we were otherwise indifferent, [. . .] then everything would be so much easier to bear; or better, it would only be the burden which weighs on our spirit and heart at the sight of how little the name of Christ is known and loved in the world after two thousand years. But these are persons who are 'related' to us, whom we love, to whom we are bound with a thousand ties of blood, of shared feelings, of life and destiny, of love, in many respects much more so than with those whom we call fellow members in the household of the faith. (Ibid.)

Rahner proceeds to detail the countless quotidian anguishes to which such a situation can give rise: loved ones' wounding mockery, family turmoil over baptisms and weddings, temptations to the believer's own faith at seeing an at times woefully deficient Church through the eyes of 'outsiders'. Then, striking at the very heart of the matter, he writes:

> But the most obscure and difficult part of these relationships is the question of the eternal salvation of those whom we love. [. . .] If we – who are baptized, nourished with the body of the Lord, living in the community of God's calling, instructed by God's word, praying – are yet admonished to work out our salvation in fear and trembling, [. . .] can we do other than think with holy fear also of the eternal salvation of others, can we then so easily reassure ourselves with the good faith of others? (Ibid.: 357–8)

Such questions spring naturally from the fault line between Christianity and an increasingly secular modern West.

Towards the end of the article Rahner offers a 'hesitant word on the most obscure part of this whole question'. And again, manifestly concrete concerns frame his disquisition:

'How is it with my father who died without the Sacraments because he did not bother about such things although he was "as such" a Catholic?' 'How am I to think of my uncle who left the Church and remained outside it until his death?' How often are such questions and many similar ones secretly asked in the most diverse circumstances of life and frequently repressed with an embarrassed shrug of the shoulders. (Ibid.: 361)

He begins by cautioning that one cannot declare *any* individual, with the special exception of those beatified or canonized by the Church, to be definitely saved. The fact that someone is a Catholic Christian is, admittedly, one reason for hope that one cannot have in the case of an unbeliever. But the tradition of the Church does not confine the *possibility* of salvation only to such persons, as attested by no less authorities than Augustine and Pius IX. Furthermore, enunciating what is by now a familiar theme from (among others) Congar and de Lubac, Rahner suggests that even those living in close proximity to the Church and its members might nevertheless be considered *invincibly ignorant* on the ground that Catholics are often 'the cause of averting the gaze of others from the true nature of the Church' (ibid.: 362). In another parallel with Congar and de Lubac – not to mention Adam, Daniélou, Blondel, and Maritain – he points out too that a real, saving faith is contained within every genuine moral decision or action, *even if* this is not consciously recognized by the agent (ibid.: 364). Thus, without becoming too mired in theological detail, he stresses that the Catholic is justified, on the firm basis of the doctrinal tradition of the Church, at least to *hope* for his or her unbelieving relations. As Nikolaus Schwerdtfeger has correctly pointed out, it is here that one finds the 'existential backdrop' to Rahner's development of the theory of anonymous Christianity (1994: 74; see also Vass 1998: 48).

ATHEISM AND ANONYMITY

Let us turn then to considering, in some detail, Rahner's understanding of how atheists may be saved – focusing, as explained above, on the fraught question of faith. As with his theology of atheism more generally, it is fair to say that Rahner's account was built up over a number of decades. He appears first to have used the *phrase* 'anonymous Christianity' in a 1960 article 'Poetry and the Christian'

([1960] 1966c). 'Anonymous Christian' was deployed the following year, in a lecture entitled 'Christianity and the Non-Christian Religions' ([1961] 1966). In these earliest outings, however, both phrases occur only incidentally. Hence in 'Poetry and the Christian', Rahner simply remarks, somewhat in passing, 'There is such a thing as anonymous Christianity' ([1960] 1966c: 366). Later in life, he was unable to remember whether he or someone else actually came up with the term(s) ([1982] 1990: 166) – evidently, it had not come to him in a memorable flash of inspiration. Only in 1963, following the publication of *The Anonymous Christian* by his friend and correspondent Anita Röper (see Röper and Röper 2009), did the phrase begin to gain any wider currency. The book is Röper's own treatment of a topic about which, as she states in her preface, 'Karl Rahner has already said many things, although only by way of hints and in a way which only professional theologians understand' ([1963] 1966: ix). Rahner's own landmark article 'Anonymous Christians' began life as a radio review of the book, which was then edited for publication in its own right, with all references to Röper removed. Only then did Rahner start to employ his own *Stichwort* with any frequency, beginning in the mid-1960s. By that time, not only was it also being used by other leading theologians (especially Schillebeeckx), but its theology, if not its phraseology, had – at least to Rahner's mind – been mandated by the Second Vatican Council.

Terminology aside, Rahner's central *ideas* had of course been gestating for rather longer. Schwerdtfeger (1994) identifies two other articles, in addition to the one discussed above, as being of especial importance: 1947's 'Membership of the Church according to the Teaching of Pius XII's Encyclical "*Mystici Corporis Christi*"', and 1957's 'On the Theology of Martyrdom'. Several others from the 1940s and 1950s might also be mentioned as already containing the main principles of anonymous Christianity, albeit at this stage in an aptly 'anonymous' way (see Gallagher 1980: 41–8; Vass 1998: 47; and Kilby 2004: 13–31). The developments in Rahner's thinking did not, moreover, stop with the publication of 'Anonymous Christians', and he continued to refine his thoughts right up until his death twenty years later. A full account of the (pre)history of anonymous Christians is, however, far beyond the scope of this chapter. For obvious reasons, the discussion below will focus on Rahner's main article dealing specifically with the salvation of atheists, and written in light of the key Vatican II texts which form the dogmatic bedrock of this study: 1967's 'Atheism and Implicit Christianity' (which incorporates and expands upon the same year's 'The Teaching of the Second Vatican Council on Atheism'). This cannot, though, be understood *in vacuo*, and a large number of other sources must also be used. Above all, before considering the 1967 piece directly, it is necessary first to grasp something of Rahner's understanding of the relationship between nature and grace. This is a huge and complex topic, of which only a brief treatment is possible here.

Nature and grace

According to Rahner, grace is, fundamentally, God's gift of *himself* to human beings:

> God does not bestow merely a certain kind of saving love and intimacy, or a certain kind of saving presence [. . .]. God does not confer on man merely created gifts as a token of his love. God communicates *himself* by what is no longer simply efficient causality. He makes man share in the very nature of God. (1975b: 588)

As he would later put it in *Foundations*: 'It is decisive for an understanding of God's self-communication to man to grasp that the giver in his own being is the gift, that in and through his own being the giver gives himself to creatures as their own fulfilment' ([1976] 1978: 120). In explaining how this self-gift of God (grace) relates to concrete human beings (nature) in 1950, Rahner positioned his own views as a *via media* between the 'extrinsicism' of the neo-scholastics, and the 'intrinsicism' of proponents of the *nouvelle théologie* (represented, above all, by de Lubac). On Rahner's assessment, the neo-scholastics err in presenting grace as something wholly extrinsic to nature: 'a mere superstructure [. . .] imposed upon nature by God's free decree, and in such a way that the relationship between the two is no more intense than that of a freedom from contradiction' ([1950] 1961: 298). On this model, grace is merely an *extra* to 'pure nature'; a supremely desirable one, to be sure, but an add-on all the same. Furthermore, since 'in the average (if not unanimous) view grace in itself remains absolutely beyond consciousness' (ibid.), it remains something external, a thing which one learns *about*, but whose presence or absence is never *felt*. On this view, as he complained in a later article, grace becomes 'a superstructure beyond the realm of consciousness', and 'the relationship between nature and grace is conceived in such a way that they appear as two layers so carefully placed that they penetrate each other as little as possible' ([1960] 1966b: 166, 167).

Though sharing these criticisms, de Lubac's counterview is also inadequate. On Rahner's assessment, de Lubac's positing of 'an unconditional and yet natural ordination of man to the supernatural' ([1950] 1961: 310),[6] that is – to put it crudely – of an *intrinsic* orientation of nature to grace, critically undermines the unexactedness of grace. If (as de Lubac claims) grace is inseparable from the concept of nature, and if therefore even the theoretical possibility of a *natura pura* (i.e. a nature devoid of grace) is inconceivable, then according to Rahner, grace can no longer be, in any meaningful sense, *gratuitous*. It is instead a necessary 'component' of nature, which God is obliged to supply. Rahner's concerns here echo those voiced earlier that same year by Pius XII who, in *Humani Generis*, rebuked those who 'corrupt the "gratuity" of the supernatural order, since they say that God cannot create beings endowed with intellect, unless he relates and calls them to the beatific vision' (art. 26; AAS 42 [1950]: 570).

Rahner in fact provides two formulations of his own solution. In doing so, he offers an illuminating insight into his theological method. The first account is avowedly 'kerygmatic':

> God wishes to communicate himself, to pour forth the love which he himself is. That is the first and the last of his real plans and hence of his real world too. Everything else exists so that this one thing might be: the eternal miracle of infinite Love. And so God makes a creature whom he can love: he creates man. He creates him in such a way that he *can* receive this Love which is God himself, and that he can and must at the same time accept it for what it is: the ever astounding wonder, the unexpected, unexacted gift. [. . .] Thus in this second respect God must so create man that love does not only pour forth free and unexacted, but also so that man as real partner, as one who can accept or reject it, can experience and accept it *as* the unexacted event and wonder not owed to *him*, the real man. ([1950] 1961: 310–11)

---

[6] It is worth pointing out that in this article Rahner is not engaging directly with de Lubac's own writings on the subject, but rather with 'a faithful summary of de Lubac's position' published by an anonymous author 'D.', usually identified as Emil Delaye SJ, in a 1950 issue of *Orientierung* (O'Sullivan 2007: 21).

Having outlined what he – a little optimistically perhaps – refers to as 'simple propositions, which every Christian can in a true sense make his own', only then does Rahner attempt to transpose them into 'theology'. While such transposition is, Rahner avers, 'necessary for the theologian and the preacher if he is to be preserved from the danger of misinterpreting them or rendering them innocuous', it is evident that he regards this as very much a *secondary* activity. This is noteworthy in itself, and further accentuates his pastoral motivations: preaching is not diluted theology; instead, theology is clarified preaching. Rahner's *theological* gloss on the above passage, then, relies on two central premises. Firstly, human beings, as they actually are, must always have a genuine receptivity to grace.

> Man should be *able* to receive this Love which is God himself; he must have a congeniality for it. He must be able to accept it (and hence grace, the beatific vision) as one who has room and scope, understanding and desire for it. Thus he must have a real 'potency' for it. He must have it *always*. He is indeed someone always addressed and claimed by this Love. For, as he now in fact is, he is created for it; he is thought and called into being so that Love might bestow itself. To this extent this 'potency' is what is inmost and most authentic in him, the centre and root of what he is absolutely. (Ibid.: 311)

Even among the damned, those who have turned *themselves* away from God's love, this 'potency' for grace remains absolutely ubiquitous. Thus Rahner describes it, borrowing Heideggerian terminology (e.g. Heidegger [1927] 2000: 83–4), as an *existential*. That is, to quote Fergus Kerr, 'an essential feature of human existence: not any particular phenomenon, certainly not anything psychological, but one of the a priori conditions in order that human existence should exhibit some phenomenon or other' (1997: 174).

Secondly, however, developing his criticism of de Lubac et al., Rahner insists that: 'The real man as God's real partner should be able to receive this Love as what it necessarily is: as free gift.' Grace must be gratuitous. As such, it follows that 'this central, abiding existential, consisting in the ordination to the threefold God of grace and eternal life, is itself to be characterized as unexacted, as "supernatural"' ([1950] 1961: 312–13). For the reasons given above, this could not be the case if the *existential*, each person's orientation towards grace, were properly a part of his or her nature. Instead, this 'elevation' of nature is a freely given, wholly gratuitous gift (hence 'supernatural'). It is, however, a gift that is given to each and every person, without exception (hence 'existential') – something which, as Rahner frequently points out, by no means compromises its gratuity.[7] This is, in essence, what Rahner means by his daunting term 'supernatural existential' (*übernaturliches Existential*).[8] In the words of Joseph DiNoia: 'Without itself being grace, the supernatural existential confirms the orientation of the human natural order to the supernatural order which God's intention to confer grace presupposes' (DiNoia 1989: 194). Furthermore, on Rahner's theory, unlike on that of de Lubac, the scholastic concept of *natura pura*, nature devoid of grace, is retained. This preserves grace's necessary gratuity. *Natura pura* is, hence, what would have been the case, had God not, in fact, freely chosen to supply nature with a receptivity to his self-gift that it would otherwise lack. As things actually are, however, this *natura pura* is only a 'remainder concept' (*Restsbegriff*) ([1950] 1961: 313–14).

The experience of grace

In 1954, the same year as 'The Christian among Unbelieving Relations', Rahner also published a short article entitled 'Reflections on the Experience of Grace'. He begins with the question 'Have we ever experienced grace?' and, after some preliminary remarks, suggests a litany of possibilities for 'our' having done precisely that (only a selection of which are reproduced here):

> Have we ever kept quiet, even though we wanted to defend ourselves when we had been unfairly treated? Have we ever forgiven someone even though we got no thanks for it and our silent forgiveness was taken for granted? [. . .] Have we ever sacrificed something without receiving any thanks or recognition for it, and even without a feeling of inner satisfaction? Have we ever been absolutely lonely? [. . .] Have we ever tried to love God when we seemed to be calling out into emptiness and our cry seemed to fall on deaf ears, when it looked as if we were taking a terrifying jump into the bottomless abyss, when everything seemed to become incomprehensible and apparently senseless? ([1954] 1967b: 87)

---

[7] 'Theology has been too long and too often bedevilled by the unavowed supposition that grace would be no longer grace if it were too generously distributed by the love of God!' ([1960] 1966b: 180).

[8] For more detailed discussions than are possible here of this crucial Rahnerian term, see Vass 1985: 59–83; Dych 1992: 35–7; or Conway 1993: 10–16.

Karl Rahner and the Salvation of Atheists 91

Note, first of all, that none of these are religious experiences in a classical, Jamesian sense. Some of them would seem to be outright irreligious (in that their primary referent is the *absence* of God), and the great majority have no obvious 'religious' bearing whatsoever. For Rahner, however, this point is immaterial. Irrespective of how such experiences seem, they are nonetheless experiences of 'the spirit in its proper transcendence':

> For the experience meant here is the experience of eternity; it is the experience that the spirit is more than merely a part of this temporal world; the experience that man's meaning is not exhausted by the meaning and fortune of this world; the experience of the adventure and confidence of taking the plunge, an experience which no longer has any reason which can be demonstrated or which is taken from the success of this world. (Ibid.: 88)

Furthermore, he continues, 'once we experience the spirit in this way, we (at least, we as Christians who live in faith) have also already *in fact* experienced the *supernatural*. We have done so perhaps in a very anonymous and inexpressible manner' (ibid.; see also [1976] 1977: 20–3). This is a crucial passage for understanding Rahner. Although he is addressing here other Christians, it is obvious that such experiences of 'the spirit', and thus of the supernatural, are not restricted only to believers. Indeed, even for Christians, the experience of the Holy Spirit at such moments may occur 'in a very anonymous and inexpressible manner'. That is, they may well not be consciously aware of the fact, or if they are, of its correct interpretation. Further, Rahner's use of the term 'anonymous' in this context is especially noteworthy. It may well be the word's first usage in this *specific* sense in Rahner's entire corpus.[9]

Needless to say, the supernatural existential is the pre-condition for such experiences of grace. And this pre-condition is, as its Heidegger-inspired name suggests, present in all human beings. Again, as was noted above, Rahner rejected the idea that the presence of grace is something 'absolutely beyond consciousness'. Grace must, therefore, be *felt* by everyone, whether they can correctly identify it or not. This is singularly important, of course, in the case of the non-believer. If Rahner is right, then even the most resolute of atheists has encountered the grace – and hence, as noted above, the *self-revelation* – of

---

[9] At least, it is the term's first such appearance in the *Theological Investigations*.

God, albeit 'in a very anonymous and inexpressible manner', precisely in his or her *transcendental experience*. This technical term requires a certain amount of explanation. In his 1957 *Lexikon* entry, for example, Rahner spoke of 'the absolute transcendency (*Transzendenz*) of man', which 'as the transcendental condition of all intellectual knowledge and free action, implicitly refers to God' (1957: 987). In Kantian philosophy 'transcendental' refers to the a priori conditions that make a particular state of affairs possible (see Kerr 1997: 173; Weger 1980: 34; and Sheehan 2005). Hence, to adapt one of Rahner's own examples, hens are *transcendental* with regard to eggs ([1969] 1974: 150). However, in Rahner's idiom, the word implies both this Kantian sense, and an actual transcending of something (Kilby 2004: 32–4). As Karen Kilby has pointed out, Rahner's explanation of transcendental experience in *Foundations* is telling in this regard:

> This experience is called *transcendental* experience because it belongs to the necessary and inalienable structures of the knowing subject itself, and because it consists precisely in the transcendence beyond any particular group of possible objects or of categories. (Rahner [1976] 1978: 20)

For Rahner, therefore, *transcendental* experience signifies both the existence of an a priori condition for its very possibility (grace, and thus ultimately God), and the fact that it points to something beyond itself (God again). This is closely allied to the notion that God, as he writes elsewhere in *Foundations*, 'is at once giver and gift and the ground of the acceptance of the gift' (ibid.: 125).

Implicit faith

What, though, does all this have to do with the salvation of atheists? Throughout his writings, Rahner frequently draws (or assumes) a distinction between a person's unthematic *awareness* of God, and his or her subsequent *conceptualization* of that basic datum. Contrasting the former with the latter, he writes:

> It is to be noted that it is not a case of a conceptual representation of God, nor of a theorem or a proposition about God constructed out of human concepts [...] It has to do with God himself, not with a concept of him. [... It] is not just a conceptual thought of God but an awareness in experience of what alone gives (implicitly [...]) such concepts their real meaning. ([1956] 1964: 149–50)

Karl Rahner and the Salvation of Atheists

Rahner envisions two epistemological strata. In the first, God is apprehended at an unconscious or subconscious level, without the mediation of human concepts: 'the original experience'. In the second, this experience is 'comprehended' in a conscious, intellectual way: 'the subsequent reflection' ([1969] 1974: 150). This is, however, never a true comprehension, since God is of course the *absolute Mystery* (cf. Vass 1985: 110–12). As Kilby has expressed it:

> It is necessary to distinguish, Rahner insists again and again, between an *original* level of knowledge, or experience, or existence, and the level on which we use words and concepts. We use concepts to verbalize, thematize, or objectify our original experience, but the latter is never fully captured, never exhausted, by these concepts. The original experience always remains richer than any articulation of it, always eludes a complete verbalization. (2004: 21)

This distinction between two mental 'levels' allows him to make a crucial move at this point. The atheist, *ipso facto*, does not believe in God at the conscious, categorical level. But this does not necessarily preclude a deeper, subconscious belief at the transcendental level. This may manifest itself in a number of ways. In his 1962 article 'Thoughts on the Possibility of Belief Today', for instance, he suggests that:

> anyone who courageously accepts life – even a shortsighted, primitive positivist who apparently bears patiently with the poverty of the superficial – has really already accepted God. [. . .] For when man accepts himself in this way wholly and entirely, he accepts this light (i.e. he believes) even though he does so unthinkingly and without expressing it. ([1962] 1966a: 7–8)

Or alternatively, from 1967's 'Atheism and Implicit Christianity':

> The person who accepts a moral demand from his conscience as *absolutely* valid for him embraces it as such in a free act of affirmation – no matter how unreflected – asserts the absolute being of God, whether he knows or conceptualises it or not, as the very reason why there can be such a thing as an absolute demand at all. ([1967] 1972: 153)

For Rahner, *implicit* within a person's belief in the meaningfulness of life is a potentially saving *faith* in the One who is the ground of that very meaningfulness. Likewise, *implicit* within a person's belief in the absoluteness of a moral demand, is a *faith* in Him without whom no absolute moral demands would be possible. And this may be so even for one who explicitly denies the existence of such a being:

It is not so important how far, in such an act, a man is or is not consciously aware of these presuppositions [...] which inform his concrete knowledge and action. It may even be that he is *not able* to reflect conceptually upon the subjective factors involved in his concrete spiritual action. (Ibid.)

Rahner supports this view by pointing out that a person may think and act in accordance with logical principles, even though 'as a simple man he would be probably quite incapable, even after instruction, of understanding the abstract principles of Aristotelian logic as such in its abstract formality' (ibid.). Evidently, the recognition and acceptance of these principles are *implicit* in his thoughts and action, even if he does not, or cannot, articulate them in a conscious, categorical manner.

Something similar may, Rahner argues, be the case with (perhaps a great many) unbelievers. As we shall see in the following chapter, there are various reasons why a person may inculpably either fail to recognize, or actively deny, the existence of God at the conscious, categorical level of her psyche. And yet, through living out her life in a certain way, she may nevertheless signal the trust and confidence in God and his providential care for humanity which she possesses, 'perhaps in a very anonymous and inexpressible manner', at the subconscious, transcendental level. *In nuce*, this is what he means by 'the possibility of coexistence of a conceptually objectified atheism and a non-propositional and existentially realised theism' (ibid.: 148).

This is, then, Rahner's solution as to how an inculpably ignorant atheist might fulfil the necessary condition of *faith* for attaining salvation. (There are, of course, two other conditions – baptism, the Church – but these are not the focus of this chapter. They will be discussed in chapters four and five.) Compared to a recitation of the Athanasian Creed, 'courageously accepting life' or bowing to an absolute moral demand may seem like very strange expressions of one's faith or belief. Recall, though, Augustine's delineation of the different senses of *credere* in chapter one. *Credere Deum*, 'to believe that there is a God', is an intellectual stance *about* God. *Credere in Deum*, 'to believe in God', is to trust and have confidence *in* God (and act accordingly). The possibility of 'practical atheism' was also explored there, which may be thought of as the possession of *credere-Deum* belief, without *credere-in-Deum* believing (and acting). Thus on Rahner's own previously quoted definition, it is 'a lifestyle in

Karl Rahner and the Salvation of Atheists

which no (discernible) conclusions are drawn from the (theoretical) recognition of the existence of God' (1957: 983). Rahner sees his anonymous or implicit Christianity as the antitype to this. His implicitly faithful atheist 'existentially' possesses belief *in* God (*credere in Deum*), without 'intellectually' believing that there is a God (*credere Deum*).

> The transcendental experience of God is present of necessity and is also freely accepted in a positive decision to be faithful to conscience, but it is incorrectly objectified and interpreted. [...] There can be such a thing as innocent atheism because of the difference between subjective transcendentality and categorial objectification in concepts and sentences, producing the co-existence of transcendental theism and categorial atheism. [...] The components of this innocent atheism are: *on the one hand* the subject's continual transcendental dependence on God and the free acceptance of this dependence, especially in the moral act which respects absolutely the demands of conscience – i.e. a transcendental theism 'in the heart's depths' – and *on the other hand* the free rejection of the objectified concept of God, i.e., a categorial atheism in the forefront of conscious reflection, a rejection which cannot in itself be regarded as culpable. ([1967] 1972: 156)

Of course, in such cases there is a profound disjunction between what the (apparent) 'atheist' *really* believes (transcendentally), and what he or she only thinks she does (categorically) – an issue to which we shall return in depth. But Rahner can, and often does, appeal here to the findings of psychology. To quote from two later articles, in defence of anonymous Christianity:

> [I]n the consciousness, in its realization, realities can be present (of a subjective but ultimately also of an objective kind) which are conscious without necessarily having to be verbally objectified as objects which have been explicitly reflected upon. This is a truism that should not be overlooked especially in the age of Freud [...]. In principle, then, a knowledge can also be present in a *fides qua* (however more precisely this may be conceived), which knowledge need not at all be an object known and verbalized in the consciousness, a knowledge which the reflexive consciousness even denies possessing. ([1982] 1988: 154–5)
>
> [W]e should have learnt enough from psychology, depth psychology and a genuine metaphysical understanding of human knowledge and freedom to realise that man does not deliberately put into practice only those things which he can state in words as objects of his conscious awareness or can freely affirm. (1979: 219; see also [1983] 1990: 126–7)

These are not, it should be said, simply apologetic attempts by Rahner to bolster his theory. As early as the 1946 sermons on prayer, for example, he was already arguing that 'the mind of man is not consciousness alone, and that below the level of consciousness are infinite possibilities, unfathomed depths, unmeasured horizons' ([1946] 1993: 31). And further:

> It is a well established psychological fact that actions deliberately and consciously performed are motivated by unconscious urges, are controlled by emotions long buried in the recesses of our being; so that, what appear to be actions done in the full light of consciousness, are but shadows and symbols of buried urges which now suddenly become active beyond the reach of our conscious will. What appeared, therefore, as straightforward acts consciously controlled, are shown to be, as it were, a mirror held up to the true inner reality of ourselves. Thus we come to realise, with a rush of panic, that what we regard as actions posited by us are in reality but aspects of our real selves: they are us. (Ibid.: 10–11)

RAHNER CRITIQUED

We are now well acquainted with, if not the entirety of Rahner's theory of anonymous or implicit Christianity, then at least one crucial aspect of it: the appeal to, and justification of, the possibility of an implicit, saving faith on the part of a justified unbeliever. As I have already argued, this is not something that is *distinctively* Rahnerian. Rahner's account is surely the most systematic, and indeed influential, but – without ignoring differences of a greater or lesser degree – an appeal to precisely this kind of implicit, or anonymous, or secret, or hidden faith was nigh-on ubiquitous among major Catholic theologians in the years surrounding the Second Vatican Council (and beyond). Arguably, such a move requires at least some distinction between mental strata; for, at the very least, the atheist must be unaware that they indeed possess such a faith. And in the writings of Maréchal, Maritain, Gilson, and de Lubac, at least, this need is met with an epistemology very similar to Rahner's. Thus Maritain, for example, posited a 'prephilosophic' knowledge of God existing 'below the threshold of reflective consciousness' ([1953] 1955: 1, 78; cf.

O'Callaghan 1986: 23–30).[10] In the above long section, I have tried to present a fair, compelling, and above all comprehensible elucidation of Rahner's main ideas. His account of implicit faith is, on any assessment, an impressive, multi-layered piece of theological reasoning, and I hope that I have done it justice.

Yet despite its virtues (and these are many and significant), I do not ultimately find Rahner's account convincing. At the very least, I think that it is open to enough doubts and questions that there is a strong justification for trying to find a different solution to the problem it addresses. In the bulk of this section, I will outline three of these: (i) a general caution against appealing to the implicit or unconscious, (ii) a specific argument, borrowed from Joseph DiNoia, against Rahner's stretching of the existing theological concept of 'implicit faith', and (iii) a criticism of the justifications which Rahner puts forward for imputing such a faith to the inculpable atheist. Before broaching these, however, it is necessary first to comment on how closely Rahner's theories fit with the relevant pronouncements of Vatican II.

Anonymous Christianity and Vatican II

As mentioned previously, both 1964's 'Anonymous Christians' and 1967's 'Atheism and Implicit Christianity' – along with pretty well all Rahner's subsequent writings on the subject – make explicit reference to the selfsame conciliar statements that form both the start and end point of this book's investigation. This is not, of course, surprising. Rahner was Cardinal König's *peritus* at the Council, and by almost all accounts, except typically his own (e.g. [1979] 1985: 81–3), he exerted a considerable influence over it. Naturally, this influence was fully reciprocal; for the rest of his life Rahner was deeply concerned with both the implications, and the implementation, of all aspects of the conciliar theology – only one of which, of course, will be investigated

---

[10] It is worth noting that, although there are a great number of similarities between Maritain and Rahner on this and other issues, I have found no evidence of any direct Maritainian influence on Rahner's thought here. Indeed, in the entirety of the *Theological Investigations* Rahner mentions him only twice – once in an extremely lengthy bibliography on the philosophy of symbols ([1959] 1966: 223 n. 3), and once as simply one name in a list of eighteen modern philosophers ([1962] 1966b: 409). As such, it is likely that both developed their theories independently, albeit working from a common source in Blondel – primarily via Maréchal in Rahner's case; and from Blondel directly, but with additional influence from Maréchal, in Maritain's.

here. It is tempting to assume, therefore, that either he or his theology exerted a cardinal influence on the evolution of LG 16 and GS 19–21. Indeed, hints of this sort are met with frequently in Rahner scholarship (e.g. O'Callaghan 1986: 1; Dych 1992: 13; Vass 1998: 51). Closer examination, however, suggests that this was not the case: despite being König's *peritus*, Rahner was not one of the drafters of GS 19–21 (unlike de Lubac and Daniélou) and, though he did work on LG, was not part of the subcommittee directly responsible for the chapter *De Populo Dei* (unlike Congar).

My purpose here is *not* to argue that Rahner's theory of anonymous Christianity, or his account of implicit faith specifically, is incompatible with the pronouncements of Vatican II. My concern is rather with the possibility that his ideas are *so* compatible with LG 16 and GS 19–21 that any other, non-Rahnerian interpretations are excluded. If this were so, then an argument against Rahner would be an argument against the Council (which, for the reasons invoked in the introduction to this book, is something I have no desire to advance). Yet the unwary reader of Rahner might assume that this is indeed the case. In 'Anonymous Christians', for example, he avers 'it is quite impossible to doubt that what is *meant* by the "anonymous Christian" (the name itself is unimportant) is compatible with the Council's teaching, indeed is explicitly stated by it' ([1964] 1969: 398). This is a puzzling statement. Recall again the relevant sentences of LG 16:

> Those indeed who are, without fault, ignorant of the Gospel of Christ and his Church, yet who seek God with a sincere heart, and who, knowing his will through the command of conscience, strive under the influence of grace to accomplish works, are able to obtain eternal salvation. Nor does divine Providence deny the assistances necessary for salvation to those who, without fault, have not yet arrived at an express recognition of God and who, not without divine grace, endeavour to attain to an upright life.

Even taking into account the rest of the document (as of course one must), it is certainly not the case that LG 16 is committed to, say, Rahner's understanding of nature and grace, his theological anthropology, or even an appeal to implicit faith – all of which, one might assume, are '*meant* by the "anonymous Christian"'. It does not rule them out, of course, and certain phrases may perhaps seem particularly conducive to a Rahnerian reading: the atheist's lack of an '*express* recognition of God' could be read as pointing to an 'inexpress' (or implicit, or anonymous) recognition, for example. However it scarcely requires it, and in the following chapter strong arguments will be given for favouring a quite different reading of the passage than that imagined by Rahner. In the words of George Vass:

> What Rahner did was a possible interpretation of the Council's position: the theory of anonymous Christianity was a hypothesis to fill a gap in the mentioned decree. In reviewing the Council texts we are by no means bound to interpret them according to Rahner's mind. (1998: 90–1)

The arguments that follow challenge Rahner and others; they are not criticisms of the magisterium.

Appeals to the unconscious

As is now clear, in the standard Catholic view of how atheists may be saved, ably represented here by Rahner, a great deal of store is set on the murky recesses of human subconsciousness. Appeals to implicit, anonymous, secret, or hidden beliefs, faiths, decisions, rejections, or acceptances all rely to a considerable degree on imputing unconscious mental states to people. These are mental states of which they are presently unaware, yet which, after death, they will recognize as among the most important that they ever held. Without denying the existence, importance, or causal efficacy of unconscious mental states per se, it is nonetheless worth expressing a few caveats in the current context. Without delving too deeply into the contemporary philosophy of mind, we might, for instance, do well to heed the warnings of some of its leading proponents. In the words of John Searle, for example:

> We have become so used to talking about the unconscious, so comfortable with the idea that there are unconscious mental states in addition to conscious mental states, that we have forgotten just how puzzling the notion of the unconscious really is. (1994: 165)

Later he adds: 'The notion of the unconscious is one of the most confused and ill-thought-out conceptions of modern intellectual life' (ibid.: 178; see also Searle 1992: 151–73). Likewise, both he and Paul Churchland caution against too readily transposing familiar psychological categories (e.g. thought, belief, etc.), with all their 'immediate intuitive appeal', into the realm of the unconscious (Churchland

1995: 182). Whatever else it might be, an unconscious mental state is unlikely to be 'exactly like a conscious mental state only minus the consciousness' (Searle 1994: 196). If nothing else, we might then be wary of setting too much salvific store against a hypothesized *implicit* faith.

Let us not, however, be unfair to Rahner. He is rightly tentative in making his suggestions. In 'Atheism and Implicit Christianity', for example, he accepts he is making 'an over-simplification which does not correspond to concrete reality', speaks of 'indefinite transitions and fluid boundaries', and admits that 'the system we have outlined is no more than a rough preliminary sketch' (Rahner [1967] 1972: 157). Furthermore, the concept of *mystery* is a central one throughout Rahner's writings, and that is no different when he is referring to 'the strange infinities within us' ([1946] 1993: 27). Indeed, as he wrote as early as 1946: 'There is indeed something more in our souls than can be revealed by daily experience, by modern psychiatry or psychology, by mystical communion with nature, by the exaltation of art or of love – in short, by any attempts of the human mind to grasp infinity' (ibid.: 28). Nor should we lose sight of the fact that Rahner's starting point is emphatically not any *theory* of the unconscious, but is rather a concern for the salvation of 'the overwhelming mass' of humanity, coupled with fidelity to the doctrines of scripture and the Church.

This is all to the good. But even so, it does not remove the troubling fact that there are serious theological problems with making this kind of move, irrespective of how tentatively this is done. One might, for instance, question the very cogency of a 'non-propositional', prelinguistic faith in *anything* – even an 'existentially actualised' one – let alone a salvifically relevant one in the triune God. This is an objection which the Dominican theologian Fergus Kerr has raised, on occasion against Rahner ([1986] 1997: 10–11), though more consideredly against de Lubac. Referring specifically to the latter's *The Discovery of God*, which was quoted at length in chapter two, and his affirmation, following Blondel, that 'Every human act, whether it is an act of knowledge or an act of the will, rests secretly upon God' (Lubac [1956] 1960: 40), Kerr contends:

> It is difficult to understand how God can be 'secretly affirmed and thought', prior to there being any of the judgement and concept formation which we normally mean by affirming and thinking. How does one 'affirm' God – even 'secretly' – prior to one's thinking about God in some way that is in principle communicable to others? [. . .] Above all, what is

this 'idea' that we have of God, 'mysteriously present in us from the beginning', which is antecedent to all our concepts? What is an 'idea', which is beyond our grasp *without the help of concepts*? An idea which is 'prior to all our argumentation, in spite of being logically unjustifiable without them [our concepts]?' [...] The idea of a concept – of God or anything else – prior to the network of concepts we inherit as we are initiated into language, needs a good deal of discussion. (2007: 79)

More troublingly still, recall Rahner's own criticism of the neo-scholastic, 'extrinsicist' view as positing grace as 'a superstructure beyond the realm of consciousness' ([1950] 1961: 298). The 'quite unexplicitated and unconscious' (1974: 226) faith of Rahner's anonymously Christian atheists runs, necessarily, counter to their own conscious, categorical experience. As such, surely then their salvation relies on a *sub*structure *beneath* the realm of consciousness. Of course, what is implicit will, in the fullness of time, become explicit. In many cases, such 'explicitation' must come after death. Even for someone with the strongest, most deeply held, implicit faith, this can only be imagined as a surprising, painful, and (if temporal categories are relevant here) lengthy process. Already having (some kind of) faith, or even already being (in some sense) a Christian, will not remove the need for extensive catechesis: a postmortem RCIA, so to speak. This will be worth bearing in mind in chapters four and five.

Fides implicita

Rahner writes in 'Atheism and Implicit Christianity': 'The concept of being "implicit" is thoroughly common in theology: it even occurs in a related context in *fides implicita*, *votum* (*baptismi*, *Ecclesiae*) *implicitum*, etc.' ([1967] 1972: 145). He has a point. Appeals to the 'implicit' have a strong pedigree and, the above considerations notwithstanding, ought not perhaps to be dismissed so hastily. Certainly, Rahner's own positing of implicit faith gains a good degree of its immediate plausibility from this fact. Since Catholics already accept the actuality of implicit faith among themselves, what is the difficulty in also extending it to virtuous, unevangelized atheists or members of other religions?

Another Dominican, the theologian of religions Joseph DiNoia, has taken exception to precisely this move. While admitting some of its advantages, he argues that: 'the concept of implicit faith [...] in fact poses intractable philosophical and theological difficulties when used as the basis for general descriptions of the religious (and moral) states and dispositions of non-Christian persons' (1983: 210). Specifically, DiNoia's main concern is that 'The application of the concept of "implicit faith" to the dispositions of persons who are not Christians represents an extension somewhat beyond the logical range of its normal use in theology' (ibid.: 224). In order to appreciate – and moreover develop – his point, it is first necessary to understand precisely this 'normal use'.

Discussing the necessity of explicit belief for salvation, Thomas explains in the *Summa theologiae* that: 'explicitness of believing is not, for all people, uniformly as much necessary for salvation since those who have the office of instructing others are held to believe more things explicitly than are others' (*Summa theologiae*, IIa IIae, q. 2, a. 5; Thomas Aquinas [1265–74] 1974: 84). His point here is not that explicit believing is less necessary for some than it is for others, but rather that the number of things that one is obliged to believe explicitly differs according to one's office *within* the Church. 'The simple' (*minores*) are not obliged to believe explicitly in, say, the hypostatic union of Christ's human and divine natures. Their teachers, however, certainly are. But for Thomas, it is not the case that the *minores* do not believe in the hypostatic union in any sense. Rather, this belief is implicit within both their explicit beliefs that, among other things, 'the Word became flesh' and Christ is 'true God and true man', and the trust which they place in their teachers, insofar as their teachers are orthodox.[11] In the earlier *de Veritate*, Thomas locates this faith not in one's teachers, but in the Church itself: 'one who believes the faith of the Church to be true, in this implicitly believes each item contained in the faith of the Church' (*De veritate*, q. 14, a. 11; Thomas Aquinas [*c.* 1259] 1925: 408). In the words of DiNoia:

> 'Implicit faith' designates in the first place the dispositions of one who is a member of the community, who accepts what is taught in it as right, true and good and who undertakes to pattern his life in accord with these teachings *even though* he may not be able fully to articulate all the teachings of his community in their totality and complexity. The

---

[11] This latter clause is significant since it protects non-experts from any doctrinal errors, intended or not, which their teachers may hold (see Thomas Aquinas [1265–74] 1974: 86).

Karl Rahner and the Salvation of Atheists 103

disposition of faith of such a person can be said to be, to a certain extent, implicit. (1983: 223)

And furthermore:

> It should be noticed that the acceptance involved in the disposition of implicit faith extends not only to an intellectual assent to the truths of faith but also to the total commitment which characterizes the life of faith. Christian faith – implicit and explicit – concerns not only the adherence to certain beliefs but also the determination to give one's entire life a certain course in accordance with the pattern of life fostered by the Christian community and sustained by its common life and worship. (Ibid.: 223–4)

To give a contemporary example (mine, not DiNoia's): suppose that I know little about the Church's teaching on, say, stem-cell research. I do, however, have a general faith in the truth of Catholicism, and moreover in the authority and reliability of the Church's moral teaching. Furthermore, in my faltering way, I strive – and probably struggle – to live my life in harmony with the Church's teachings, as far as I understand them. For Thomas, this explicit faith, which is both intellectual and existential, contains within it an implicit faith in the Church's teaching on stem cells, even though I do not actually know what that teaching is (and am, perhaps, even incapable of ever fully understanding it).

Turning now to Rahner and others, DiNoia points out that, whereas on the traditional view, 'implicit faith' heavily relies upon – indeed, is *implied* by – an explicit faith in the Church, on Rahner's and others' 'extended usage', this essential link is severed.

> [T]hey prescind from a condition which the standard theological use of the notion generally involves, viz., a potentially explicable and publicly identifiable body of teachings implicitly held (on the whole) on the authority of competent or official teachers. Versions of this extended usage which seek to incorporate relational aspects of our dispositions and actions as they are directed to God in addition prescind from a condition of 'implicit faith' in its ordinary use, viz., explicit knowledge of the reliability of some existent in view of which confidence about its conduct in given circumstances is reasonable. (Ibid.: 225)

The inculpably ignorant non-Christian does not, of course, believe in the veracity of the gospel or the teachings of the Church. Indeed, it is quite probable that he or she has quite definite views to the contrary.

In the case of non-Christian theists, the traditional solution here has been to argue that such belief may nevertheless be contained in a general belief in both the existence of God and his providential care for humanity. From a Christian perspective, of course, God's providence implies, among much else, Christ's incarnation, crucifixion, and resurrection. Thomas, for example, argues that Hebrews 11.6 defines the absolute minimum that must be *explicitly* believed by those invincibly ignorant of the gospel: 'For whoever would approach him must believe that he exists and that he rewards those who seek him' (*De veritate*, q. 14, a. 11; Thomas Aquinas [c. 1259] 1925: 408–9). But even here, it is fair to say, with DiNoia, that the meaning of *fides implicita* is being stretched fairly far from its origins.

> The intrinsic logical connection between 'implicit' and 'explicit' when the distinction is used to describe the disposition of Christian faith is loosened here to allow for the possibility of a partial or otherwise inadequately articulated adherence on the part of non-Christians to the doctrines knowledge of which is regarded as necessary for salvation as Christianity defines it. (1983: 225)

DiNoia refers only to members of non-Christian religions, but his point applies all the more forcefully in the case of atheists, who naturally do not even meet the Hebrews-defined criteria for explicit believing. For Rahner, as we have seen, an atheist's faith in the Christian God may be implicit within, say, his or her acceptance of absolute moral norms, or in facing up to life in the face of 'the sense of vacuum, the deadly loss of meaning and purpose, the metaphysical lassitude' ([1964–5] 1973: 68), which (he affirms) characterize the modern situation. The validity of these arguments will be explored presently, but note here how minimal is this *explicit* faith: indeed, it is highly likely that its possessors would not regard it as 'faith' at all. This is, it is worth noting, a very long way from the traditional understanding – from which, as we have seen, the appeal to an atheist's 'implicit faith' derives its immediate credibility. For Rahner, unlike for Thomas, it is not simply the acceptance of certain doctrines (*fides quae*) that may be implicit within a person's (explicit) act of faith (*fides qua*). Rather, the very act of faith *itself* may be implicit within a person's thoughts and actions. This sense of 'implicit faith' is, at the very most, analogical to the traditional, Thomistic one.

Once again, such concerns are not necessarily fatal to Rahner's account. But still, they do weaken it, and make its automatic

Karl Rahner and the Salvation of Atheists

acceptance far less attractive an option for the dogmatic theologian. Even without the above considerations concerning atheists (to whom his own arguments apply a fortiori), DiNoia argues that 'the concept of implicit Christian faith be retired from general use in the field of Catholic theology of religions' (1983: 211). But that said, DiNoia and I myself are committed to both the strictures of LG 14 regarding the necessity of faith (and baptism, and the Church) for salvation, and the optimism of LG 16 regarding the possibility of salvation for non-Christians. Rahner perceived both poles of the 'problem' decades before the Council, and proposed implicit faith as a crucial element in reconciling them. Certainly, one may depart from Rahner here, and plead ignorance as to the actual solution, safe in the knowledge that God has 'ways known to himself' (*Ad Gentes* 7; AS IV/vii: 677). But, for good or ill, this is not the way of dogmatic theologians. If, therefore, one has no (more) satisfactory replacement, then whatever problems Rahner's own solution might pose, it should perhaps be given the benefit of the doubt. For DiNoia, however, this is not the case:

> In view of the difficulties posed by theological formulations of this sort, I suggest that Christians express their confidence in the possible salvation of non-Christians by speaking of their future or 'prospective' affiliation with the Christian community rather than of their present but 'hidden' membership in it. In this alternative formulation the Christian valuation of the present dispositions and conduct of non-Christians is projected into the eschatological future. (1983: 235–6)

He continues:

> Rather than attributing an implausible implicit faith in Christ to the members of other religious communities, a theology of religions employing the concept of prospective affiliation could assert that non-Christians will have the opportunity to acknowledge Christ in the future. This opportunity may come to them in the course of their lives here on earth or in the course of their entrance into the life to come. Recent discussions of the theology of death and purgatory suggest that the postulation of such an opportunity is more compatible with central Catholic doctrines than has sometimes been thought in the past. (Ibid.: 240)

DiNoia is, I believe, most definitely 'onto something' here, and a postmortem solution to our *problemata*, though differing from DiNoia's own in key respects, will be developed in the following two chapters.

Before this, however, there is one last difficulty to lay at Rahner's door.

Morality and meaningfulness

Earlier in this section, several arguments were offered regarding the problematic nature of implicit and unconscious beliefs, and the need for caution when faced with overly simplistic appeals to them – especially when used to justify claims of implicit faith on the part of self-conscious atheists. But even if, as Searle argues, 'the notion of the unconscious is one of the most confused and ill-thought-out conceptions of modern intellectual life', that does not mean that one can simply dispense with it. The reason for this is in fact very simple: appeals to unconscious beliefs, desires, and dispositions have proven invaluable in explaining human behaviour. Thus Alasdair Macintyre, commenting on the popular reception of 'the unconscious', has remarked:

> [T]his essentially simple notion seems able to relate a far wider range of disparate human phenomena and to subsume the wildly abnormal and the tediously normal activities of human beings under the same headings far more easily than any other explanatory concept advanced so far. ([1958] 2004: 43)

And as Searle himself admits: 'It is because we want to explain our behaviour that we postulate the unconscious at all' (1994: 173). In this regard, though slightly tangentially, it is worth mentioning the growing body of empirical research into unconscious mental phenomena (see Uleman 2005). Perhaps the most famous and philosophically interesting aspect of this concerns *blindsight*, a phenomenon observed in subjects who, due to brain damage, are blind in a certain area of their visual field. Despite not being consciously aware of 'seeing' anything, and indeed being certain that they are not, they are nonetheless able to 'guess' the shape or movement of stimuli presented to this area with a degree of accuracy well above chance. In such cases as these, the explanatory utility of at least unconscious perception is plain (see Dennett 1991: 322–3; and Searle 1997: 199).

Historically at least, the same explanatory impulse holds for Catholic theologians in justifying their imputations of unconscious beliefs to (apparent) non-Christians. In chapter one, the traditional view that atheists logically ought to lead immoral and meaningless lives was introduced. And in chapter two, the process was narrated by which Catholic priests and theologians, led initially by the French priest-workers, discovered that many atheists did not, as a matter of fact, lead such lives. This curious realization was, of course, explained by positing unconscious theistic or Christian beliefs. Even then, however, such ideas were not wholly novel. Claeys-Bouuaert, writing in 1921 on the subject of 'apparent atheism', observed (in Riccardo Lombardi's paraphrase):

> Without even perceiving the contradiction, the atheist generally avoids [. . .] absolute independence of any law, whereas, logically speaking, he should boast of these things if he really were an atheist; therefore, fundamentally he acknowledges himself to be dependent on something outside and above himself and thus is no true atheist! ([1942] 1956: 171)

Similar appeals to morality as evidence of an implicit belief in God occurred frequently in the preconciliar decades, as for example in the writings of Blondel, Adam, Daniélou, de Lubac, Maritain, and Schillebeeckx.

For Rahner, of course, an atheist might demonstrate his implicit faith through (among other things) 'courageously accept[ing] life' ([1962] 1966a: 7–8), or accepting 'a moral demand from his conscience as absolutely valid for him' ([1967] 1972: 153). And while Rahner does not deduce his account of implicit faith from such attitudes or actions, they nonetheless serve as key evidences for his theory: that many atheists do indeed lead subjectively meaningful and morally serious lives is, he thinks, strong support for anonymous Christianity. Rahner states his arguments most explicitly in interviews given in his later years, when he is trying to enunciate his ideas in simple terms, divorced from their usual, dauntingly theological carapace. In these, it is clear that Rahner takes the necessary meaninglessness and absurdity of an atheistic universe to be a basic datum. Thus when asked in 1979 what he would do if he ceased believing in God, he bluntly replied:

> If once I were to be really convinced in an absolute way that all we live, do, and think is circumscribed by an absolute, meaningless nothingness, then and there, I think, it would be better to cease to live. ([1979] 1986: 212)

Unless this were a complete *non sequitur*, Rahner evidently regarded the non-existence of God as co-extensive with the universe being encompassed by 'an absolute, meaningless nothingness'. And if one were to believe that this was actually the case, then a despairing death would be preferable to life. Rahner expanded on this theme in an interview from March 1984, given in Budapest, where he had been attending a joint Marxist–Christian conference on 'The Responsibility of Human Beings in the Contemporary World'. There he affirms that the Marxist, *qua* atheist, 'ultimately grants that this entire human life, which is like a gleam on a small planet in a world made up of billions of galaxies, is really nothing' ([1984] 1990: 134). As such, Rahner draws the corollary:

> [I]n the atheistic world the question arises: How are ultimate values absolutely binding? [. . .] Imagine you are sitting in front of a piece of equipment and you know: if I press this button, my enemy who has insulted me dies and I know with absolute certainty that no one will be able to prove that I killed him. Ask the Marxist: 'What keeps you ultimately from pressing the button?' He could respond that his humanitarianism commands it. But then I would ask: 'Why must one act humanely?' I don't know how a Marxist would answer now. His reason must be realistic, of course, and not idealistic. And yet the reality which he or she presents would have to be able to ground the absolute demand of the postulate. (Ibid.)

However, 'a reality that is heading toward destruction on its own' (which the atheist believes to be actual state of our universe) 'can't come up with the demand for absolute respect, on its own' (ibid.: 135). Rahner's interviewer ripostes with the obvious objection that many atheists do, as matter of fact, adhere to such moral absolutes. At this juncture, Rahner makes the key move in his argument for anonymous Christianity:

> This just raises the question as to why. If one really knew that human beings are only a biological reality, then one could not do it. [. . .] I see no problem that this false theory [i.e. atheism] is not realized by people in practice. [. . .] To be sure, the atheist doesn't say 'God,' but 'I may never destroy humankind; I may not be so egoistic that another person has no place, and so on.' In making the norm absolute, the atheist has basically affirmed God, even if he or she denies God in reflexive, conceptual, and articulated theory. (Ibid.)

In both interviews, Rahner is making a number of key assumptions regarding both meta-ethics and the meaningfulness of life, and a great deal – far more than is either possible or desirable here – could be said in exploring them. Briefly, though, I would like to pick up on a point touched upon in chapter one. There, it may be remembered, atheistic justifications were quoted for accepting certain moral absolutes – e.g. Nielsen's 'Torturing human beings is wrong [...] exploiting or degrading human beings is vile. If we know anything to be wrong, we know these things to be wrong and to be just as wrong in a godless world as in a world with God' (2001: 98–9) – and for leading certain kinds of morally committed lives – e.g. Camus' 'Perhaps we cannot prevent this world from being a world in which children are tortured. But we can reduce the number of tortured children' ([1948] 1964: 52). As I suggested there, even *if* these arguments are ultimately false, they are plausible *enough* to explain why an atheist might 'courageously accept life', or accept a moral demand as absolutely binding. No doubt, such things are possible only through God's grace-full self-gift (i.e. they are 'objectively' theistic), but one need not have faith in God, explicit or implicit, in order to do them (i.e. they can be 'subjectively' atheistic).

To illustrate this basic point: suppose I erroneously believe that the Sun orbits the Earth. Now I believe, quite correctly, that when it is nighttime in Britain it is daytime in Australia. Though my geocentric reasons for believing this are false, there is no need to impute to me any *implicit* belief that the Earth, in fact, orbits the Sun – for my erroneous theory suffices to explain my correct belief in the relative day and night times on opposite sides of the world. The same applies, I argue, to Rahner's anonymously Christian atheist. Even though there is, in fact, a God, and even *if* morality and meaningfulness are, at bottom, illogical without one, the fact remains that the kind of life lived by Camus' Dr Rieux is perfectly possible, without supposing it to demonstrate any 'existentially actualised theism'. In the fullness of time, perhaps Rieux will come to realize that his heroic life was, objectively, not possible without God. But this need not involve the 'explicitation' of a hitherto-implicit faith.

Alexei Kirillov, anonymous Christian

Once again, it seems that the case for imputing implicit faith to sincere, virtuous atheists has been weakened yet further. In addition to the conceptual difficulties attending implicit or unconscious mental states *in toto*, and the problems in extending the Thomistic principle of *fides implicita* to incorporate unbelievers, we can now add the dubiety of Rahner's primary empirical evidence. None of this *prevents* a person from being a Rahnerian (or early-Schillebeeckxian, or Maritainian, or de-Lubacian) 'implicitist', but these are far from insubstantial difficulties – especially if, like Rahner and myself, one has *hope* that LG 16 applies to a very large number of people indeed. Yet for all my criticisms of Rahner, I wish to end this section with a qualified defence of the *hypothetical* possibility of an atheist who not only possesses a salutary, genuinely implicit faith, but who even perhaps 'can and should yet be called [a Christian] in a meaningful sense' (Rahner [1964] 1969: 391). While this is indeed a defence of Rahner's views, I must however admit that in another certain sense it is but a further critique. A comparison between Rahner's account, and what I take to be a *plausible* model of an implicitly believing atheist, should highlight just how great is the difference between them.

Chapter two alluded briefly to Dostoevsky's Kirillov, the nihilist engineer from *Demons* who so impressed de Lubac. Despite professing atheism, and being convinced that by committing suicide he will himself become God, Kirillov is indeed one in whom 'extreme atheism joins hands with sainthood' (Lubac [1944] 1995: 316; see also Frank 1995: 482; Berdyaev [1923] 1934: 81; and Ivanov 1959: 66). He is protective towards (the *virgin*) Marya, and gives the money saved for his last meal to the impoverished Shatov. Admitting that 'God has tormented me my whole life' (as, famously, did Dostoevsky himself), he keeps a candle lit before an icon of 'the Saviour', and spends his nights reading scripture, which he also quotes frequently. Moreover, Dostoevsky endows him with several characteristics of another of his creations, *The Idiot*'s Christ-figure Prince Myshkin: his love of children, his 'remarkably deep understanding of people', his epilepsy. Yet more strikingly, Kirillov is overcome with feverish rapture when telling Pyotr Verkhovensky of 'a big idea':

> There was one day on earth, and in the middle of the earth stood three crosses. One on a cross believed so much that he said to another: 'this day you will be with me in a paradise.' The day ended, they both died, went, and did not find either paradise or resurrection. [. . .] Listen: this man was the highest on all the earth, he constituted what it was to live for. Without this man the whole planet with everything on it is – madness only. (Dostoevsky [1872] 2000: 618)

Now in a case such as this, the imputation of an implicit faith in God – indeed, *pace* Balthasar, perhaps even of a genuinely anonymous Christianity – would indeed be a plausible explanation of Kirillov's startling behaviour. And nor, as I have argued elsewhere, is Kirillov alone in Dostoevsky's *oeuvre* (Bullivant 2008b).

In real life, the French psychologist and priest Ignace Lepp published a number of case studies of what he termed 'neurotic atheists' in his 1961 book *Atheism in Our Time*. These fully live up to their name, exhibiting genuinely pathological behaviour which, after psychoanalysis, is found to rest on repressed beliefs about God or religion. Despite this, Lepp disdains more general, contemporary appeals to unconscious beliefs:

> But it would be a serious mistake to conclude that all atheists would be believers if they were psychoanalyzed, or that depth psychology confirms the slogan so dear to a special breed of preachers: 'The unbeliever is a believer at heart.' ([1961] 1963: 60)

The difference is, of course, that in the case of Lepp's 'neurotic atheists', as indeed with Dostoevsky's Kirillov, the imputation of implicit theistic or specifically Christian faith serves a legitimate and perhaps irrefragable explanatory function. There seems, quite simply, to be no other reasonable explanation one can give. Against such examples as Lepp's, but most obviously against Dostoevsky's fictional depiction, the other objections to implicit faith outlined above lose much of their force. Against Searle's and Churchland's general caveats, one may point to the overwhelming explanatory benefits in imputing such a faith to such 'neurotic atheists'. And to DiNoia's qualms about extending *fides implicita* beyond its traditional scope, one may cite Kirillov's asceticism, works of mercy, scripture reading, and icon veneration, as exhibiting, in some sense, a 'determination to give [his] entire life a certain course in accordance with the pattern of life fostered by the Christian community' (1983: 225). This is, at the very least, no mere substructure beneath the realm of consciousness.

Kirillov, however, is a fictional character, and Lepp's pathological cases are truly exceptional. Implicit believers of *this* sort, fascinating though they are to speculate upon, are largely irrelevant to the 'existential backdrop' which motivated Rahner's impressive and influential – though, as I have argued, by no means immune to reasonable doubt – theory of anonymous Christianity:

> But can the Christian believe even for a moment that the overwhelming mass of his brothers, not only those before the appearance of Christ right back to the most distant past (whose horizons are being constantly

extended by palaeontology) but also those of the present and of the future before us, are unquestionably and in principle excluded from the fulfilment of their lives and condemned to eternal meaninglessness? He must reject any such suggestion, and his faith is itself in agreement with his doing so. For the scriptures tell him expressly that God wants everyone to be saved (1 Tm 2:4); the covenant of peace which God made with Noah after the flood has never been abrogated: on the contrary, the Son of God himself has sealed it with the incontestable authority of his self-sacrificing love embracing all men. ([1964] 1969: 391)

CONCLUSION

A great deal of ground has been covered in this and the previous chapter. In chapter two, the crucial shifts in Catholic understandings of both atheism and the salvation of non-Catholics, which were ultimately enshrined in the documents of Vatican II, were narrated at some length. Despite numerous individual differences, a *standard view* of mainstream Catholic theologians regarding the possible salvation of atheists was identified, positing the existence of implicit, unconscious, hidden, or anonymous faith on the part of well-disposed atheists. Evidence of this kind of approach was identified in the writings of (in no particular order): Adam, Claeys-Bouuaert, Blondel, Maréchal, Maritain, de Lubac, Daniélou, Congar, Schillebeeckx, Balthasar, Ratzinger, and Rahner.

Taking the latter's famous formulations to be, contrary to popular perception, broadly representative of this grand tradition, this chapter first offered a detailed exposition of Rahner's theology of anonymous Christianity, focusing on the crucial issue of implicit faith. Having argued that Rahner's solution is only one possible reading of LG 16, a series of difficulties with Rahner's ideas were then proposed. These were: (i) the general uncertainty of appeals to the implicit or unconscious in the human psyche, and the need therefore to be cautious; (ii) the problems involved in 'stretching' the traditional understanding of 'implicit faith' to non-Christians, and (going beyond DiNoia at this point) especially to atheists; and (iii) the implausibility of the evidences which Rahner offers for imputing implicit faith to virtuous, life-accepting unbelievers. While the *possibility* of an atheist with a genuine, sufficiently robust implicit faith was indeed admitted, with

Karl Rahner and the Salvation of Atheists

reference to Dostoevsky's Kirillov and some of Ignace Lepp's patients, these are far from the 'anonymous Christians' of Rahner's speculations. Since there are – to put it mildly – a great many sincere, virtuous, and (hopefully) inculpably ignorant atheists who are neither fictional nor pathological, one must look elsewhere to hypothesize how these might ultimately attain salvation.

As I have mentioned several times now, the above arguments are not necessarily insuperable to the committed Rahnerian (or de-Lubacian, Maritainian, Adamian, early-Schillebeeckxian, etc.!). Taken together, however, I do believe that they cast sufficient doubt on the widespread appeal to implicit faith to meet one of LG 14's three pre-conditions as to encourage the active exploration of other orthodox possibilities. Hints as to the direction this will take in the following two chapters were given in our discussion of DiNoia. As a further foretaste of what is to come, it is worth quoting from two theologians who, as we have seen, both once subscribed to 'implicit faith'. According to Congar, commenting on his own conciliar contribution in a 1988 interview:

> I once held the theory of implicit faith, for which moreover I could find good authority, notably the text from the Holy Office in the Feeney case, which arose in the United States in 1947 or 1948, but this position has been criticized, in particular by my colleague and friend Fr Liégé. His position was more bound up with eschatology: God will recompense each and every one on the basis of what he or she has done and what he or she has received. (1988: 14)

And, quoting from a 1982 interview with Schillebeeckx:

> According to what is said in Mt 25, you are in the end judged by what you have done for the least of the brethren. You are not judged by how you justify your actions in the religious or ethical sense.
>   If you read that chapter in Matthew about the eschatological judgement, you can really get a hold of what Jesus was about. In the end we are judged by whether we have given water to the thirsty or whether we have helped the poor. In one sense, a purely atheistic judgment! [. . .] That whole passage sounds quite horizontal, even atheistic – what have you done for the poor? That is the appeal that is made to you. Then, at the end of the text, we have the interpretation: what you have done to your fellow-man, you have done to me. The poor man is identified with Jesus himself. (1983: 31–2)

These texts reveal the general direction in which this book is heading – albeit with several crucial qualifications. Chapter five will argue for a specific interpretation of Mt 25.31–46, understood within its proper scriptural and dogmatic context, as holding the key to the salvation of atheists. Firstly, however, since doubt is now cast upon the Rahnerian solution, a new framework is required for explicating LG 16. Secondly, more thought must also be given to two words that ring like a refrain throughout the Council's pronouncements on the salvation of non-Christians: *sine culpa*. These two subjects, necessary prolegomena to a renewed Catholic understanding of the salvation of unbelievers, are considered in the next chapter.

4

The Salvation of 'Jane' and the Problem of Ignorance

As mentioned in the introduction, recent decades have witnessed several significant attempts by theologians at explicating the Church's optimism for the salvation of non-Christians. In these, however, 'non-Christians' is typically a cipher for 'members of the world religions', with little mention either of the existence of millions of non-religious unbelievers, or of the fact that these too are unambiguously included in LG 16's assurances. For example, Gerald O'Collins' excellent chapter on 'The Salvation of Non-Christians' in *Jesus Our Redeemer: A Christian Approach to Salvation* directly addresses only the salvation of religious people (2007: 218–37). This approach is also reflected in the preface to his *Salvation for All: God's Other Peoples*: 'With many others I dislike such negative labels as "non-Christian" and "non-evangelized." But how are we to name en bloc those of other religious traditions?' (2008: vii). The common elision of 'non-Christian' with 'non-Christian religious' is unfortunate. Atheists are thus the forgotten subjects of LG 16. And given the *sui generis* nature of atheism (as argued in chapter one), little of the very valuable research by Catholic theologians into the salvation of 'non-Christians' is directly applicable to this monograph's *problemata*.

Gavin D'Costa's *Christianity and World Religions: Disputed Questions in the Theology of Religions* (2009) constitutes a welcome exception to this trend, however. (Throughout this chapter, bare page numbers given parenthetically in the text refer to this book.) In its final two chapters, which substantially critique and develop a theme pioneered by George Lindbeck and Joseph DiNoia (e.g. Lindbeck 1984: 55–63; DiNoia 1992: 103–8), D'Costa addresses the question: 'how is it intelligible that the just who have not been evangelized might nevertheless be saved, without denying the necessity of Christ for salvation?' (xiii). Although the focus here is squarely on members of the world religions, atheists are not wholly forgotten. (Indeed, in earlier chapters several interesting comments are made on 'those individuals, communities, and social structures that might be described as agnostic, atheist, and indifferent to the question of God' [107].) Significantly, D'Costa develops his account of how, in principle, a non-Christian may be saved with reference to the test case of a Buddhist, whom he calls Jane. Jane signifies a *type*, rather than any specific individual. Her adherence to Buddhism specifically is, moreover, largely illustrative; D'Costa is directly concerned not with how Buddhists might be saved, but with how sincere adherents of non-Christian religions, in general, might be. To this end, at least, Jane might just as well be a practising Muslim, Sikh, or Hindu.[1]

Yet for my purposes, the choice of Buddhism is of central importance, since as D'Costa himself points out in justifying his choice, 'it is not theistic' (162). Hence Jane's salvation cannot, for example, be founded on her having an explicit, though in some ways misguided, belief that God 'exists and that he rewards those who seek him' (Heb 11.6). D'Costa also rejects the standard solution of implicit faith (163–4), although for different reasons to those which I have advanced in chapter three. His enquiry is, furthermore, framed in terms of the same dogmatic constraints that I outlined in my introduction. D'Costa's own statement of these, with particular reference to Jane, is worth quoting at length:

> The Catholic church teaches explicitly that a non-Christian can be saved with the following qualifications, which I shall take as granted from now on. First, it is assumed that Jane [. . .] has not known the gospel; it is assumed that she cannot make new decisions after death, for death represents the final summation and end of the person's life; it is assumed that baptism is required both to bring about and signify Jane's regeneration – the church is a necessity of means and precept; it is assumed that Jane has lived a good life, following the truth to the best of her ability, in the light of her conscience; it is assumed that possibilities of the good, true, and beautiful life might be found in positive elements within her religion (let us say Buddhism as it is not theistic), and in this

---

[1] The case of Jews is more (or perhaps less) complicated, owing to Judaism's special relationship with Christianity (see e.g. D'Costa 2007: 443; D'Costa 2009: 174–5).

way Jane is acting in response to the promptings of the Holy Spirit who is the foundation of our freedom and search for truth. (162)

As will become clear in the following section, there is a great deal in D'Costa's ensuing account that is useful and germane to the present *quaestio*. So much so, in fact, that the ideas developed in the following chapter are done so explicitly in light of the 'D'Costan paradigm'. Nevertheless, despite the general agreement that this implies, my own views will diverge on a number of points. In the main, this is due to our difference of subjects: the salvation of a conscious, non-religious atheist raises certain questions not raised by that of a non-theistic Buddhist. But on two specific issues, I will highlight more substantive problems in D'Costa's account – at least, as it stands in the text itself.[2] One of these, a 'sin' of omission by no means exclusive to D'Costa, I will attempt to rectify at length in the remaining sections of this chapter. The other will be taken up in chapter five.

SAVING JANE

D'Costa's account, which may be synopsized only briefly, centres on the doctrine of Christ's descent into hell, as affirmed, for example, in the Apostles' Creed: *descendit ad inferos*, 'he descended to the dead (i.e. to hell)' (cf. Pitstick 2007: 9–13). Importantly, note here that 'hell' does not refer primarily to *Gehenna*, the abode of the damned. Rather it means, more generally, *Sheol*, the abode of the dead (see CCC 633). Importantly for us, this includes the *limbus patrum*, or 'limbo of the Fathers/just' – of which, much more later.

Appealing to LG 16, D'Costa rightly affirms that 'explicit recognition of God is not required in this life ("not yet attained") for the possibility of salvation' (162). Such an 'explicit recognition' is, however, ultimately required for this possibility to become an actuality. This is so because 'final salvation' – that is, the attainment of the beatific vision – 'requires not only an ontological and causal, but also an epistemological, relationship to Christ' (24). For D'Costa, this

---

[2] I have been fortunate enough to discuss these issues with Prof. D'Costa, and he has clarified several points for me. All that follows, regarding both his ideas and my own, has been greatly illuminated by these exchanges. Here, however, I will be explicitly engaging only with D'Costa's ideas in their published form.

'final epistemic necessity of faith (*fides ex auditu*)' (24) implies recourse to a post-mortem solution to the problem of Jane's salvation. This is so because (i) in the wake of Vatican II 'there has been no developed answer as to how the good non-Christian is actually saved'; and (ii) the 'descent into hell' teaching provides resources to answer this question in terms of a post-mortem solution (162).

Now Christ's Descent is a rich and difficult doctrine; a full appraisal of its history and significance is not possible here.[3] Yet several elements must be highlighted in order to appreciate D'Costa's argument. While not the only supportive text (cf. Ps 68.18; Eph 4.9–10), 1 Peter provides the Descent's scriptural *locus classicus*:

> For Christ also suffered for sins once for all, the righteous for the unrighteous, in order to bring you to God. He was put to death in the flesh, but made alive in the spirit, in which also he went and made a proclamation to the spirits in prison, who in former times did not obey, when God waited patiently in the days of Noah, during the building of the ark, in which a few, that is, eight people, were saved through water. [. . .] For this is the reason the gospel was proclaimed even to the dead, so that, though they had been judged in the flesh as everyone is judged, they might live in the spirit as God does. (1 Pet 3.18–20, 4.6)

The interpretation of this passage is admittedly not straightforward. As John Sanders points out, though, the word translated in the NRSV as 'made a proclamation' (*ekēruxen*) is a standard New Testament term for the preaching of the gospel (e.g. Mk 1.14). This reading is confirmed by 4.6, which literally states 'the dead have been evangelized' (*nekrois euēngelisthē*) (Sanders 1994: 187). The identity of 'the spirits in prison' (3.19) is more problematic. Taken by itself, 4.6's generic 'the dead' might perhaps imply *all* the dead, whether Jew or gentile, righteous or unrighteous. On the other hand, the gnomic reference to 'the days of Noah' in 3.19 suggests a rather more restricted referent. As one might expect, 1 Pet 3.18–4.6, in conjunction with other texts, generated a diverse array of interpretations in the patristic period (see Dalton 1989: 27–66). While noting some of these 'disparate and overlapping traditions', D'Costa traces one major trajectory, in which he includes Clement of Alexandria, Origen,

---

[3] See Pitstick 2007: 9–85. I am, however, inclined to demur from Pitstick's contention that the tradition 'speak[s] with one voice' (ibid.: 85) concerning Holy Saturday.

Cyril of Alexandria, John Damascene, and Augustine, and which 'by the fifth century, [...] had become more consolidated into a single teaching that remained unquestioned with staggering continuity until the time of the Reformation' (169). For the present purposes, it is necessary only to discuss Clement and Augustine. While following D'Costa's account, I have elaborated upon certain aspects of Clement's and Augustine's texts. To preserve his exegetical nuances, where D'Costa himself quotes a text, I will follow the translation which he uses. Where not, I shall rely on other translations (in Augustine's case, my own).

Clement (c. 150–215) was a leading representative of Alexandrian theology, and a key influence on Origen. In *Stromata* 6, he ostensibly understands 1 Peter's 'spirits in prison' to be 'those that perished in the flood' ([c. 200] 1983: 490). However, judging from the rest of the chapter, it seems that this is a synecdoche for 'the Jews' in general. At least, no further allusion to 'the days of Noah' is made, and Clement speaks simply of 'the Jews' or 'the Hebrews'. But while, for Clement, Christ preached only to the Jews in Hades, in *Stromata* 2 he has already argued that the apostles, upon their own deaths, had preached to the gentiles as well. This startling claim is justified not from scripture, but rather from the *Shepherd of Hermas*, a text that was accorded great weight among the early Fathers:

> The apostles and the teachers who preached the name of the Son of God, after they had fallen asleep in the power and faith of the Son of God, preached also [...] to them that had fallen asleep before them, and themselves gave unto them the seal of the preaching. Therefore they went down with them into the water, and came up again. [...] So by their means they were quickened into life, and came to the full knowledge of the name of the Son of God. (170)

Returning to book 6, on D'Costa's reading, Clement suggests that Christ himself preached both to the righteous Jews in *Sheol* (i.e. those who would later be identified as inhabiting the *limbus patrum*), as well as to the unrighteous ones, in case God's 'saving and disciplinary' punishments had led the latter to repentance, and thus to conversion (169).[4] In death, as in life, the disciples extend Christ's mission in

---

[4] A different interpretation is, I think, also sustainable from Clement's (not wholly transparent) text. On this reading, both the 'righteous' and the 'unrighteous' are subjected to God's 'saving and disciplinary' punishments, which are proper to being 'in prison' (1 Pet 3.19). This is so because – as Clement seems to think – *all* are

preaching to the gentiles in Hades. Thus the *Church* (i.e. the apostles) continues Christ's evangelizing work among the dead: 'the entire church shares in the reality of the "body of Christ," which would mean, to use later terminology, that in the descent into the limbo of the just we see the instrumental causality of both Christ and his church as the means to salvation' (170). Admittedly, Clement's account is not devoid of problems. Chief among these is his suggestion of the possibility of post-mortem repentance and conversion – something which, as will be discussed presently, the later, Augustine-inspired tradition would prohibit.[5] Nevertheless, D'Costa is correct in stressing Clement's significance:

> In a single stroke Clement solves many of the problems I want to address: the necessity of Christ and his church as a means of salvation and the explicit relationship of the unevangelized to the Blessed Trinity that is a precondition of salvation are both addressed through the descent into the limbo of the just. Analogically, this is a very promising avenue for our problematic. (171)

Writing over two centuries later, Augustine exhaustively explored the difficulties presented by 1 Pet 3.18–4.6, in Epistle 164 to bishop Evodius of Uzalis. Unlike Clement, Augustine is repulsed by the idea that Christ genuinely *preached* to those in Hades, presenting them with an opportunity to believe in him that they had (due to having lived before his advent) lacked on earth. He considers this idea to be abhorrent, not least because it implies that 'those who did not believe while they lived, are able to believe in Christ among the dead' (*Ep.* 164, 4, 13; PL 33: 714). He thus rejects any possibility of

---

(objectively) guilty of the sin of unbelief, despite the fact that, because they had never heard the gospel, they are not subjectively guilty. When confronted by Christ's proclamation, however, it is the 'righteous' who are brought to repentance and conversion. The 'unrighteous', meanwhile, do not repent – although, due to Christ's proclamation, they now know that they have been (justly) condemned. Whatever its other faults, this reading (*pace* D'Costa) makes better sense of Clement's assertion that: '[Christ] should *bring to repentance* those belonging to the Hebrews, and [the apostles] the Gentiles; that is, *those who had lived in righteousness according to the Law and Philosophy, who had ended life* not perfectly, but *sinfully*' ([c. 200] 1983: 490; my emphasis). See also Clement's rhetorical question: 'Did not the same dispensation obtain in Hades, so that even there, *all the souls, on hearing the proclamation, might either exhibit repentance, or confess that their punishment was just,* because they believed not?' (Ibid.: 491; my emphasis).

[5] In fact, if my reading of *Stromata* 6 is correct (see previous footnote), then the problem is even greater than D'Costa realizes.

The Salvation of 'Jane' and the Problem of Ignorance   121

post-mortem conversion. As D'Costa notes, his view on this issue became accepted as definitive (172; cf. Sanders 1994: 46; Trumbower 2001: 140).[6] Because of this, Augustine, despite affirming the reality of Christ's Descent on other grounds, denies that 1 Pet 3–4 has any bearing on this doctrine. Instead, he takes 'the days of Noah' literally, arguing that, through the person of Noah, the pre-existent Christ preached to Noah's (living) contemporaries, calling them to repentance. On Augustine's construal, 'spirits in prison' (3.19) refers simply to 'souls which were at that time enfleshed, and were shut up in the shadow of ignorance as if "in prison"' (*Ep.* 164, 5, 16; PL 33: 715). Likewise, 'the dead' (4.6) may 'denote unbelievers, as being spiritually dead' (ibid.: 7, 21; PL 33: 717).

At this juncture, D'Costa comments:

> Thus the passage refers to those who responded positively to Noah's/ Christ's teachings just before the flood. Augustine's argument continues that since some of these sinful contemporaries had repented but were drowned in the flood and died without being on the ark, this means that Christ descends only to those who are already 'saved,' like those who responded to Noah, but who had appeared to be damned in the flood narrative. This is an ingenious argument that attends to the difficult references to Noah. According to Augustine all such people must await Christ for the completion of the process that started in their positive response to Noah/Christ. (172–3)

D'Costa errs, however, in attributing this view to Augustine; there is no suggestion in Epistle 164 that some of those to whom Christ/Noah preached may have repented prior to drowning. Rather, this reading belongs to the sixteenth- and seventeenth-century Jesuit cardinal (and later saint and Doctor of the Church) Robert Bellarmine (see Pitstick 2007: 50). But irrespective of whose interpretation it originally was, the use to which D'Costa puts it remains valid. Most particularly, it is indeed true that, following Augustine's pronouncements on the subject elsewhere, the Descent came generally to be viewed:

> as Christ's coming to set the just free, rather than his preaching the gospel to those who had earlier rejected God. Preaching comes to be understood as an announcement of Christ's lordship, his proclaiming

---

[6] The principle is not, however, an Augustinian innovation. See e.g. the second-century author of 2 Clement's 'For after we have departed from this world, we can no longer make confession, or repent any more in that place' (quoted in Fairhurst 1981: 313).

> that what they have secretly desired is now here: the entry into heaven has finally come. This Augustinian [i.e. Bellarminean] reading explains how Christ is involved in the explicit redemption of those who would in fact accept him when they meet him in the limbo of the just. (173)

He continues:

> This also means that it is possible to see the limbo of the just as providing a solution that overcomes the prohibition on 'conversion,' a new decision in the next life, for in one sense no conversion is required but a completion of the person's life and their destiny. There must be adequate continuity in the person's life for them to 'qualify' for being present in the limbo of the just. Allied with Clement's insight that the church is co-present with Christ, we have an answer to the question of Jane coming clearly into focus. (Ibid.)

D'Costa's appeal to the limbo of the just (*limbus patrum*) – traditionally, 'Abraham's bosom' (Lk 16.22–3), that region of Hades where the righteous of the Old Testament resided prior to Christ's leading them into heaven – is of crucial significance. Since they had lived prior to the incarnation, these 'holy dead' could not have had the explicit 'epistemological relationship to Christ' that is absolutely necessary for salvation. This is rectified, however, in Christ's Descent, and specifically, by his preaching of the gospel. *But*, technically speaking, they are not 'converted' by this proclamation. This is so because they are already, in God's sight, 'just'; those in the *limbus patrum* have no need for genuine conversion, that is, that 'radical new direction of the whole of life, a return, a conversion to God with all our heart, an end of sin, a turning away from evil, with a repugnance toward the evil actions that we have committed' (CCC 1431). For this reason, Augustine rejects the suggestion (*à la* Clement) that the Old Testament patriarchs and prophets – 'to whose justice and piety, in God's scripture, such signal testimony is exhibited' – were subjected to punishments while in Hades (*Ep.* 164, 3, 7; PL 33: 711). Hence on this view, as D'Costa explains, Christ's proclamation to the dead: 'comes to be understood as an announcement of Christ's lordship, his proclaiming that what they have secretly desired is now here: the entry into heaven has finally come' (173). This is effectively the same as Pitstick's argument that 'the "preaching" of Christ need not be an exhortation, but may be the announcement that redemption has been accomplished through His death on the cross, i.e., a proclamation of a fact' (2007: 50).

The Salvation of 'Jane' and the Problem of Ignorance   123

It is here that D'Costa's own theology comes to the fore. He proposes that Jane's post-mortem fate be understood *by analogy* (albeit with important qualifications) with that of the holy dead in the limbo of the just. This solution must not, however, be misunderstood:

> Remember, we must not imagine this solution as a celestial waiting room under the earth, but a conceptual theological datum based on the tradition that provides an answer uniting the ontological and epistemological to explain the case of Jane's salvation, as it did for the just before the time of Christ. (174)

He is well aware, of course, that it has traditionally been thought that, following Christ's once-for-all liberation of its inhabitants, the limbo of the just's function is obsolete; even if it still exists, it is necessarily empty (178). This was based, explicitly or not, on the widely held assumption that, after Christ's coming, all people have been evangelized, and thus have either accepted, or culpably rejected, the gospel. However, 'This ancient assumption is no longer tenable as we now know that, throughout Christian history, there have been billions of people and cultures who have not heard the gospel' (ibid.). And so therefore:

> There are epistemologically and ontologically possibly millions of unevangelized who are in the same state as those in the limbo of the just [. . .] Clearly, the limbo of the just will not persist and is temporary, but *it will continue to analogically operate in teaching that the just are never lost and await the Lord's coming after their death*, just as do Christians. (Ibid.; emphasis added)

This is, then, how the *limbus patrum* functions as a 'conceptual theological datum'. In the case of the pre-incarnation just, Christ's Descent was necessary both for (i) 'opening' heaven; and for (ii) bringing them to an *epistemological* relationship with himself (which, in D'Costa's words, 'does not require "conversion," but a coming to maturation and completion' [179]). D'Costa characterizes these two aspects as 'objective' and 'subjective', respectively. On the one hand, then, 'objectively speaking, Christ's resurrection means that the gates of heaven are now open and one objective sense of the descent doctrine has now objectively changed the nature of reality' (179). But on the other hand, 'there are many who subjectively still exist in the state of those who entered the limbo of the just' (ibid.).

One is thus justified in positing a post-mortem proclamation, *analogous* to that provided by Christ himself in the limbo of the just (or even by 'the Church', as on the Clementine schema), for those in Jane's situation.[7]

Two further, important points are added to this basic insight. First of all, one need not assume that the newly evangelized Jane enters immediately into heaven, as the Fathers of the Old Testament are traditionally thought to have done. D'Costa points here to the thief on the cross, known since the twelfth century as 'Dismas', to whom Christ promised 'today you will be with me in Paradise' (Lk 23.43). Within the Catholic tradition at least, this 'Paradise' has traditionally been understood as the *limbus patrum*. D'Costa persuasively argues, however, that Dismas might well not have entered heaven with the rest of the holy dead since, despite his profession of faith, 'the accumulated venial sin of a lifetime would still require purgation' (176). Moreover,

> the same could be said of the righteous recently converted, in Augustine's [i.e. Bellarmine's] reading of 1 Peter 3–4, who then immediately drowned in the flood. Would not those who had responded positively to Noah's teaching still require 'time' to mature into the new life of faith that they had begun? Might they not be like most humans, 'on the way,' but not fully purified? The point here is not that God is unable to bear sin and imperfection in us, but that we are unable to bear the fullness of glory without purification. (176–7; on this latter point, see Ratzinger [1977] 1988: 230–1)

Since souls in purgatory are, already, *saved* – or, at least, 'are assured of their eternal salvation' (CCC 1030) – Jane's post-mortem evangelization must occur either prior to, or coterminously with, her purification. (That is, if she is in need of it: D'Costa does not deny 'the possibility that some will enter heaven immediately without this purgatorial cleansing, however difficult that might be to imagine' [177]).

This leads neatly into the second point. Since baptism is necessary for salvation, this too must be supplied before Jane enters into either

---

[7] Also relevant here are D'Costa's arguments for the descent into hell being represented, along with the crucifixion and resurrection, in the Eucharist. Thus: 'the Eucharist enacts, celebrates, and makes present the cross, the descent into hell, and the resurrection, so that the fruits of this sacrifice may become available to all. This means that the descent is a liturgical reality present in the life of the church, not an arcane and embarrassing doctrine' (186).

The Salvation of 'Jane' and the Problem of Ignorance   125

purgatory or heaven. This need not, however, be sacramental baptism (*in re*). As mentioned in chapter two, since at least the time of Ambrose and Augustine, the Catholic tradition has recognized the efficacy of a baptism by desire (*in voto*). The baptism of blood (*sanguinis*), accorded to those martyred before receiving sacramental baptism, has also long been affirmed. In light of these considerations, the International Theological Commission's 2007 report *The Hope of Salvation for Infants Who Die Without Being Baptised*, to which D'Costa closely refers, notes: 'While considering sacramental Baptism necessary inasmuch as it is the ordinary way established by Jesus Christ to configure human beings to himself, the Church has never taught the "absolute necessity" of sacramental Baptism for salvation' (2007: art. 66). And later in the same document, there is a remarkable passage deserving to be quoted in full:

> God does not demand the impossible of us. Furthermore, God's power is not restricted to the sacraments: '*Deus virtutem suam non alligavit sacramentis quin possit sine sacramentis effectum sacramentorum conferre*' (God did not bind His power to the sacraments, so as to be unable to bestow the sacramental effect without conferring the sacrament). God can therefore give the grace of Baptism without the sacrament being conferred, and this fact should particularly be recalled when the conferring of Baptism would be impossible. The need for the sacrament is not absolute. What is absolute is humanity's need for the *Ursakrament* which is Christ himself. All salvation comes from him and therefore, in some way, through the Church. (Art. 82)

On D'Costa's account, it will be remembered, the instrumental causality of the Church (and thus of Christ, as its head) in the *limbus patrum* has already been affirmed, with reference to Clement. He also offers other arguments (e.g. 180–6). In effect, though, the point could simply be answered, yet again, by analogy with the limbo of the just: in whatever manner the Old Testament Fathers, or indeed Dismas, received baptism (or, alternatively, were dispensed from its necessity), that too could suffice for Jane.[8]

---

[8] Interestingly, Dismas' salvation proved problematic for Augustine. In his earlier writings, Augustine accepted that he was saved despite having neither been baptized nor martyred (hence receiving a *baptismus sanguinis*) – e.g. *De baptismo contra Donatistas* 4, 22 (PL 43: 173). In later, anti-Pelagian mode, however, Augustine rejected this possibility, speculating that the thief may have already been baptized (his repentance thus being that of a lapsed Christian), or that, due to the water issuing

THE D'COSTAN PARADIGM: *PRO* AND *CONTRA*

Now the above paragraphs represent only a summary of D'Costa's position; much of its richness and detail, for brevity's sake, has been omitted. Nevertheless, I hope, this summary is a fair reflection of the cardinal elements of the D'Costan schema. It will serve as the framework for my own constructive account of how atheists may be saved – after, that is, the qualifications to be made below. Before these, however, I wish to add one further argument in its favour to those offered by D'Costa himself.

The hypothesis of a post-mortem proclamation (properly understood) for the righteous unevangelized who, from God's perspective, were already on the way to final salvation in their telluric lives – such that their acceptance of this proclamation does not require a full *conversion* – coheres very closely with the linguistic subtleties of LG 16 itself.[9] The Latin speaks not of those who have 'not accepted (*non acceperunt*)' the gospel, but rather of those who have '*not yet* accepted (*nondum acceperunt*)' it (AS III/viii: 796). The implication of *nondum* here, in line with LG 14's earlier affirmation of the trifold necessity for faith, baptism, and the Church for salvation, is that such people must, at some unspecified future time, accept the gospel. There is no suggestion that this will occur during their earthly lives, and indeed, 'Such an interpretation would deprive the texts of any serious meaning' (Rahner [1967] 1972: 150). Some manner of post-mortem solution (if not necessarily of the sort outlined above) thus seems to be required by LG 16. Moreover, D'Costa's solution gains further credence from LG 16's use of *present* verbs in describing the situation vis-à-vis salvation for those who will only accept the gospel in the *future*. For example, 'Those who seek God with a sincere heart [...] *are* able to obtain (*consequi possunt*) eternal salvation' (AS III/viii: 797). And, '*Nor does* divine Providence *deny* (*Nec...denegat*) the assistances necessary for salvation to those who, without fault, have

---

from Christ's side on the cross, he had been 'washed with a baptism of this most sacred kind' (*De anima et eius origine* 3, 9 [PL 44: 517]). See also Trumbower 2001: 135. Augustine also believed that the Old Testament Fathers' circumcision would suffice as a pre-advent proxy for baptism – which would not, of course, help with solving Jane's problem. Even if Augustine is basically correct, though, by no means all of even the male members of the holy dead were circumcised Jews.

[9] This basic point is alluded to, but only very briefly, by D'Costa himself (162).

The Salvation of 'Jane' and the Problem of Ignorance

not yet (*nondum*) arrived at an express recognition of God' (ibid.). Some of those who have not yet accepted the gospel (but, of course, who will in the future) are, in their *current* state, able to be saved. Likewise, God is *presently* helping towards salvation some of those who have *not yet* come to an express recognition of him (but who, again, will in the future). Although these individuals must, necessarily, come to an acceptance of God and/or the gospel before they are ultimately saved, they are nonetheless now on the way to salvation. Note that this dynamic between 'present' and 'future' coheres well with the definition of 'salvation' offered in my introduction: 'a present and ongoing process of human transformation and growth, which is begun in this life [. . .] and comes to maturation and completion – i.e. *final* salvation – in the post-mortem entry into heaven'. It also fits in very closely with D'Costa's assertion that:

> it is possible to see the limbo of the just as providing a solution that overcomes the prohibition on 'conversion,' a new decision in the next life, for in one sense no conversion is required but a completion of the person's life and their destiny. There must be adequate continuity in the person's life for them to 'qualify' for being present in the limbo of the just. (173)

Lest it be thought my exegesis of LG 16 is overly literal, consider the considerable change in meaning had it read 'Those who have *not accepted* (*non acceperunt*) the Gospel [. . .] are able to obtain eternal salvation'. This would imply acceptance of the gospel to be optional, contradicting LG 14 and a great deal else. Alternatively, suppose it had read 'Those who have not yet accepted the Gospel [. . .] *will be able* (*poterunt*)' – i.e. once they have accepted it – 'to obtain eternal salvation', and 'Nor *will* divine Providence deny (*Nec . . . denegabit*) the assistances necessary for salvation'. These would suggest that God's salvific activity will begin only *after* they have accepted it, which if this were to occur after death, arguably implies a radical disjunction of the sort forbidden by Augustine. It would also ignore the fact that God's salvific activity is the ground and condition for this acceptance in the first place (see CCC 2023).

D'Costa's theory is not, though, devoid of difficulties, whether intrinsic or when adapted to the specific problems posed by (non-religious) atheism. Three in particular are identified here. Solutions to each will, however, be offered in the course of this chapter and the next.

First of all, LG 16's extension of the possibility of salvation to non-Christians is predicated on the condition that they are 'without fault, ignorant (*sine culpa ignorantes*) of the Gospel of Christ and his Church'; and also, in the case of atheists, that they 'without fault (*sine culpa*), have not yet arrived at an express recognition of God'. Likewise, *Ad Gentes* 7 asserts that 'in ways known to himself God is able to lead men who are, without fault of their own, ignorant (*sine eorum culpa ignorantes*) of the Gospel to that faith without which it is impossible to please him (Heb 11.6)' (AS IV/vii: 677). Sensibly enough, the Council Fathers passed no comment on what such *inculpable ignorance* actually connotes. More surprising, however, is the fact that recent Catholic theologians have exhibited a similar reticence. Neither Gerald O'Collins nor Jacques Dupuis, for example, offers a sustained exposition.[10]

For his part, D'Costa directly mentions the 'inculpably ignorant' twice in an early chapter. While explicating John Hick's pluralism, he writes: 'There are many millions who have never heard of Christ through no fault of their own, before and after the New Testament period – the *inculpably ignorant*' (9). And then, discussing Rahner's ideas: 'Rahner maintains that Israel remains a lawful religion for those who have never been confronted historically and existentially with the gospel – in effect, the inculpably ignorant' (20). These descriptions are, of course, not synonymous: one can have *heard of* Christ, without having been 'confronted historically and existentially with the gospel'. And D'Costa himself, when presenting his own theory in the later chapters, speaks not of the 'inculpably ignorant', but rather of the 'unevangelized'. But this term is itself ambiguous. Does it mean those who have never been preached *to* ('the objectively unevangelized')? Or those who, even if they have been preached to, were not *successfully* evangelized ('the subjectively unevangelized')? At times, it appears as though D'Costa has the first sense in mind (e.g. 178). Yet it is said of Jane that she 'has not known the gospel', which intimates something more nuanced than simply not having heard. Although a

---

[10] At least, not in Dupuis 1997: 158–79; Dupuis 2002: 195–217; or O'Collins 2007: 218–37 – all sections where one might have expected, or hoped for, such a treatment. To these, one may also add Knitter 1985: 120–44; and DiNoia 1992: 94–108. (It must be said, however, that I have conducted no exhaustive exploration of these authors' impressive *oeuvres*.) More attention has been given to these issues by Protestant writers, although typically without direct reference to LG. See Sanders 1994: 15 n. 2; Strange 2002: 33–5; and Tiessen 2004: 126–36.

The Salvation of 'Jane' and the Problem of Ignorance   129

Buddhist, Jane has a Western name. As such, she has presumably *heard* of Christ (and/or his Church), even if she has never been confronted 'historically and existentially with the gospel'. Pedantic though these points may be, they highlight just a few of the issues raised by LG 16's stipulation of an *ignorantia sine culpa*. If indeed 'Theological expertise is now turned to [the salvation of non-Christians], in order to understand it more deeply' (*Dominus Iesus* 21; AAS 92 [2000]: 762), then to do this comprehensively, more attention must be paid to exploring quite what this might mean. As it currently stands, therefore, there remains a significant *lacuna* in D'Costa's theory (as there also is in those of O'Collins and Dupuis). My own, necessarily preliminary, attempt at rectifying this will follow in the next section.

Secondly, D'Costa's schema both upholds Augustine's strictures against any 'new decision in the next life' (173), and requires that those who hitherto did not believe in Christ and his Church (if not also, as with Jane, in God), be brought to this belief in limbo in order to attain the beatific vision. For D'Costa, the latter does not contravene the former since it does not constitute a genuine conversion, but rather 'a coming to maturation and completion' (or, more accurately, the *beginnings* of completion; purgatory, which would ordinarily follow limbo, is itself part of this process of maturation). Furthermore, he can appeal here to the strong precedent within the tradition of the Old Testament righteous, for whom Christ's proclamation in Hades must have served a similar end.

Leaving aside the troubling question of whether Jane, not to mention the multitudes whom she represents, can truly be understood (even analogically) as a latter-day Abraham or Moses,[11] it could be argued that D'Costa minimizes here what one might call the *necessary newness* of faith. This may be seen most clearly if Jane's post-mortem 'coming to maturation and completion' is instead extrapolated backwards into her earthly life. Suppose, then, that she is 'existentially' confronted with the gospel proclamation while still alive, and hence leaves Buddhism in order to be baptized into the Catholic Church. In this case, one would surely be justified in speaking of 'conversion'. This need not imply a complete rupture with her (Buddhist) past.

---

[11] Note that this is not simply an issue of conflating 'the status of the pre-messianic Jews with post-messianic non-Christians' (174). As noted in chapter two, not all of the 'holy dead' were Jews, including Enoch, Job, Abel, and the Queen of Sheba.

Jane herself may well view her becoming a Christian as 'a fulfillment of what was already present [...] coming to its full maturation' (172). Yet she would almost certainly regard it as being *something more besides* (perhaps incalculably so), and as very much 'a new decision'. And if so, then how could it be any different in limbo? *Pace* D'Costa (23), Rahner avoids this difficulty in appealing to implicit faith, since he can argue that the post-mortem 'explicitation' of hitherto-implicit attitudes and beliefs is indeed a 'coming to maturation and completion' requiring no genuinely new decision. But both D'Costa and I reject Rahner's solution. Certainly, it can be argued that there is a tension inherent within the dogmatic tradition on this point (especially if, as I have argued, LG 16 implies a post-mortem solution to the problem of the salvation of non-Christians). If so, then theologians would be well-advised to preserve, rather than domesticate, this tension in their hypotheses. Bearing this in mind, a hesitant answer to this problem will nevertheless be suggested in chapter five, both in light of the Augustinian and Bellarminean understandings of 1 Peter, and a number of key ideas yet to be discussed.

Thirdly and finally: relevant though Jane is to many of the issues discussed herein, this book ultimately concerns not the salvation of non-theistic Buddhists, but the salvation of non-religious atheists. As such, certain important aspects of D'Costa's account of how Jane might be saved do not obviously apply here (although this is not, of course, a deficiency in D'Costa's work itself). In particular, one important way through which Jane might receive and respond to grace is through her own religious tradition. Thus:

> possibilities of the good, true, and beautiful life might be found in positive elements within her religion [...], and in this way Jane is acting in response to the promptings of the Holy Spirit who is the foundation of our freedom and search for truth (162)

Furthermore, within the world's various religious traditions 'there may be sufficient elements of *preparatio evangelica* that allow God's grace to work toward the final salvation of such persons' (211). This was also affirmed in *Dominus Iesus* 21: 'The various religious traditions certainly contain and offer elements of religiosity which come from God' (AAS 92 [2000]: 763). Such *preparatio evangelica* is, however, presumably not accessible to the typical atheist. Now admittedly, Jane has other means at her disposal for encountering grace, whether she knows it or not, which are also available to the atheist:

adhering to the (God-given) dictates of her conscience, for example. But if Jane's participation in her own religious tradition is indeed a significant contributing factor to her being 'on the road to salvation', then this is a significant contributing factor that the non-religious atheist, *ipso facto*, lacks. It appears the atheist is presented with far fewer opportunities for encountering and responding to grace than does, say, a practising Buddhist. Despite LG 16's affirmations of the *possibility* of an atheist being saved, this appears to be a further cause for pessimism as to its actuality. Yet again, a possible solution to this will be developed in the course of the next chapter. But before that, let us return to the subject of ignorance.

THE PROBLEM OF IGNORANCE

As argued above, the notion of *ignorantia sine culpa* ('inculpable ignorance') is pivotal to a proper understanding of Vatican II's pronouncements regarding the salvation of non-Christians. Thus the phrase *sine culpa* qualifies the key conciliar expressions of optimism for those who have 'not yet accepted the Gospel'. *Ignorantia* and its cognates are also prominent. This fact is, however, largely obscured in the standard English translations. The Latin of LG 16 speaks of those who 'without fault, are ignorant (*ignorantes*) of the Gospel of Christ of his Church'.[12] The choice of terms here is underlined by the fact that LG 14 also literally reads 'those men cannot be saved, who not being ignorant (*non ignorantes*) [of the fact that] the Catholic Church has been founded as necessary by God through Jesus Christ, are nevertheless unwilling either to enter it, or to persevere in it.' Significantly, the use of the awkward phrase *non ignorantes* was a deliberate decision by the Council Fathers: in earlier drafts of LG, referring to a single non-believer, the more natural *sciens* ('knowing') is used.[13] It seems that those drafting these paragraphs intended to

---

[12] Cf. Abbot and Gallagher 1967: 35; Flannery 1975: 367; Tanner 1990b: 861; and the official version on the Vatican's website: <http://www.vatican.va/archive/hist_-councils/ii_vatican_council/documents/vat-ii_const_19641121_lumen-gentium_en. html>. Accessed on 23 February 2009. All of these read 'do not know' for *ignorantes*.

[13] The switch from *sciens* to *non ignorantes* occurred in the course of the Theological Commission's revising of the unofficial draft text by the Belgian theologian Gerard Philips (written in autumn 1962), following the Council's rejection of the

highlight the importance of ignorance to the question of salvation, hence this apparent *inclusio* between LG 14 and 16.

Vatican II's emphasis on ignorance and inculpability raises a great many questions – none of which it answers. Most obviously, what counts as inculpable ignorance, whether of God, 'the Gospel of Christ and his Church', or the fact that 'the Catholic Church has been founded as something necessary by God through Jesus Christ'? Must one never have even heard of Christianity, or would a merely superficial acquaintance with the gospel also count? What about those brought up in supposedly Christian countries, and who have perhaps even been baptized – might even some of these be inculpably ignorant? It will be remembered from chapter two that Pius IX introduced the Thomistic principle of *invincible* ignorance into Catholic discussions of those *extra Ecclesiam* (see also Morali 2004: 201). This teaching was reiterated in the Holy Office's 1949 intervention in the Boston Heresy Case, which is cited in a footnote to LG 16. Is inculpable ignorance, then, the same as invincible ignorance? If so, why does Vatican II depart from the established terminology? If not, what material difference do the two terms signify? The issue is still more problematic in view of the fact that 'invincible' ignorance was retained elsewhere in the conciliar corpus (e.g. GS 16), and continues to be used in magisterial pronouncements on moral issues.

In addressing these questions, my argument will proceed in four interrelated movements. Firstly, I shall examine the classical, Thomistic understanding of invincible ignorance, its roots in scripture, and its subsequent employment by Pius IX. Next, I shall consider how, following the discovery of the New World in 1492, the application of the Thomistic understanding was significantly reappraised. This *ressourcement* will especially focus upon two sixteenth-century Spanish Dominicans, Francisco de Vitoria and Bartolomé de Las Casas. The third section will return to Vatican II, and will argue that the new emphasis on *ignorantia sine culpa* significantly mirrors the Vitorian and Lascasian developments of the doctrine of *ignorantia invincibilis*. The fourth and final section will unite the foregoing analyses, elucidating Vatican II's understanding of inculpable

original schema. Like the rejected official draft, both Philips' original and the modified version which the Commission began work on in March 1963, read *sciens*. By the time the Commission's new version was sent to the bishops in May, *non ignorantes* had replaced it (see Alberigo and Magistretti 1975: 57, 72).

ignorance as both a rediscovery of elements already present in the tradition, and (in light of insights from the sociology of knowledge) as justifying a wide-ranging 'presumption of ignorance' (Sullivan 1992: 151) on the part of contemporary unbelievers.

General support for the mitigating nature of ignorance may, ultimately, be derived from scripture. The Lukan Jesus' gloss on the parable of the watchful slaves (Lk 12.35–40), for instance, prescribes that: 'That slave who knew what his master wanted, but did not prepare himself or do what was wanted, will receive a severe beating. But one who did not know and did what deserved a beating will receive a light beating' (12.47–8). A similar idea is behind James' admonition: 'Anyone, then, who knows the right thing to do and fails to do it, commits sin' (Jas 4.17) – the implication being, of course, that sin is not committed by someone who fails to do the right thing out of ignorance. Strikingly, 1 Timothy imputes to Paul the belief that: 'even though I was formerly a blasphemer, a persecutor and a man of violence [...] I received mercy because I had acted ignorantly in unbelief' (1.13). Paul's speech at the Areopagus states that 'God has overlooked the times of ignorance' (Acts 17.30). And at Rom 10.14, Paul famously asks: 'But how are they to call on one in whom they have not believed? And how are they to believe in one of whom they have never heard? And how are they to hear without someone to proclaim him?' The fact that Paul apparently does believe that 'all' have heard (cf. 10.18) does not nullify the importance of the question. Elsewhere, Mk 16.16's grave warning that 'The one who believes and is baptized will be saved; but the one who does not believe will be condemned' – a favoured proof-text of the dogmatic tradition for affirming the absolute necessity of faith for salvation (e.g. LG 16; *Dominus Iesus* 3) – is dependent on the previous verse's command: 'Go into all the world and proclaim the good news to the whole creation' (16.15). Thus this stark condemnation of non-believers seems to assume that they have heard the gospel, and (culpably) rejected it. Finally, the Johannine Jesus says even of those who actively persecute the Church: 'If I had not come and spoken to them, they would not have sin; but now they have no excuse for their sin. [...] If I had not done among them the works that no one else did, they would not have sin. But now they have seen and hated both me and my Father' (Jn 15.24). Once again, Christ's condemnation explicitly presupposes a lack of ignorance, and hence a culpable rejection.

Much later, these biblical precedents became crystallized in the moral theology of Thomas Aquinas. He writes in the *Summa theologiae*:

> Now it is manifest that whosoever neglects to have or do those things that he is obliged to have or do, sins by a sin of omission. Thus because of negligence, ignorance of those things which someone is obliged to know is a sin.
>
> However, negligence is not imputed to a man if he is not able to know those things which he does not know. Thus ignorance of these things is called invincible: because it obviously cannot be overcome [even] by effort. Because of this, this kind of ignorance is not a sin, since it is not voluntary, and it is not in our power to repel it.
>
> Thus it is obvious that invincible ignorance is never a sin: vincible ignorance is a sin, if it is of those things which someone is obliged to know, but not if it is of those things which he is not obliged to know. (*Summa theologiae*, Ia IIae, q. 76, a. 2; Thomas Aquinas [1265-74] 1969: 148)

Thomas draws an important and influential distinction between two kinds of ignorance. *Vincible* ignorance is such that a person both could and should have overcome it. Such ignorance, born from negligence, does not excuse sin. Conversely, *invincible* ignorance is such that the person is not able, even by diligence, to overcome it. Hence there is no sin to excuse. In the *Summa*, this is presented as a general principle, and is not applied to the question of salvation. In his *Quaestiones disputatae de veritate*, however, Thomas had already considered the situation of someone being (albeit *avant la lettre*) invincibly ignorant of the gospel. Writing in the mid-1200s, it is noteworthy that Thomas was only able to envisage this scenario in terms of someone having been brought up 'in the woods or among brute animals' (the assumption being that the gospel had, by now, been preached throughout the whole world). Given the exceptional nature of this case, Thomas is justified in positing an exceptional solution:

> For if someone was brought up in such a way, provided that he had followed his natural reason in seeking good and avoiding evil, it is certainly to be held that God would either reveal to him by an internal inspiration the things which are necessarily to be believed, or would direct some preacher of the faith to him, just like he sent Peter to Cornelius (Acts 10). (*De veritate*, q. 14, a. 11, ad. 1; Thomas Aquinas [*c*. 1259] 1925: 409)

Note that, in this thought-experiment, the subject literally could not even have heard *of* Christ. Thomas does not, for example, pick a pious Muslim or Jew who, despite having heard of Christ and the Church, has no particular reason for wanting to find out more about them. Rather, this person's ignorance is 'invincible' in a very strong sense of the word. When, several centuries later, Pius IX adopted Thomas' later terminology in order to qualify what is in fact a very robust defence of *Extra Ecclesiam nulla salus*, it is therefore tempting to assume that he had in mind a similarly narrow frame of application. This interpretation would gain support from the pessimistic position, evinced in his 1864 *Syllabus of Errors*, impugning the opinion that: 'Good hope at least is to be considered regarding the eternal salvation of all those who are not in the true Church of Christ' ([1864] 1867: 705). Yet in *Singulari Quadem* Pius' application of the principle is conspicuously wider than that apparently envisaged by Thomas. Indeed, as we have seen, Pius resolutely refuses to set definitive limits to its application:

> Now truly, who would arrogate so much to himself, as to be able to designate the limits of this kind of ignorance, due to the reason and variety of peoples, regions, natural dispositions, and a great many other things? ([1854] 1864: 626)

This is a startling admission, and constitutes a major landmark on the road to LG. But, as so often with the development of doctrine, in order to move forwards, one must first look backwards. For as we shall see, such a nuanced comprehension of invincible ignorance's possible extent was by no means a nineteenth-century innovation.

Christopher Columbus discovered the Indies in 1492, and promptly claimed them for the Spanish crown (later confirmed by Pope Alexander VI's 1493 bull *Inter Caetera*). The ensuing gold rush was disastrous for the continent. The population fell vertiginously within thirty years, primarily from disease, but also, to quote Nathan Wachtel, from 'murderous oppression' (1984: 212–13). Even leaving aside the infamous encomienda,[14] we may quote Las Casas, writing fifty years after Columbus' discovery:

---

[14] This was an 'institutionalized form of slavery' (Bradstock and Rowland 2002: 62), whereby whole communities were often forcibly 'entrusted' to Spanish soldiers or *conquistadores* and required to pay tribute in exchange for instruction in the Spanish language and Catholicism. Not surprisingly, abuses were rife (see Poole 1992: 80).

> The pattern established at the outset has remained unchanged to this day, and the Spaniards still do nothing save tear the natives to shreds, murder them and inflict upon them untold misery, suffering and distress, tormenting, harrying and persecuting them mercilessly. ([1542] 1992: 11)

Las Casas' indictment is confirmed by Gonzalo Fernández de Oviedo, appointed official historian of the Spanish Crown in 1523, and no friend either to Las Casas or the Amerindians:

> If all were written in detail as it was done, there would be neither time nor paper to enumerate all that the captains did to destroy the Indians and to rob and ravish the land. (Quoted in Hanke 2002: 34–5)

It is against this background that the Vitorian and Lascasian developments of invincible ignorance must be understood.

As the destruction of the Indies continued unabated, members of the Spanish intelligentsia began to question whether or not these overseas campaigns constituted 'just wars'. Vitoria broached the issue in his professorial 'relection' *De Indis* (*On the Indies*), delivered in Salamanca in 1539. He counters the opinion that war against the Indians is morally and legally justified because 'they refuse to accept the faith of Christ, although it has been proposed to them, and they have been insistently admonished to accept it' (*De Indis*, q. 2, a. 4; Vitoria [1539] 1952: 68), arguing instead that, due to certain mitigating factors, the Indians remain invincibly ignorant of the Christian proclamation. He contends, on the authority of Rom 10.14, that 'If the faith has not been preached to them, they are invincibly ignorant (*ignorant invincibiliter*), because they are not capable of knowing [it]' (ibid.: 74). So far, so Thomasian. But Vitoria goes further:

> The barbarians are not bound to believe from the first announcement of the Christian faith, in the sense of sinning mortally by not believing due to this alone: because it is merely announced and proposed to them that the true religion is Christian, and that Christ is the saviour and redeemer of the world, without miracles or any other proofs or arguments. (Ibid.: 76)

If unbelievers are preserved from guilt by never having heard of Christianity (as in Thomas' thought-experiment), then equally: 'they are not obligated by this kind of simple statement and announcement. Such an announcement is no argument or motive for believing'. Moreover, as he quotes from Cardinal Cajetan, 'it is rash

The Salvation of 'Jane' and the Problem of Ignorance 137

and imprudent of anyone to believe something (especially in matters such as these, concerning salvation) unless one knows it to be from a trustworthy source' (ibid.). Now of course, if Christianity is preached in a plausible fashion, supported by rational arguments, and by people whose behaviour concurs with what is taught, then the Indians are indeed 'obliged to accept the faith of Christ under pain of mortal sin'. With regard to the current situation, however:

> It is not sufficiently clear to me that the Christian faith has thus far been proposed and announced to the barbarians so as to obligate them to believe it [. . .] It does not appear that the Christian religion has been preached to them suitably and piously, so as to obligate acquiescence. (Ibid.: 80)

Hence Vitoria insists that ignorance remains fully invincible (and therefore morally inculpable) when Christianity is presented only very superficially, unaccompanied by any more persuasive catechesis.[15]

Las Casas concurs on key points with his Dominican confrère, railing in book after book against the *conquistadores*' failures to present Christianity in any remotely convincing manner. Due to the sheer volume of his writings on this topic, it is worth concentrating on his critique of one especially notorious example: the *Requerimiento*, devised by the celebrated jurist Juan Palacios López de Rubos in 1513. This text, 'one of the strangest documents in Spanish history' (Poole 1992: 81), was intended to be declaimed in Latin upon first contact with Indian nations. It outlines the history of the world from Creation, noting especially the establishment of the papacy and the pope's donation of the Indies to Spain. It then '*requires*' that those listening submit to the Church, the pope, and the Spanish Crown, and that they allow the Christian faith to be preached to them, before explaining what will happen if they do not so consent:

> We shall take you and your wives and children, and shall make slaves of them, and as such shall sell and dispose of them as their Highnesses may command; and we shall take away your goods, and shall do all the

---

[15] It is worth noting, however, that Vitoria is not at all concerned here with the Indians' possible salvation. Indeed, he is quite emphatic on this point: 'The barbarians, to whom an announcement of the faith or the Christian religion has never come, will be damned on account of their mortal sins or idolatry, but not for the sin of unbelief' (ibid.: 76). The same applies to Las Casas (cf. [1542] 1992: 6, 126).

harm and damage that we can [...]. (Quoted in Hanke 2002: 33; see also Gutiérrez 1993: 110–25)

Las Casas, not surprisingly, confesses in his *History of the Indies* not to 'know whether to laugh or cry at [its] absurdity' ([1552] 1971: 196), and asks 'what credit should a people who lived at peace in its territory without harming anyone be expected to give to such a bill of sale?' (ibid.: 195). Naturally, he does not dispute the *Requerimiento*'s truth-claims concerning the Church and the papacy. But importantly, he denies their authority for those who have only just been informed of the *existence* of these institutions, especially when delivered by 'bearded messengers armed to the teeth with terrible weapons' (ibid.: 194). Indeed, as he quotes elsewhere from Sirach 19.4: 'Being too ready to trust shows shallowness of mind' ([c. 1550] 1974: 134). Needless to say, such a skeletal presentation does not constitute *evangelization* in any meaningful sense and, therefore, does not nullify any hitherto-present invincible ignorance.

Yet the inadequacy of the proclamation was not the severest grievance of Vitoria and Las Casas. Rather, both object most vociferously to the *defamation* of the Faith by (in the phrase of the latter) 'the devils of the New World who masquerade as Christians' ([1542] 1992: 124). Thus Vitoria complains that he hears 'only of many scandals, cruel atrocities, and multiple impieties' ([1539] 1952: 68), and exasperatedly exclaims 'would that the sins of some Christians were not much worse [...] than those among these barbarians!' (ibid.: 90). And for Las Casas, the conduct of those who 'are not warriors for Christ, but for anti-Christ' ([1552] 1992: 144) has brought it about 'that nothing is more odious nor more terrifying to the people than the name *Christian*' ([1542] 1992: 82). Such people have damned 'those who grew to hate our faith because of the awful example you gave, grew to ridicule the universal Church, grew to blaspheme God' ([1552] 1992: 150). In his *In Defense of the Indians* (c. 1550), Las Casas directly links this experience with invincible ignorance. After asserting that the invincibly ignorant 'are not obliged to believe unless the faith is fully presented and explained to them by suitable ministers', he declares:

> [A] great many unbelievers are excused from accepting the faith for a long time and perhaps for their whole lifetime, no matter how long it lasts, so long as they see the extremely corrupt and detestable conduct of the Christians. ([c. 1550] 1974: 133–40)

Taking their writings together, it is possible to identify three, interrelated Vitorian/Lascasian reasons why invincible ignorance may perdure *after* someone has not only heard of Christ and the Church, but has perhaps even been (objectively) evangelized. The first of these is that the proclamation may itself be intrinsically inadequate: at its most extreme, the simple assertion of the mere *existence* of Christ or the Church is not sufficiently persuasive as to oblige assent. The second is that certain social factors, while extrinsic to the proclamation itself, may undermine its claims to authority. (This 'sociological' point, which Las Casas only hints at, will be explained in more detail below.) And the third – which is, properly speaking, a notably conspicuous example of the second – recognizes that the misconduct of Christians (acting either singularly or collectively) may so defame Christianity as to prolong invincible ignorance over a long period of time, and perhaps indefinitely. It will be recognized that these constitute a considerable widening of invincible ignorance's application compared to Thomas' 'in the woods or among brute animals' thought-experiment (framed as it was by his reasonable, but nonetheless false, assumptions regarding the extent and adequacy of evangelization up to that point). On that note, let us return to Vatican II.

As noted above, neither LG 14, LG 16, nor *Ad Gentes* 7 explains quite what inculpable ignorance might entail. A revealing clue may, however, be found in GS 19. It avers, first of all, that 'those who wilfully try to drive God from their heart and to avoid religious questions, not following the dictate of their conscience, *are not devoid of fault* (*culpae expertes non sunt*)' (AS IV/vii: 743; my emphasis). This is an important and necessary qualification to the Council's (and my own) 'salvific optimism': inculpability is by no means a foregone conclusion.[16] Yet the very same sentence continues: 'however, believers themselves often bear a certain responsibility for this.' More strikingly, this claim is soon elaborated with reference to both the first ('inadequate proclamation') and third ('Christian misconduct') of the Lascasian/Vitorian criteria:

---

[16] This bears on a point raised in chapter one, concerning the 'salvifically relevant differences' between, say, an agnostic and a militant anti-theist. Although both atheists, it may well be that the latter's ignorance, due to her wilfully trying to drive God from her heart, is culpable, whereas the agnostic's is not. This might gain credence from LG 16's specific mention of those 'who seek God with a sincere heart'. That said, of course, it is certainly possible for an agnostic's ignorance to be culpable due to avoiding religious questions.

[B]elievers can have no small part in the rise of atheism, since by neglecting education in the faith, teaching false doctrine, or through defects in their own religious, moral, or social lives, they may be said rather more to conceal than reveal the true countenance of God and of religion. (Ibid.)

The Council Fathers' deliberations on this issue make for interesting reading. At the Third Session (1964), Cardinal Suenens of Mechelen, Belgium, urged that while:

Atheism is certainly a terrible error, [...] it would be too easy simply to condemn it. It is necessary to examine why so many men profess themselves to be atheists, and whom precisely is this 'God' they so sharply attack. Thus dialogue should be begun with them so that they may seek and recognize the true image of God who is perhaps concealed under the caricatures they reject. On our part, meanwhile, we should examine our way of speaking of God and living the faith, *lest the sun of the living God is darkened for them*. (AS III/v: 271; my emphasis)

Similarly, during the Fourth Session (1965), Cardinals Šeper and König expressed the opinion that Christians are largely to blame for the rise and spread of atheism (AS IV/ii: 436, 455; see Ratzinger 1969: 144; McNicholl 1968: 23). Patriarch Maximos IV Saigh went yet further, asserting that atheists 'are often scandalized by the sight of a mediocre and egoistical Christendom absorbed by money and false riches'. He adds: 'is it not the egotism of certain Christians which has caused, and causes to a great extent, the atheism of the masses?' (AS IV/ii: 452; quoted from Hebblethwaite 1967: 81). While these statements were made during the discussions of Schema XIII, rather than of what would become LG, they nevertheless shed a great deal of light on what the Council meant by *ignorantia sine culpa*. Furthermore, although referring specially to atheists, there is no reason why these considerations do not also apply, *mutatis mutandis*, to other groupings. The 'egotism of certain Christians' may just as easily scandalize Muslims, Sikhs, and Buddhists – or, for that matter, other Christians (and in fact, perhaps these most of all) – as they do atheists. If so, then this would also be a factor in maintaining their inculpable ignorance regarding Catholic truth-claims about the gospel and the Church, even if not necessarily with regard to the existence of God. Similar concerns were also, it will be remembered from chapter two, voiced by many theologians (including, of course, de Lubac and Daniélou, who were among the drafters of GS 19–21) in the decades leading up to the Council.

What Vatican II seems to have intended by inculpable ignorance is, therefore, in substantial agreement with what, in the sixteenth century, Las Casas and Vitoria meant by invincible ignorance. That is not, of course, to ignore the major disparities between their respective *Sitze im Leben*: Vatican II's *ignorantes* would, by and large, have been brought up within at least nominally Christian societies; Las Casas and Vitoria were not directly concerned with the salvation of the invincibly ignorant.[17] Differences aside, however, both Vatican II and the great Dominicans accept that (i) inculpable/invincible ignorance prevents unbelief from being sinful; and (ii) this kind of ignorance may be prolonged, even after acquaintance with Christianity and the Church's proclamation, if this is either intrinsically insufficient or if Christians themselves fail *scandalously* (in the full, scriptural sense of the term) to live up to the name. This constitutes, as we have seen, a significant development over Thomas' own, apparently restricted application of *ignorantia invincibilis*.[18] And this fact explains the Council Fathers' avoidance of the term. For those schooled in (neo-) Thomism, as were the vast majority of at least the Latin-rite Council Fathers and *periti*, the phrase invincible ignorance may well have carried overtones of its earlier, far narrower applications. Pius IX, however, had *already* departed from these by acknowledging the 'variety of peoples, regions, natural dispositions, and so many other things'. Thus, with its doctrine of inculpable ignorance, the Second Vatican Council both authentically developed Pius IX's teaching on invincible ignorance, and (apparently unwittingly) rediscovered an understanding of invincible ignorance already firmly present in the non-magisterial tradition of the Church, while

---

[17] At least, not insofar as they remained invincibly ignorant. But that said, Las Casas' primary ire at the Spanish presence in the Antilles was the 'infinite number of souls despatched to Hell', due to the fact that 'the local people have died and still die in the blackest ignorance of the faith and without the benefit of the Sacraments' (Las Casas [1542] 1992: 6, 126).

[18] Too much should not, perhaps, be read into Thomas' single example: he is not necessarily committed to the view that *only* someone brought up 'in the woods or among brute animals' could fulfil the criteria for being invincibly ignorant. The passage in the *de Veritate* (written before his use of the phrase itself in the *Summa*) might just as easily be read as offering, for didactic purposes, the clearest and most extreme example. To the best of my knowledge, there is nothing in either *de Veritate* or the *Summa* to suggest that, faced with the same situation as Las Casas and Vitoria, he would have found their applications of his principle inimical.

at the same time avoiding the phrase itself as something potentially misleading.[19]

In addition to the Council's own deliberations, a number of post-conciliar developments are germane for a contemporary understanding of inculpable ignorance. Firstly, the inadequate presentation of Christianity by the Church(es) and other ecclesial communities is a leading theme of several important enquiries into the rise and spread of modern atheism. Most famously, Michael Buckley has argued that the concept of God presented in seventeenth- and eighteenth-century apologetic works, in which the 'intellectual credibility of the existence of God had been made to depend fundamentally upon the inference in philosophy or natural philosophy or mechanics' (Buckley 2004: 36), sowed the seeds for the rise of modern unbelief. What began as an intellectual exercise against chimerical opponents soon, by its very insufficiency, engendered the very phenomenon which it set out to disprove (Buckley 1987: 37–67). From this foundation, wave and counter-wave of apologetic writing from both sides has proceeded dialectically, in the words of Dostoevsky's Prince Myshkin, 'eternally [...] talking *not about that*' ([1868] 2001: 221). In an analogous vein, Mikhail Epstein's seminal work on the fall, rise, and transformation of Russian religion over the past two centuries argues that the prevalence of Orthodox apophatic and hesychastic theology led inexorably to the 'Russian nihilism of the nineteenth century and the Soviet atheism of the twentieth, in which negative theology becomes the negation of theism itself' (1999: 351). That is to say, it was 'the anti-intellectual stance of Orthodoxy' that prepared the way 'for atheism as a spiritual neurosis' (ibid.: 351–2). Whether accurate or not, it is beyond the scope of this enquiry to adjudicate. Nevertheless, these studies lend further theoretical support to the statement that 'believers can have no small part in the rise of atheism'.

Secondly, Las Casas' remarks about the dubitable authority of the *conquistadores*' proclamation, due to certain extrinsic factors, can be significantly elaborated and developed in light of insights from the sociology of knowledge, as first developed in Peter Berger and

---

[19] This latter claim is admittedly difficult to substantiate. However, given the fact that the traditional phrase *ignorantia invincibilis* was frequently used in theological writings of this time, and is prominent in the Holy Office's Letter to the Archbishop of Boston cited in LG 16, its absence is noteworthy. A different explanation to the one I am offering is that this reflects the drafters' desire to avoid overly technical terms.

The Salvation of 'Jane' and the Problem of Ignorance 143

Thomas Luckmann's 1966 book *The Social Construction of Reality*. Putting it very simply, they argue for the necessity of social 'plausibility structures' for the construction and maintenance of any given 'reality'. Hence:

> Subjective reality is thus always dependent upon specific plausibility structures, that is, the specific social base and social processes required for its maintenance. One can maintain one's self-identification as a man of importance only in a milieu that confirms this identity; one can maintain one's Catholic faith only if one retains one's significant relationship with the Catholic community; and so forth. ([1966] 1971: 174)

This is brought out most obviously when a person switches from accepting one 'reality', or worldview, to a different one – as, paradigmatically, in the case of religious conversion:

> To have a conversion experience is nothing much. The real thing is to be able to keep on taking it seriously; to retain a sense of its plausibility. *This* is where the religious community comes in. It provides the indispensable plausibility structure for the new reality. In other words, Saul may have become Paul in the aloneness of religious ecstasy, but he could *remain* Paul only in the context of the Christian community that recognized him as such and confirmed the 'new being' in which he now located this identity. (Ibid.: 177–8)

This general principle does not, however, apply only in conversion situations. Rather, such 'plausibility structures' (which, concretely, may simply be regular contact with 'significant others' who share the same beliefs) are necessary for sustaining a person in a given worldview. To quote from Berger's follow-up *The Sacred Canopy*, where he specifically applies this theory to the case of religion:

> [I]t can be said that *all* religious traditions, irrespective of their several 'ecclesiologies' or lack of the same, require specific communities for their continuing plausibility. In this sense, the maxim *extra ecclesiam nulla salus* has general empirical applicability, provided one understands *salus* in a theologically rather unpalatable sense – to wit, as continuing plausibility. The reality of the Christian world depends upon the presence of social structures within which this reality is taken for granted and within which successive generations of individuals are socialized in such a way that this world will be real *to them*. When this plausibility structure loses its intactness or continuity, the Christian world begins to totter and its reality ceases to impose itself as self-evident truth. ([1967] 1990: 46)

Importantly, Berger singles out pluralism as posing a particular threat to such structures: 'the pluralistic situation *ipso facto* plunges religion into a crisis of credibility'. His twofold justification for this is worth quoting at length:

> The pluralistic situation, in demonopolizing religion, makes it ever more difficult to maintain or to construct anew viable plausibility structures for religion. The plausibility structures lose massivity because they can no longer enlist the society as a whole to serve for the purpose of social confirmation. Put simply, there are always 'all those others' that refuse to confirm the religious world in question. Put simply in a different way, it becomes increasingly difficult for the 'inhabitants' of any particular religious world to remain *entre nous* in contemporary society. Disconfirming others (not just individuals, but entire strata) can no longer be safely kept away from 'one's own.' (Ibid.: 151)

And furthermore:

> The pluralistic situation multiplies the number of plausibility structures competing with each other. *Ipso facto*, it relativizes their religious contents. More specifically, the religious contents are 'de-objectivated,' that is, deprived of their status as taken-for-granted, objective reality in consciousness. (Ibid.)

Now, it is precisely pluralism which many sociologists identify as a key catalyst in European secularization (e.g. Bruce 2002: 220–6). In the words of Stephen Hunt: 'the pluralist situation relativizes competing religious worldviews and their matter-of-fact acceptance. Moreover, the pluralistic situation where one can choose one's religion is also a situation where one can choose to disbelieve' (2002: 19). A similar idea is behind Pope Benedict XVI's comment on American Catholics' drifting away from the Church: 'Certainly, much of this has to do with the passing away of a religious culture, sometimes disparagingly referred to as a "ghetto," which reinforced participation and identification with the Church.'[20] Arguably, therefore, Berger and Luckmann's theories open up new vistas for the understanding of inculpable ignorance – at least, with regard to modern, secularized societies (where, of course, a large proportion of the world's atheists reside). Now the two sociologists, true to their discipline's 'methodological a-theism', refuse

---

[20] Text available online at: <http://www.vatican.va/holy_father/benedict_xvi/speeches/2008/april/documents/hf_ben-xvi_spe_20080416_response-bishops_en.html>. Accessed on 1 October 2010.

to be drawn on the *actual* truth-value of the myriad (perceived) 'realities' or 'truths' which have, in one or another time and place, been accepted by social groups (Berger and Luckmann [1966] 1971: 14; Berger [1967] 1990: 179–80). But I, true to my own 'methodological Catholicism', need not be so coy. Nevertheless, there is no reason to suppose that acceptance of *the* Truth (even when assisted by grace) is any less contingent upon appropriate plausibility structures than is the acceptance of mere 'truths'. And as such, inculpability becomes far more complicated.

It is no longer simply a question of not having heard the gospel, nor even of not having heard an (intrinsically) plausible presentation of it. One must rather speak, with Rahner, of not having been *existentially* confronted with the gospel ([1961] 1966). But in a modern pluralist society, which relativizes all truth- (let alone Truth-) claims, it may be that a great many people, and perhaps even an overwhelming majority, are never so confronted (especially when considered in conjunction with the other factors identified by both Vitoria/Las Casas and GS 19). Note that this could well, moreover, include a large number of baptized Christians. Certainly, there is no a priori reason why a person could not be (nominally) brought up as a Christian, attend Christian schools, get married in a church, and live out his or her whole life within a (historically) Christian society, without ever truly *hearing* the gospel.[21] Indeed, as GS 19 itself recognized: 'Contemporary civilization itself, not intrinsically, but inasmuch as it is too engrossed with the things of this world, can often make it more difficult to approach God' (AS IV/vii: 743).

---

[21] In fact, one could even argue that in societies such as Britain many people are (to adapt a metaphor used very differently by Richard Dawkins – e.g. [1993] 2003) 'inoculated' against the 'virus of Christianity' in much the same way as one is against real viruses – that is, by being subjected to small doses of 'dead' Christianity in one's youth, preventing one's contracting a 'live strain' later on. Thus acquaintance with fairly shallow aspects of Christianity (hymns in assembly, harvest festivals, evangelical youth clubs) may make people believe that they 'know' Christianity, making it all the more easy to ignore and dismiss later in life. LG 14's warning is perhaps relevant here: 'those men cannot be saved, who not being ignorant [of the fact that] the Catholic Church has been founded as necessary by God through Jesus Christ, are nevertheless unwilling either to enter it, or to persevere in it'. Although perhaps not the drafters' (primary) intention, this seems to allow at least the possibility of salvation for a baptized Catholic who fails to persevere in the Church, on the condition that he or she be ignorant of its divinely ordained necessity.

Of course, this is certainly not to imply that it is impossible in such societies to be confronted with the gospel in such a way that one is, on pain of damnation, obliged to enter the Church, and to persevere in it (cf. LG 14). And nor does it imply that all those who have neither entered nor persevered *are*, as a matter of fact, inculpably ignorant (GS 19 is quite clear on this point). How many, if any at all, are in fact excused from pre-mortem belief due to the above considerations is not something for theologians to judge. But what it *does* do is reinforce, on the basis of a strong theoretical foundation, Vatican II's 'presumption of innocence' (Sullivan 1992: 151) when encountering, or theologizing about, contemporary unbelievers.

CONCLUSION

Two main things have been accomplished in this chapter. In the first place, Gavin D'Costa's recent contribution to understanding how non-Christians may attain salvation was expounded and interrogated in some depth. His rediscovery of Christ's descent into hell, and certain strands of its interpretation in the Catholic tradition, constitutes an important new departure for theologians such as myself, who are seeking to explicate Vatican II's salvific optimism concerning 'those who have not yet accepted the Gospel [but who] are related to the People of God in diverse ways'. For reasons already given (especially its close correlation to the letter of LG 16), I substantially accept D'Costa's proposal, and my own account of the salvation of atheists will be developed within its broad framework.

Yet though adopting the D'Costan paradigm, I shall also be adapting it. Specifically, three points needing further attention and/or qualification were identified and explained – the second two of which will be dealt with in chapter five. However, the first of these, D'Costa's lack of a clear account of whom 'the unevangelized' includes, was addressed at length in the foregoing section. This is the chapter's second main accomplishment. The Council's notable emphasis on *ignorance*, which is rarely brought out in the documents' translations, was first examined in light of the history of doctrine. This was then entered into dialogue with a specific sociological theoretical perspective: Berger and Luckmann's 'sociology of knowledge'. On the basis of all this, it was argued that Vatican II's pronouncements, both developing the teaching of Pius IX and recovering (knowingly or not) the crucial insights of Vitoria and Las Casas, justify a very wide *hope* that many of today's unbelievers are indeed inculpably ignorant of the gospel, the Church, and perhaps even of God himself.[22] The foolishness of 'Christ crucified' is as evident to today's gentiles, not least those living amid the ruins of Christendom, as it was for those in Paul's time (cf. 1 Cor 1.23). 'This teaching is hard; who can accept it?' (Jn 6.60) is often an honest response to what is sincerely perceived as a scandalous proposition.

---

[22] Note that this last point does not contradict chapter one's argument against the opinion that atheists necessarily only reject *false* Gods. Certainly, it is possible to have a reasonable (theoretical) knowledge of 'what' God is supposed to be, while at the same time being inculpably ignorant of the fact that such a God exists.

5

Extra minimos nulla salus

At the close of chapter three, certain hints were made concerning the centrality of the description – it is not a parable[1] – of the Last Judgement given at Mt 25.31–46 (which, hereafter, I shall refer to simply as 'Mt 25') for resolving this study's problematic. Although a familiar passage, its significance for what follows requires that it be quoted here in full:

> When the Son of Man comes in his glory, and all the angels with him, then he will sit on the throne of his glory. All the nations will be gathered before him, and he will separate the people one from another as a shepherd separates the sheep from the goats, and he will put the sheep at his right hand and the goats at his left. Then the king will say to those at his right hand, 'Come, you that are blessed by my Father, inherit the kingdom prepared for you from the foundation of this world; for I was hungry and you gave me food, I was thirsty and you gave me something to drink, I was a stranger and you welcomed me, I was naked and you gave me clothing, I was sick and you took care of me, I was in prison and you visited me.'
>
> Then the righteous will answer him, 'Lord, when was it that we saw you hungry and gave you food, or thirsty and gave you something to drink? And when was it that we saw you a stranger and welcomed you, or naked and gave you clothing? And when was it that we saw you sick and in prison and visited you?' And the king will answer them, 'Truly I tell you, just as you did it to one of the least of these my brothers, you did it to me.'

---

[1] 'Unlike the preceding parables, however, this narrative is based not on a fictitious story but on the description of a very real, though future, event. Despite some clear parabolic elements, the passage with its future tense forms is more properly categorized as an apocalyptic revelation discourse' (Hagner 1995: 740; see also Cope 1969: 34).

> Then he will say to those at his left hand, 'You that are accursed, depart from me into the eternal fire prepared for the devil and his angels; for I was hungry and you gave me no food, I was thirsty and you gave me nothing to drink, I was a stranger and you did not welcome me, naked and you did not give me clothing, sick and in prison and you did not visit me.' Then they will also answer, 'Lord, when was it that we saw you hungry or thirsty or a stranger or naked or sick or in prison, and did not take care of you?' Then he will answer them, 'Truly I tell you, just as you did not do it to one of the least of these, you did not do it to me.' And these will go away into eternal punishment, but the righteous into eternal life.

It is not surprising that this pericope is often cited, by theologians and non-theologians alike, as crucial for comprehending how anybody, but especially non-Christians (including atheists), will be saved: Schillebeeckx and Congar, quoted earlier, are by no means alone (e.g. Torres [1964] 1973: 272; Boff [1972] 1980: 95). In simply repeating Mt 25, it might therefore seem that the problem of this investigation has already been solved: atheists can and will be saved according to what they have done for Christ's *minimi* (or indeed *minimae*), his 'least ones'.

Properly understood, this is – as I am about to argue – indeed true. Yet things are not quite so straightforward. Taking such an unrestricted interpretation of Mt 25 at face value, then with regard to the Catholic dogmatic tradition, it leaves much to be desired. Gone, most obviously, is the necessity for faith, baptism, and the mediation of the Church. These are infallible, *de fide* doctrines, and were insisted upon just as strongly at Vatican II as they were at, say, Trent. Now, of course, *if* Matthew's pericope does indeed represent the *ipsissima vox Jesu*, *if* 'the least' includes Christians and non-Christians alike, and *if* this interpretation is overwhelmingly attested in the Church's tradition (especially among the Fathers), then the established teaching would run here into major difficulties. So much so, in fact, that a powerful, prima facie case could be constructed for favouring Mt 25 over and against it. But this is not so.

Firstly, the pericope's Jesuanic provenance, while perhaps probable, has not been definitively established (Luz [1989] 2005: 267). Secondly, this unrestricted interpretation rests squarely on taking verses 40 and 45's 'the least' (*hoi elachistoi*) to refer to *all* human beings who are in need. Yet *elachistos* is the superlative form of *mikros*, meaning little or insignificant. At Mt 10.42, *oi mikroi* refers unambiguously to the apostles, where they are also told, paralleling Mt 25, 'whoever welcomes you, welcomes me'. Furthermore, contemporary exegetes argue that the passage must be interpreted in light of the Great Commission (Mt 28.16–20), where the eleven are sent to 'all the nations' (*panta ta ethnē*). At Mt 25.31, of course, it is *panta ta ethnē* who are gathered before the Son of Man. According to the Jesuit exegete Daniel Harrington, therefore:

> Those being judged are Gentiles. The issue at the judgment scene is: 'By what criterion are Gentiles to be declared just or condemned by the Son of Man? The answer is: By their deeds of mercy done to the disciples of Jesus (missionaries or ordinary Christians), because such deeds have been done to the Son of Man. The basis for this criterion is the identification between Jesus and his disciples: 'Whoever receives you receives me, and whoever receives me receives him who sent me' (Matt 10:40). (1991: 358)

Finally, regarding the reception of Mt 25 within the patristic (and subsequent) tradition, witness Ulrich Luz's damning critique of the unrestricted reading:

> This interpretation [...] whose central point is the identification of the 'lowliest brothers' with *all* persons who are in need, is not old. Contrary to other opinions, it was seldom held in the ancient church, in the Middle Ages, and during the Reformation. Thus on the tree of the history of the interpretation of 25.31–46 it is a young, and in my judgment typically modern, branch. ([1989] 2005: 271)

Although arguably overstating the case, Luz is correct that an unambiguously inclusive interpretation is *not* the majority report of the early tradition. Sherman Gray's exhaustive study of the sources reveals that, in many cases, patristic authors took no obvious interest in the identity of 'the least'. Among those who did explicitly comment, a number of important Fathers, including Origen, Cyprian, Jerome, Hilary of Poitiers, and Bede, explicitly understood it as applying only to Christians (1989: 337–8). Likewise, in the medieval period, 'The overwhelming majority of [...] commentators interpret "the least" in a narrow way, especially in the west' (ibid.: 340). Thomas, for instance, quoted the interpretation of Jerome in his *Catena Aurea*, implying that he too shared this restrictivist view (*In Matthaeum* 25, 3; Thomas Aquinas [*c.* 1262–7] 1953: 371).

Such considerations militate, very strongly, against setting up a naïve reading of Mt 25 in *opposition* to the established teaching of the Church. But that does not occlude this pericope being, in fact, absolutely critical for conceiving how atheists may be saved (not to mention everybody else, Christian or non-Christian alike – although, aside from some hesitant remarks in the conclusion, little further will be said about these groups). Indeed, that is the whole point of this chapter's title: 'Apart from the least ones, no salvation' (cf. Sobrino 2008). I would also argue that, while in no way denying what is already there, Mt 25 has not (yet) been accorded sufficient weight in the *dogmatic* strand of the Catholic tradition's teaching on salvation. Howsoever one interprets its minutiae, the fact remains that it is one of scripture's clearest and most vivid descriptions of eschatological judgement, and that it appears emphatically to prescribe at least one criterion (if an ambiguous one) according to which human beings either will, or will not, be saved. And yet, Denzinger–Hünermann records only *one* direct quotation of Mt 25 in a soteriological context before the late nineteenth century. Thus the Council of Florence's *Bull of Union with the Copts* quotes verse 41 to assert that pagans, Jews, heretics, and schismatics will 'depart "into everlasting fire which was prepared for the devil and his angels"', if they remain outside the Church (DH 1351; Tanner 1990a: 576). Beginning with Leo XIII's great social encyclical *Rerum Novarum* in 1891, however, the magisterium seems finally to have noticed the rest of this pericope – albeit not yet directly applied to the question of salvation. Leo affirms that Christ will count what is done to the poor as having been done to him, quoting verse 40 (ASS 23 [1890/1]: 651–2). Likewise, article 8 of *Apostolicam Actuositatem*, Vatican II's Decree on the Apostolate of the Laity, avers: '[It is] Christ the Lord to whom is truly offered whatever is given to the needy' (AS IV/vi: 616). And most recently, Benedict XVI's 2005 encyclical *Deus Caritas Est* emphasizes:

> Jesus assumes the persona of those in need (*Personam induit Iesus indigentium*[2]): that is, the hungry, the thirsty, strangers, the naked, the

---

[2] Note the strength of the claim made in Benedict's Latin *editio typica* (*induo* means 'to assume', 'to put on', or 'to cover oneself'), compared to its enervated, official English translation: 'Jesus identifies himself with those in need'. See: <http://www.vatican.va/holy_father/benedict_xvi/encyclicals/documents/hf_ben-xvi_enc_20051225_deus-caritas-est_lt.html>. Accessed on 17 June 2009.

Extra minimos nulla salus 153

sick, those in prison. 'Insofar as you did it to one of the least of these my brothers, you did it to me' (Mt 25.40). Love of God and love of neighbour are thus forged together: in the least we meet Jesus himself, and in Jesus we meet God (*in minimis ipsum Iesum et in Iesu Deum invenimus*). (Art. 15; AAS 98 [2006]: 230)

Encouraged by these dogmatic precedents, I believe that Mt 25 has rather more than 'everlasting fire' to contribute to Catholic inquiries concerning the post-mortem fate of non-Christians.

In what follows, I shall be focusing on a specific strand of Mt 25's reception within the Catholic tradition. Its hallmarks are: (i) an unrestricted understanding of the *minimi*; and (ii) a strong, literal construal of 'just as you did (not do) it to one of the least of these, you did (not do) it to me' (vv. 40, 45). In light of the foregoing considerations, I concede that this interpretation may not represent the evangelist's authorial intention – although this position is by no means foreclosed (Schweizer 1976: 479; O'Collins 2008: 94–5). I accept also that it does not represent the overwhelming witness of the tradition. Nevertheless, this interpretation, as shall be demonstrated, *is* firmly embedded within the Church's polyphonic tradition. I maintain, therefore, that this reading is a permissible and orthodox one. (This latter point is further secured by the apparently unrestricted interpretations given in the above quotations from Leo XIII, Vatican II, and Benedict XVI.) Very importantly, I do not suggest that Mt 25, so interpreted, can by itself answer the *problemata* of this study. Rather, it must be understood in conjunction with, and integrated within, the D'Costan paradigm. But this works both ways. In due course, it will become clear that this reading of Mt 25 points to a resolution of my two outstanding quibbles with D'Costa's account: (i) the problem of post-mortem conversion; and (ii) the atheist's lack of opportunities for encountering grace.

In the following sections, I first of all identify instances of the particular interpretation for which I am arguing, paying particular attention to the testimonies of those formally venerated by the Church, and to the hagiographical tradition. This is not, be it noted, a mere display of pious deference. Rather it is a recognition of what John Paul II termed 'the patrimony that is *the theology lived by the saints*' (*Novo Millennio Ineunte* 27; AAS 93 [2001]: 283; emphasis in original). Saints, blesseds, venerables, and servants of God *incarnate* theology (as also, of course, do countless others whom the Church has not [yet] formally recognized). Of course, none is infallible. But through 'living as though the Truth were true'[3] they have much to teach Catholic theology. This is especially clear in the case of Bl. Teresa of Calcutta, with close reference to whose writings and witness my own sustained theological reading of Mt 25 will be advanced. Although a number of possible objections will be addressed as I go along, a defence against two in particular will form the focus of the final section of this chapter.

'THE THEOLOGY LIVED BY THE SAINTS'

Although not ubiquitous, unrestricted interpretations are by no means absent from the patristic period. St John Chrysostom, for example, despite believing that verse 40 refers *primarily* to fellow Christians, nonetheless affirms it to have a wider application also. In the words of Gray:

> With Chrysostom we have a true universalism with regards to the identity of 'the least'; he has every needy human being in mind. However, like Paul (cf. Gal 6:10), Chrysostom has that specifically Christian perspective that sees a believer as a brother in a narrower sense than the nonbeliever. (1989: 52)

Certainly, a very strong sense of identity is manifest in Chrysostom's works. This is most striking in his fiftieth sermon on Matthew, where he admonishes those who, having oppressed the poor, have the temerity to approach Christ in the Eucharist:

> Therefore may neither a Judas nor a Simon come to this table; for both perished due to avarice. Hence may we flee from this abyss; and may we not think it sufficient for our salvation, if having despoiled widows and orphans, we offer to the table a golden and ornately bejewelled cup. (*In Matthaeum Homil.* 50, 3; PG 58: 508 – translated from the Latin version included by Migne)

Such an action would not merely be inappropriate. Rather, according to Chrysostom, it is outright contradictory.

---

[3] A phrase used by, and of, Dorothy Day (e.g. Berrigan 1981: xxiii).

Extra minimos nulla salus 155

Do you wish to honour the body of Christ? Then do not despise him when he is naked; while honouring him [on the altar] with silken clothes, do not then neglect him perishing outside, freezing and uncovered. For he who said 'This is my body' (Mt 26.26), and has confirmed the statement, also said 'Insofar as you did it to one of the least of these, you did it to me' (Mt 25.42, 45). (Ibid.)

This startling mode of interpretation – also reflected in the *praxis* of the early Church (see Finn 2006: 183–4) – will be elaborated upon later on. In the later patristic period (431–553), Gray identifies seven Fathers who adopt an unrestricted interpretation of 'the least': St Cyril of Alexandria, St Valerian of Cemele, Pope St Leo the Great, Salvianus, St Faustus of Riez, St Caesarius of Arles, and – perhaps most significantly – St Benedict of Nursia (1989: 334). According to the latter's vastly influential *Rule* (in many ways, the founding text of Western monasticism):

> Let all guests arriving [at the monastery] be received like Christ, because he himself will say: 'I was a stranger and you received me.' Let due honour be exhibited to all, especially to those of the household of faith and travellers. Thus as soon as a guest is announced, let the prior or the brethren meet him with all the kindness of charity; first let them pray together, and then be peacefully associated with each other. The kiss of peace is not to be offered if not preceded by prayer, on account of the devil's illusions. In the salutation itself let all humility be exhibited. By bowing the head or prostrating the body on the ground to all guests, whether coming or going, may Christ be adored in them in whom he is received. (*Regula* 52; PL 66: 749–50)

The genuine presence of Christ in those who are in need is expressed, in a strikingly direct and literal way, in patristic and medieval hagiography. Pope St Gregory the Great, for example, relates the story of St Martyrius, who, happening upon a derelict leper, carried him to a nearby monastery. Once there, the leper revealed himself to be 'the Redeemer of the human race, God and man, Christ Jesus'. Before disappearing, he blessed Martyrius, and assured him: 'You were not ashamed of me on earth; I shall not be ashamed of you in heaven' (*Homilia* 39; PL 76: 1300). Similar episodes are imputed, sometimes many centuries after their death, to the biographies of many saints and blesseds, including Pope St Leo IX, Bl. Jordan of Saxony, and Bl. John Colombini. Such incidents are, moreover, frequently the best-remembered and most-cherished details of the individual's life – as, most obviously, with St Martin of Tours and St Christopher. Sulpicius Severus' early fifth-century *Life of St Martin* famously narrates how, in the dead of winter, the then-catechumen encountered a naked beggar whom others were ignoring. Clad only in a cloak himself, Martin divided it between the two of them. That night, Christ appeared to him in a dream, wearing the half-garment, and testifying that 'Martin, still a catechumen, clothed me with this cloak.' Sulpicius continues:

> The Lord, truly mindful of his own words (who had before said: 'Insofar as you did it to one of the least of these, you did it to me'), declared himself to have been clothed in that poor man. And to confirm his testimony to so good a deed, he deemed it worthy for himself to appear in the same dress which the pauper received. Following this vision, this most saintly man was not elated with human glory, but acknowledging the goodness of God in his deed – and since he was now twenty years old – he hastened to baptism. (*De Vita Beati Martini* 1, 3; PL 20: 162)

Note that here, as in the above quotation from Benedict, Mt 25 is directly quoted. Another episode from the *Life*, that of Martin miraculously curing a Parisian leper with his kiss, grew by the Middle Ages into the popular belief that a holy person's kiss could abate the disease. In the twelfth century, St Hugh of Lincoln answered remarks about his own kisses' inefficacy with the riposte: 'Martin, by kissing the leper, cured him in body; but the leper with a kiss has healed me in soul' (*Vita S. Hugonis* 8; Gerald of Wales [*c.* 1213] 1877: 108). Given the well-known story of Martyrius, this too is surely to be taken in light of Mt 25.

The fantastical tale of Christopher is given in Bl. Iacopo da Varazze's thirteenth-century compendium the *Legenda Aurea* (or *Golden Legend*). Christopher is said to have been ordered by a hermit, to whom he had gone for catechesis, to carry travellers across a treacherous river. One day, a child asked for his assistance, whereupon Christopher took him on his shoulders and began the crossing. However, as the water rose and swelled, and the child became increasingly heavy, Christopher feared that he would drown. Upon eventually reaching the other shore, the child reveals:

> Wonder not, Christopher, for you not only had the whole world upon you, but also he who created it on your shoulders. For I am Christ, your king, whom you have served in this work. And in order that you may confirm these words are true, when you set your staff in the ground near

Extra minimos nulla salus 157

your house, in the morning you will see it bearing flowers and fruit. And instantly he [Christ] vanished from his sight. Hence Christopher set his staff in the earth, and arose the next morning to discover his staff bearing leaves and dates in the manner of a palm. (*Legenda Aurea* 96; Iacopo da Varazze [*c*. 1260] 1998: 666)

Interestingly, the *Legenda* does not narrate Christopher's baptism, despite later referring to it. It is thus tempting, and not altogether fanciful, to view this episode *as* Christopher's baptism – he is, after all, immersed in water by Christ himself, nearly dying in the process (cf. Rom 6.3–7). The famous episode of St Francis kissing the leper also belongs to this hagiographical trope. Thomas of Celano's version, given in his second *Life of St Francis* (and later elaborated by St Bonaventure in his *Legenda Major*), has the leper then – as in the Martyrius and Christopher narratives – miraculously disappear (*Vita Secunda*, 1, 5; Thomas of Celano [1247] 1927: 136). Likewise St Elizabeth of Hungary, another exemplar of early Franciscan piety, is said to have lain a leper down to rest in the bed of her and her husband, Ludwig IV of Thuringia. Learning of this, the king threw off the bedclothes, and found not a leper, but Christ crucified (see Strohm 2000: 76).

In citing these sources, I am not, of course, making any claims as to the historicity of what they relate. After all, the *Legenda Aurea* also claims that the (possibly fictional) Christopher was eighteen feet tall, and Thomas of Celano's earlier account of Francis' leper-kissing makes no mention of a miraculous disappearance (*Vita Prima*, 1, 7; Thomas of Celano [1229] 1926: 16; see Wolf 2003: 12). Instead, these narratives evince, in their own way, an important *theological* idea: that Christ is truly encountered in the poor, afflicted, and needy. Even if *all* of these accounts are fictional (though I am certainly not claiming this either), considerable weight must still be given to the sheer popularity of this trope. This applies not only to the texts themselves (the *Legenda*, in particular, was wildly successful), but to the resonance which this motif has within the *sensus fidelium*. As mentioned above, this is especially so with Christopher and Martin, whose encounters with Christ, so often represented in Christian art and iconography, are that for which they are chiefly remembered. The same is also true, albeit to a lesser extent, of Francis and Elizabeth. Furthermore, note that the sources in which these episodes are recounted were themselves often written by saints and blesseds (and even, in the cases of Pope Gregory and Bonaventure, Doctors of the Church), lending further, strong support to the orthodoxy of this notion.

Considered in themselves, these stories are liable to misinterpretation. No doubt many people have taken their moral to be that one should aid a person in need, *in case* he or she is Christ in disguise. Understood in light of their scriptural roots, however, it is clear these episodes are illustrations of a rather more radical principle: that each and every person in need *is* Christ (or at least, that Christ is genuinely present in them in a special way). The same applies, of course, to Eucharistic visions and miracles in which the Host visibly bleeds or becomes flesh. Rightly, these are not taken to signify that the sacrament should be venerated *in case* it is the body of Christ, but rather, because it always *is*. This analogy is specially fitting given the sacramental intimations of some of the above sources, whether explicit (Chrysostom's comparison between 'this is my body' and 'you did it to me'), or implicit (Hugh's soul being 'healed' by a leper's kiss; Christopher's 'baptism'). This intriguing possibility will be developed in the following section.

This interpretation gains compelling support from two further sources. Firstly, there are the magisterial statements of Leo IX, *Apostolicam Actuositatem*, and Benedict XVI quoted previously. And secondly, one has the testimony of countless other heroic figures from the Catholic tradition who, in living out their lives, have demonstrated their own accedence. Needless to say, these include many whom the Church formally recognizes, such as (to name only three) St Vincent de Paul, St Jeanne Jugan, and Bl. Pier Giorgio Frassati. Another of their number, Mother Teresa, will be discussed anon. Before that, it is worth quoting from Dorothy Day, the twentieth-century co-founder of the Catholic Worker movement, whose own cause for canonization was opened in 2000:

> It is no use saying that we are born two thousand years too late to give room to Christ. Nor will those who live at the end of the world have been born too late. Christ is always with us, always asking for room in our hearts. [...] But now it is with the voice of our contemporaries that He speaks, with the eyes of store clerks, factory workers, and children that He gazes; with the hands of office workers, slum dwellers, and suburban housewives that He gives. It is with the feet of soldiers and tramps that He walks, and with the heart of anyone in need that He begs and longs for shelter. And giving shelter or food to anyone who asks for

it, or needs it, is giving to Christ. [...] Not because it might be Christ who stays with us, comes to see us, takes up our time. Not because these people remind us of Christ [...] but because they *are* Christ, asking us to find room for Him, exactly as He did at the first Christmas. ([1945] 2005: 94, 97)

And from another of Day's essays: 'The mystery of the poor is this: That they are Jesus, and what you do for them you do for him' ([1946] 2005: 330).

'JESUS IN HIS DISTRESSING DISGUISE'

The Albanian-born Agnes Bojaxhiu, later known as Mother Teresa, joined the Sisters of the Institute of the Blessed Virgin Mary (the Loreto Sisters) in 1928, at the age of eighteen. She began her novitiate the following year in Darjeeling, India, and was later sent to teach at the Loreto convent school in Calcutta. In September 1946, she experienced what she came to describe as 'the call within the call':

> I was going to Darjeeling to make my retreat. It was on the train that I heard the call to give up all and follow Him into the slums – to serve Him in the poorest of the poor. I knew it was His will and that I had to follow Him. There was no doubt that it was to be His work. [...] The message was quite clear. I was to leave the convent and work among the poor while living among them. It was an order. (Quoted in Egan 1985: 28)

Her response to this second vocation is well known, and its full details cannot be recounted here. Among a great deal else, this led to her founding the Missionaries of Charity in 1950, the original branch of which currently has over 4,000 active Sisters, working in 133 countries (later branches of contemplative Sisters, active and contemplative Brothers, and Fathers are also flourishing). In 1979, she was awarded the Nobel Prize for Peace 'in recognition for [her] work in bringing help to suffering humanity'.[4] Following her death in 1997,

---

[4] This is a quotation from the Norwegian Nobel Committee's original press release: <http://nobelprize.org/nobel_prizes/peace/laureates/1979/press.html>. Accessed on 19 June 2009.

with a swiftness unprecedented in modern history, she was beatified in 2003.

I am focusing on Teresa for several reasons. Most importantly, her life and teachings exemplify the interpretation of Mt 25 traced in the foregoing section. At the same time, she both amplified and developed certain, crucial aspects of it. Her understanding of the text is, moreover, essential for comprehending Teresa herself, and the special charism of the Missionaries of Charity. As such, the approbation that Teresa has received within the Church, from hierarchy and laity alike, reinforces and confirms the validity of this reading. Witness, for instance, John Paul II's homily at the Mass for her beatification:

> 'As you did to one of the least of these my brethren, you did it to me'. This Gospel passage, so crucial in understanding Mother Teresa's service to the poor, was the basis of her faith-filled conviction that in touching the broken bodies of the poor she was touching the body of Christ. It was to Jesus himself, hidden under the distressing disguise of the poorest of the poor, that her service was directed. Mother Teresa highlights the deepest meaning of service – an act of love done to the hungry, thirsty, strangers, naked, sick, prisoners is done to Jesus himself. (AAS 96 [2004]: 142–3)

Recent revelations concerning Teresa's spiritual life – 'this terrible sense of loss – this untold darkness – this loneliness – this continual longing for God' (quoted in Kolodiejchuk 2008: 210) – also make her particularly relevant to a study of atheism. Even while still a Loreto sister she suffered acute feelings of desolation, and these deepened and continued, with few and fleeting respites, throughout her life. Teresa's darkness must not however be misunderstood, and glib statements regarding either her 'atheism', or conversely the atheist's own 'dark night' or 'apophasis', must certainly be avoided. Consider, for example, one of her most startling expressions of (perceived) abandonment – one which is, crucially, written as a prayer:

> Lord, my God, who am I that You should forsake me? [...] I call, I cling, I want – and there is no One to answer – no One on Whom I cling – no, No One. – Alone. The darkness is so dark – and I am alone. – Unwanted, forsaken. – The loneliness of the heart that wants love is unbearable. – Where is my faith? – Even deep down, right in, there is nothing but emptiness & darkness. – My God – how painful is this unknown pain. – It pains without ceasing. – I have no faith. (Quoted in ibid.: 187)

Leaving aside many interesting questions regarding Teresa's 'atheism' and its significance, of special importance here is the fact that, not feeling the presence of Christ in her inner life (as once she had), Teresa sought him instead in two locations: in the Eucharist, and in the destitute and dispossessed.

Teresa was not, of course, a *theologian*. Nevertheless, her published talks and writings,[5] not to mention her life itself, contain a number of profound theological insights. These, I contend, hold important implications for the salvation of atheists. I refer to these as 'implications' since, for the most part, the conclusions drawn from Teresa's comments are mine, rather than hers. Although Teresa herself often (correctly) connected Mt 25 with salvation, the brief accounts she gave were, while true enough in themselves, overly simplistic. For example:

> To help us be worthy of heaven, Christ put as a condition that at our hour of death, you and I, regardless of whom we were (Christian or non-Christians, each human being has been created by the loving hand of God in his own likeness), will stand before God and be judged according to how we have acted toward the poor (Matthew 25:40). (1980: 36)

Teresa was not, of course, attempting to make a constructive contribution to Catholic dogmatic theology on this point; she had better things to be doing. However, it is precisely this that is my intention here, and Teresa's logia provide the raw materials to do just that. Thus drawing heavily on her ideas (in addition, of course, to those of D'Costa), I will develop and defend a new account of how, in light of LG 16, atheists may indeed be saved.

Before turning to what is most striking in Teresa's understanding of Mt 25, it is worth demonstrating how firmly she fits into the trajectory delineated above. This may be established very easily, with a number of quotations. Hence:

> Actually we are touching Christ's body in the poor. In the poor it is the hungry Christ that we are feeding, it is the naked Christ that we are clothing, it is to the homeless Christ that we are giving shelter. (1975: 47)

---

[5] It is worth pointing out here that, from the scholar's point of view, these leave a lot to be desired. For the most part, Teresa's ideas must be gathered from quotations in either biographies or devotional compilations. These are often (especially in the latter) given without proper context, and with little or no information as to their provenance.

And:

> Our work calls for us to see Jesus in everyone. He has told us that He is the hungry one. He is the naked one. He is the thirsty one. He is the one without a home. He is the one who is suffering. These are our treasures. They are Jesus. Each one is Jesus in His distressing disguise. (Quoted in Egan 1985: 56)

Note that Teresa appeals to Mt 25 in a literal way. Indeed, she is quite explicit on this point: 'We should not serve the poor like *they were* Jesus. We should serve them *because they are* Jesus' (1980: 30; emphasis in original). Note also that this is not merely her own personal conviction, but is the guiding principle of her Order: 'The Missionaries of Charity are firmly convinced that each time we offer help to the poor, we really offer help to Christ' (ibid.: 24).

In the quotations from Chrysostom and Hugh of Lincoln, as well as perhaps in the *Legenda Aurea*'s life of Christopher, we have already witnessed the groundwork for a (quasi-) sacramental interpretation of Mt 25. In Teresa's teachings, however, such ideas acquire their boldest expression. She is not at all coy in equating Christ's real presence in the Eucharist, with his presence in the 'poorest of the poor'. On the contrary, this is a central and repeated aspect of her overall message. For example: 'In Holy Communion we have Christ under the appearance of bread. In our work we find him under the appearance of flesh and blood. It is the same Christ' (1975: 92). And variously:

> To those who say they admire my courage, I have to tell them that I would not have any if I were not convinced that each time I touch the body of a leper, a body that reeks with a foul stench, I touch Christ's body, the same Christ I receive in the Eucharist. (1980: 105)
>
> To be able to do what we do, and live the kind of life we live, every Missionary of Charity has to have her life united with the Eucharist. In the Eucharist, we see Christ in the appearance of bread. Then in the poor, we see Christ in distressing disguise. The Eucharist and the poor are but one love. (1991: 73)
>
> Because it is a continual contact with Christ in his work, it is the same contact we have during Mass and in the Blessed Sacrament. There we have Jesus in the appearance of bread. But here in the slums, in the broken body, in the children, we see Christ and we touch him. (Quoted in Muggeridge 1971: 114)

Intriguingly, so radical is this unity for Teresa that it works both ways: 'it is at the altar we meet our suffering poor' (1975: 28). And again, these are not simply Teresa's private beliefs, but ones intrinsic to her Missionaries' charism. This is evident in an anecdote Teresa once told, about a new arrival at the Calcutta motherhouse:

> So I told this girl: 'You saw Father during Holy Mass, with what love and care he touched Jesus in the Host. Do the same when you go to the Home for Dying, because it is the same Jesus you will find there in the broken bodies of our poor.' And they went. After three hours the newcomer came back and said to me with a big smile – I have never seen a smile quite like that – 'Mother, I have been touching the body of Christ for three hours.' And I said to her: 'How – what did you do?' She replied: 'When we arrived there, they brought a man who had fallen into a drain, and been there for some time. He was covered with wounds and dirt and maggots, and I cleaned him and I knew I was touching the body of Christ.' (Ibid.: 69)

This principle is also enshrined in the Order's *Constitutions*, which state that their 'particular mission' lies in both the works of mercy and in adoration of the Blessed Sacrament, and that 'In so doing we prove our love for Jesus under the appearance of bread and under the distressing disguise of the poorest of the poor' (quoted in Egan 1985: 124). For this reason Teresa described the Missionaries as 'contemplatives in the heart of the world, for we are twenty-four hours then in His presence' (ibid.: 477).

Let us, then, follow Teresa in her reading of 'sacred scripture': one which is, at the very least, consonant with the (admittedly polyphonic) witness of 'sacred tradition', and with key statements of 'the teaching authority of the Church' (cf. *Dei Verbum* 10). In what ways does this aid our understanding of the salvation of atheists?

Sub gratiae influxu

It need hardly be said – although it has been in chapter one – that there are untold numbers of unbelievers who are 'driven by a demanding and often a noble cause, fired with enthusiasm and idealism, dreaming of justice and progress', and who are 'endowed with great breadth of mind, impatient with the mediocrity and self-seeking which infects so many aspects of human society in our times' (*Ecclesiam Suam* 104; AAS 56 [1964]: 652–3). It is these who, in the words of LG 16, 'strive [...] to accomplish works', and who 'endeavour to attain to an upright life'. Furthermore, as argued in chapters one and three, one need not impute to them any implicit or anonymous beliefs or faith in order to explain such behaviour. To put it bluntly, to do so is like saying: 'Atheists can indeed lead moral and meaningful lives – but only insofar as they are not *really* atheists at all.' Our fictional example of Dr Rieux is both a genuine atheist, and a heroically virtuous human being. *Subjectively* – that is, from his own perspective, conscious and subconscious – his is a thoroughgoingly atheistic meta-ethics.

Yet viewed from the perspective of LG 16, and from that of Christianity in general, Rieux's moral commitment and self-understanding occur within, and presuppose, an *objectively* theistic – in fact, Christocentric – universe. Quite unbenownst to him, Rieux's subjectively-atheistic works are prompted by God 'through the command of conscience', and are possible only 'under the influence of grace'. This is a crucial clarification; without it my arguments to follow may justifiably be dismissed as Pelagian.

Pelagius (*c.* 354 – *c.* 420) was a rigoristic British monk, for whom human beings were capable of freely choosing to do good, even to the point of leading wholly sinless lives, without the assistance of grace:

> The just Lord wanted man to execute his righteousness voluntarily, uncoerced. For that reason, he relinquished him into the hands of his own decision. He placed before him life and death, good and evil; and the one which he chooses, will be given to him. (*Ad Demetriadem* 2; PL 30: 17: see Rees 1988: 34)

Naturally, Pelagius was well aware that humans do not always choose good over evil. But that does not imply that they cannot: 'We have, implanted by God, the possibility to choose either part' (Augustine, *De gratia Christi et de peccato originali*, quoting Pelagius' lost *De libero arbitrio*; PL 44: 369; see also the texts quoted in Segundo [1968] 1980: 18–19). Under the primary influence of Augustine, such ideas were soon definitively repudiated by the Church (e.g. DH 227, 377). These condemnations were later ratified, and elevated to the status of a dogmatic definition, at the Council of Trent:

> If anyone should say that divine grace is given through Jesus Christ solely so that man can more easily live justly and merit eternal life, as if free will were capable of both things without grace, albeit perhaps more

difficultly, let him be anathema. (*Canons on Justification* 2; Tanner 1990b: 679)

Obviously, like so much else in this book, such claims would be vociferously denied, if not outright ridiculed, by any self-respecting atheistic humanist. But that is not my concern. Rather, I wish to stress that nothing in my support for at least the plausibility of a (subjectively) atheistic meta-ethics entails a rejection of the (objective) presence and operation of divine grace in all human moral strivings.

Lord, when was it...?

By itself, this realization does not necessarily take us very far. After all, included among the Jansenist propositions condemned by Pope Clement XI's *Unigenitus Dei Filius* (1713) are: 'No graces are granted except through faith' and 'Outside of the Church, no graces are granted' (DH 2426, 2429). The idea that unbelievers cooperate with grace in their moral strivings is not, in itself, enough to ground Vatican II's optimism for their ultimate salvation. Armed also with Teresa's interpretation of Mt 25, however, one is able to go much farther: moral atheists such as Rieux do not only act *sub gratiae influxu*, but they also – and again, *objectively* – encounter Christ himself. Obviously, they will not be aware of this fact at the time. But then that is, after all, precisely the situation envisaged in the gospel:

> Lord, when was it that we saw you hungry and gave you food, or thirsty and gave you something to drink? And when was it that we saw you a stranger and welcomed you, or naked and gave you clothing? And when was it that we saw you sick and in prison and visited you? (Mt 25.37–9)

In this regard, Teresa's emphasis on the Eucharist is of especial importance (developing an idea already present in Chrysostom).

Every one of the Church's sacraments is, according to the classical definition, 'a visible form of an invisible grace' (Trent, *Decree on the Most Holy Eucharist* 3; Tanner 1990b: 694). And Christ may rightly be said to be present in each of them, at least insofar as they embody his actions (Schillebeeckx [1960] 1963: 71; O'Collins 2007: 212). Thus, in the words of Augustine, 'When Peter baptizes, it is *he* [i.e. Christ] who baptizes; when Paul baptizes, it is *he* who baptizes; when Judas baptizes, it is *he* who baptizes' (*Tract. 6 in Ioannem*, 7; PL 35:

1428). And relatedly, quoting Pius XII's *Mystici Corporis*, 'it is he who through the Church baptizes, teaches, rules, looses, binds, offers, sacrifices' (AAS 35 [1943]: 218). Christ's presence in the Eucharist, however, is of a wholly different order. According to Schillebeeckx:

> In both cases we have a personal presence of Christ himself, but the principle of the presence differs; in the Eucharist Christ himself is present by the power of transubstantiation; in the other sacraments Christ is present only in virtue of his redemptive *act* sacramentally embodied. ([1960] 1963: 72)

For this reason, in the judgement of Thomas, 'absolutely speaking, the sacrament of the Eucharist is the greatest among sacraments [...] because in this one Christ Himself is contained substantially' (*Summa theologiae*, III, q. 65, a. 3; Thomas Aquinas [1265–74] 1975: 152). Not surprisingly, since it contains 'the Author of Sanctity himself' (Trent, *Decree on the Most Holy Eucharist* 3; Tanner 1990b: 694), this sacrament is pre-eminently linked to salvation. As John Paul II expressed it in his 2003 encyclical *Ecclesia de Eucharistia*:

> The Eucharist is a striving towards the final end, a foretaste of the fullness of joy promised by Christ (cf. Jn 15.11); certainly, it is in some sense an anticipation of paradise, 'the pledge to us of future joy'. [...] He who is nourished by Christ himself in the Eucharist need not wait until after death in order to receive eternal life: *he already possesses it on earth*, as the first-fruits of a future plenitude which embrace this whole man. For in the Eucharist we also receive confirmation of bodily resurrection at the end of the world. (AAS 95 [2003]: 445)

Against this background, it is all the more striking that Teresa should correlate Christ *sub specie panis* with Christ *sub specie minimi*,[6] that is, 'Jesus in His distressing disguise'. Moreover, she is quite categorical that the Missionaries' encounter with Christ 'in the slums, in the broken body, in the children' is '*the same* contact we have during Mass and in the Blessed Sacrament' (quoted in Muggeridge 1971: 114; my emphasis). If so, then the outstanding problem of the non-religious atheist's necessarily lacking sufficient opportunities for receiving grace (compared, say, to a practising non-theistic Buddhist such as Jane) dissolves away. In place of D'Costa's Jane, let us once again

---

[6] Note that Gregory the Great, in the homily quoted earlier, explicitly states that Christ met Martyrius '*sub leprosi specie*' (PL 76: 1300).

take Camus' Dr Rieux. In tending the sick, visiting the dying, or even attempting (in the words of his author) 'to reduce the number of tortured children' – that is, in performing what Catholics call the corporal 'works of mercy' – Rieux may not only receive sanctifying grace, but stands in the presence of 'the Author of Sanctity himself'.

This sacramental, indeed Eucharistic, interpretation of Mt 25.40 must not, however, be taken too far (cf. Saward 2005: 92–3). Specifically, it should not be taken to imply that the graced encounter with one of Mt 25's *minimi* is itself a sacrament in the full and proper sense of the term. Indeed, a number of important sacramentological considerations weigh against this possibility. Firstly, a sacrament is generally regarded as being 'a visible act of the Church' (Schillebeeckx [1960] 1963: 140). Secondly, the sacraments, as Vatican II reiterated, 'presuppose faith' (*Sacrosanctum Concilium* 59; AS II/vi: 423): a faith that the atheist does not yet possess, whether explicitly or otherwise. Despite a sacrament being an *opus operatum*, its effects may, even among baptized and believing Christians, be frustrated through 'unbelief or obstinacy in sin' (Rahner and Vorgrimler [1976] 1983: 350; see also Schillebeeckx [1960] 1963: 96–7; Béguerie and Duchesneau [1989] 1991: 32). Finally, and most obviously, there are only seven sacraments of the Church (Trent, *Canons on the Sacraments in General* 1; Tanner 1990b: 684). One ought not to speak, therefore, of any 'sacrament of the *minimi*' or 'sacrament of one's neighbour', unless in a figurative or analogical sense (cf. Congar [1959] 1961: 124). Strictly speaking, this eighth (!) sacrament, as a 'sacrament of faith' (cf. *Sacrosanctum Concilium* 59), would be efficacious only for Christians, thus undermining the entire thrust of Mt 25. Obviously, this would be useless for the present purposes. Arguably, it would also rival (and could perhaps *replace*) the Eucharist. If Christ is indeed present in both 'in the same way', then one could arguably pick and choose under which species to receive him. Obviously, such a suggestion cannot be countenanced by Catholic theology. Nor, it must be stressed, would it have been by Teresa, who never suggested Christ 'disguised in the broken body of the poor' could *substitute* for Christ 'in the living Bread of the Eucharist' (quoted in Egan 1985: 298). As Chrysostom also recognized, no 'either/or' is justified by the correlation of 'this is my body' and 'you did it to me'.

Such considerations do not, however, prevent Mt 25.40 being interpreted *on analogy with* the sacraments, and with the Eucharist in particular. This allows one to retain the full force of those elements of the tradition that have been emphasized in this chapter – most notably, the full and real presence of Christ in his *minimi*, and thus the potential of his imparting grace to those who, regardless of their religious beliefs (or lack of them), perform the works of mercy. Christ is, after all, the *Ursakrament*. Schillebeeckx writes:

> The man Jesus, as the personal visible realization of the divine grace of redemption, is *the* sacrament, the primordial sacrament, because this man, the Son of God himself, is intended by the Father to be in his Humanity the only way to the actuality of redemption. ([1960] 1963: 16; see also International Theological Commission 2007: art. 82)

And as Thomas rightly recognized: 'God has not bound his power to the sacraments, so as not to be able, outside of the sacraments, to confer the effect of the sacraments' (*Summa theologiae*, III, q. 64, a. 7; Thomas Aquinas [1265–74] 1975: 124).

A pledge of future joy?

In this light, it becomes clearer how Rieux's helping 'Christ in His degradation, in His most hidden guise' (Day [1949] 2005: 101), while not itself a sacrament, can nevertheless confer the *effect* of the sacraments: one of which is, of course, in the case of the Eucharist, 'the pledge to us of future joy'. Assuming that the atheist Rieux is inculpably ignorant, then this 'pledge' could be brought to fruition in the D'Costan *limbus patrum*. (Note though, that for the *culpably* ignorant, as for actual Christians, while the same grace may be conferred, this would not, in itself, suffice to place them on the road to salvation. They would still be obliged to enter the Church and/or persevere in it.) It should be stressed at this point that I am presenting a general principle, and nothing more. In short, the principle is this: for an atheist who is inculpably ignorant of the gospel, the objective encounter with Christ in his *minimi* is the pre-eminent *locus* for him or her receiving the grace necessary for (eventually) attaining salvation. Obviously, I pass no comment as to how *many* works of mercy such a person would need to perform to 'qualify': a pointless, if not outright sacrilegious, question. Hope might perhaps be gained from the medieval legend of the miser who, for want of a better missile, throws a loaf of bread at a beggar. Upon his death, Mary wields the loaf – his nearest thing to a good deed – to drive off the devil and save his soul

(Duffy 2005: 358).[7] But one should not be too complacent. It must not be forgotten that Mt 25 promises not only salvation for what has been done for 'one of the least of these', but damnation for what has not been done (a key point too in the parable of Dives and Lazarus at Lk 16.19–31). On this basis, who is not both a 'sheep' and a 'goat'; both 'blessed by my Father' and 'accursed'?[8]

That said, Teresa's teachings permit this principle to be fleshed out in certain other respects. Mt 25 need not, for example, refer exclusively to the materially poor.

> God has identified himself with the hungry, the sick, the naked, the homeless; hunger, not only for bread, but for love, for care, to be somebody to someone; nakedness, not of clothing only, but nakedness of that compassion that very few people give to the unknown; homelessness, not only just for a shelter made of stone, but that homelessness that comes from having no one to call your own. (1975: 32–3)

And again:

> The poor may be in our own families. Maybe you have plenty to eat. Maybe you have wonderful things and beautiful houses. But what if your father, your mother, your wife, your husband or your child feels lonely? (1991: 3)

Here too, Teresa's teachings resonate with ideas already present in the tradition: works of mercy towards the 'spiritually homeless, naked and hungry' were counselled in the early Church. These were eventually schematized into seven 'spiritual works of mercy', paralleling the seven corporal ones (i.e. the six actions identified in Mt 25, plus burying the dead): instructing the ignorant, counselling the doubtful, comforting the afflicted, admonishing the sinner, forgiving offences, bearing wrongs patiently, and praying for the living and the dead (Keenan 2005: 61–2).

A further perspective on who, in addition to Christ, 'the least' might be can be advanced on exegetical grounds. Above, I rehearsed the common argument that 'the least' (*hoi elachistoi*) refers solely to

---

[7] See also Grushenka's story in *The Brothers Karamazov*, suggesting that the gift to a beggar of a single onion may be enough (Dostoevsky [1880] 2004: 352–3). Though compare Primo Levi's critique: 'This fable has always struck me as revolting: what human monster did not throughout his life make the gift of a little onion, if not to others, to his children, his wife, his dog?' ([1986] 1989: 40).

[8] Rahner is, once again, probably helpful here, with his notion of a person's 'yes' or 'no' to God being built up over the course of his or her entire life (see Craigo-Snell 2008: 11).

the disciples, or at most to Christians in general, on the basis of 10.42 so designating 'the little ones' (*oi mikroi* – *elachistos* being, as may be remembered, the superlative form of *mikros*). Yet elsewhere in the gospel, it is actual children who are called 'little ones' (*mikroi*), accompanied by dire warnings to any who would 'put a stumbling-block before' one of them (18.6–7). Most of Mt 25's works of mercy – 'I was hungry and you gave me food, I was thirsty and you gave me something to drink, [...] I was naked and you gave me clothing, I was sick and you took care of me' – apply naturally to the care of *all* infants, rich or poor. The remaining two – 'I was a stranger and you welcomed me [...] I was in prison and you visited me' – could also, tragically, apply to countless minors. This interpretation of the *minimi/elachistoi* as children points, in addition, to the Matthean material relating to the massacre of the Holy Innocents (2.16–18), whose murders in the place of Christ proleptically imply Mt 25.40's 'you did it to me'. Likewise, as James Keenan points out in his study of the works of mercy, 'Is it not striking that the first two infancy narratives of the Gospels concern the need to shelter the Christ child?' (2005: 21). This points also to the possibility of a Mariological, and indeed Josephological, dimension. In feeding, giving drink to, clothing, and nursing their own 'least one', Joseph and Mary too, also in a literal sense, 'did it to [him]'.

This mention of Mary leads into a further, and final, aspect of Teresa's thought. I repeat here the account by her biographer, Eileen Egan, of a talk given at the forty-first Eucharistic Congress, held in Philadelphia in 1976:

> She began by reminding her hearers that Mary, the Mother of the Church, could say of Jesus, 'This is my body,' and that it was by surrendering herself that she became the Mother of God. When His followers deserted Jesus, she went on, it was Mary who stayed with Him. She remained when He was spat upon, treated like a leper, disowned by all and crucified.
>
> 'Do we remain with our people when they are disowned, thrown out, when they suffer? Do we give them understanding and love?' she asked. 'Do we have the eyes of compassion of Mary? Do we understand their pain? Do we recognize their suffering?' (1985: 316–17)

As we have seen, Teresa repeatedly emphasized Christ's presence in those who suffer. Here, however, the focus is not on Christ's presence, but on the human being's. For Teresa, *we* must be present with those

Extra minimos nulla salus 171

who suffer, just as Mary was present at the foot of the Cross. The point is not that Mary did anything, materially, to alleviate her son's sufferings. Rather, she simply remained with him; she was *there*. Applying this to others, Teresa's suggestion seems to be that just as Christ is present with – is *there* with – those who suffer, so too (like Mary) ought we to be there too. This too, of course, has very definite Eucharistic overtones. Indeed, to quote the *Catechism*: 'In the Eucharist the Church is, with Mary, in a certain way at the foot of the Cross, united with the offering and intercession of Christ' (CCC 1370).

An answer to my remaining difficulty with the D'Costan schema (i.e. the tension between the need for a post-mortem coming to faith, which seems to require something genuinely 'new', and the Augustinian principle of the fixity of death, prohibiting any new decisions after death) may at last, tentatively, be broached. This will not, I readily admit, dissolve the tension entirely; but nor, as noted in chapter four, need it try to. It may be recalled that Augustine understood Christ's preaching 'to the spirits in prison' (1 Pet 3.19) as referring not to Christ's descent into hell, but rather to his historical, antediluvian proclamation in the person of Noah. Bellarmine later added the suggestion that some of these had repented, prior to drowning in the flood, and it is these to whom Christ descends, in order to bring their earthly conversion to completion. Crucially, these people are understood as having, in their earthly lives, already encountered, and responded to, (the pre-existent) Christ. Now, the inculpably ignorant atheist has not, presumably, been preached to by Christ himself. But in light of what I have presented in this chapter, the Catholic is justified in believing that, insofar as she has helped Christ's least ones, she too has encountered, and responded to, him. This is not, of course, something of which she was aware. But according to the gospels, this is not unusual when meeting the post-resurrection Christ, with or without 'His distressing disguise'. In the words of Béguerie and Duchesneau:

> Here we have one of the recurring themes of the account of the appearances of the Risen Christ. Mary Magdalene believed him to be the gardener, the apostles in the upper room thought that he was a ghost. On Lake Tiberias, Peter and his friends had difficulty in identifying their mysterious companion. The end of Mark's Gospel even says: 'He appeared to them in other forms.' In this way, the first witnesses wanted to alert us to the difficulty we always come up against in recognizing this presence of the Lord. ([1989] 1991: 27)

This is most clearly evident with the two disciples on the road to Emmaus (Lk 24.13–32). Despite spending several hours in the presence of Jesus, only at the end of the day do they recognize him (or rather, does he allow himself to be recognized). This disclosure thence casts their journey in a wholly different light: 'Were not our hearts burning within us while he was talking to us on the road [...]?' (v. 32). One might well say that these too, while still on the road, had 'not yet arrived at an express recognition of God' (LG 16).

There is, of course, a great deal of difference between 'accepting something' and 'accepting something *as the thing that it actually is*'. The same fundamental distinction applies, naturally, to 'encountering Christ (*sub specie minimi*)' and 'encountering Christ *as* Christ (*in limbo patrum*)'. In feeding a hungry person, there is indeed a genuine sense in which one is feeding Christ. Yet this need not imply that the feeder has any *implicit* knowledge, recognition, or even love of Christ, qua Christ. *Anonymous Christs do not entail anonymous Christians.*[9] My contention is that Dr Rieux aids a suffering child, and is fully justified in doing so, precisely because it is a suffering *child*. Only after death, in the limbo of the just, is it revealed who was co-present, both in solidarity with the sufferer, and as a co-recipient of Rieux's charity. And perhaps then, as with the Emmaus road disciples, might some long-forgotten inkling of grace be stirred. The crucial point here is that Christ is revealed, and *accepted*, not as some totally new reality, but rather, as one in whose presence Rieux has already been. In his mundane life, he has already encountered Christ in performing the works of mercy (D'Costa's 'ontological relationship'); but he only encounters him *as* Christ in the limbo of the just (D'Costa's 'epistemological relationship'). What is more, Christ is encountered there not only *as* the one who has 'in a certain way united himself with every human being' (GS 22), but who has, in a special and particular manner, united himself with all who suffer. This latter point cannot be stressed enough, for on it hangs the entire possibility of an atheistic *humanist*, who may have perhaps defined his or her whole life in opposition to (what he or she understands to be) God and Christianity, in accepting God, Christ, and the Church after death, and for this genuinely to be 'a coming to maturation and completion'. The feasibility of this, I believe, hangs on the fact that God is (with due

---

[9] *Contra* Leonardo Boff, who refers to Mt 25 as 'the parable concerning anonymous Christians' ([1972] 1980: 95).

apologies to Schillebeeckx, and to elegant users of the Latin language) a *Deus Humanist-issimus*.[10] I will explain this idea a little more in the following section.

There I will also address a number of further possible objections to the account I have developed. Before that, it will be helpful to recapitulate exactly in what that account consists. First of all, I accept the genuine possibility of an atheist being *inculpably ignorant* of the existence of God, the general truth of Christianity, and the necessity of him or her entering and persevering in the Church. (Although my account does not strictly depend upon it, I have offered reasons for thinking that such inculpable ignorance may be very widespread indeed, even among those brought up in supposedly Christian societies, and who have perhaps even been baptized, confirmed, and/or communicated as Christians.) According to LG 16, such people both exist and can be saved. This cannot, however, be fulfilled without their coming to faith and being baptized (or, at least, receiving the effect typically conferred by sacramental baptism). But how is this possible? The letter of LG 16 appears to imply a post-mortem solution. In the case of the righteous who lived before Christ, this was accomplished through Christ's proclamation to them in the *limbus patrum* on Holy Saturday. An analogous possibility may be hypothesized, therefore, for bringing subsequent non-Christians to the requisite 'epistemological relationship' with Christ, in order for them ultimately (almost certainly following further purification) to attain the beatific vision. This preserves the *limbus patrum*, not necessarily as an actual *place*, but rather as a 'conceptual theological datum'. Two further points: firstly, it is not *every* inculpably ignorant non-Christian who will ultimately – followed by sojourns in limbo and (probably) purgatory – be saved. Only those who have endeavoured to lead good and moral lives, following the truth insofar as they are able, and (in the case of members of the world religions) receiving grace through religious practices, will be so privileged. And secondly, their eventual coming to faith in limbo cannot be construed as any 'new decision after death', or as a genuine *conversion*, since this would contravene the established teaching of the Church. Suppose, though, that an inculpably ignorant atheist, as (say) a good Marxist or humanist, has devoted much of her life to alleviating the sufferings of her

---

[10] My inspiration for this (wholly serious) pun is the title of Philip Kennedy's study of Schillebeeckx: *Deus Humanissimus* (1993), or 'The Most Human God'.

fellow human beings. This may well have included some or all of the 'works of mercy'. Her rationale for doing these neither had, nor needed to have, any theistic element at all. Nonetheless, on the basis of a particular (and thoroughly orthodox) interpretation of Mt 25, a Catholic is permitted to believe that in doing these things for her fellow human beings, she was *also* doing them for Christ himself. Therefore, although she did not know it at the time (and may have regarded any such suggestion with derision, if not offence), she was in the presence of 'the Author of Sanctity himself', and was receiving grace, in an analogous manner to the way in which Christians do from Christ's presence in the sacraments, and pre-eminently from his real presence in the Eucharist. Because of this she (i) does not suffer from the lack of opportunities for encountering grace that one might expect of a person who neither receives the Christian sacraments, nor encounters the Spirit through the practice of a non-Christian religious tradition; and (ii) arguably need not undergo any radical *metanoia* in limbo, if she comes finally to recognize the one in whose presence she has passed significant moments of her life, and moreover, to recognize him *as* one who has allied himself, in compassionate solidarity, to all who undergo suffering. Her eventual, post-purgatorial attainment of the beatific vision would, then, be a genuine maturation and coming to completion of a relationship that was *already* present, in a truly significant way, in her earthly existence. As such, I feel able to make my own the following statement of Rahner's (my various debts to whom were, it may be remembered, duly acknowledged in chapter three):

> In order to understand our central thesis in this reflection, the doctrine of grace and the doctrine of the final vision of God must be understood within Christian dogmatics in the closest possible unity. For the themes in the doctrine of grace, namely, grace, justification and the divinization of man, are understood in their real nature only in the light of the doctrine of the supernatural and immediate vision of God, which according to Christian dogmatics is man's end and fulfillment. [...] What grace and vision of God mean are two phases of one and the same event which are conditioned by man's free historicity and temporality. They are two phases of God's single self-communication to man.
> ([1976] 1978: 118)

This paragraph presents, *in nuce*, my understanding of how it is that atheists may be saved.

POSSIBLE OBJECTIONS

In developing the above account, I have already identified and countered a number of objections. Chief among these are the three that I formulated in response to D'Costa's text. In addition, a brief defence of my position against the likely charge of Pelagianism (inevitable, it would seem, for theologians who advocate the importance of Mt 25) was given, as was a rebuttal of my views being misconstrued as implying any implicit or unconscious faith on the part of the righteous, works-of-mercy-performing atheist. Two further objections must now be engaged. The first relates to the role of the Church (or rather, its apparent lack of much of a role) in my explanation of how atheists may be saved. The second, and most important, challenges my reading of Mt 25, asking whether it corrupts genuine, interhuman morality. Both objections can, however, be satisfactorily met.

My account cannot, I believe, be accused of denying the letter of *Extra Ecclesiam nulla salus* (at least, not in the sense in which it has gradually come to be understood within the Church). I follow D'Costa in his 'Clementine' affirmation of the Church's instrumental causality in limbo. Elsewhere in the book, D'Costa emphasizes the Church's liturgical intercession, especially in the post-conciliar prayers for Good Friday, for the salvation of non-Christians:

> The liturgical reality, like the Eucharistic sign, effects the grace it signifies, so that these prayers bring about an instrumental relation of efficacy to the unevangelized non-Christians, like Jane and her entire community (past, present, and future). (2009: 186; cf. Sullivan 1992: 169)

On this point too, I am happy to concur. But even so, my account could be (mis)construed as being ecclesially deficient in less obvious ways. I have titled this chapter *Extra minimos nulla salus*. It should be clear by now, in light of the arguments advanced, that I understand this phrase to be, in effect, synonymous with *Extra Christum nulla salus*. Much has been made of Christ's presence in those who suffer, as it also has of the atheist's encounter with, and reception of grace from, him when performing the works of mercy. But since I have denied that this constitutes a sacrament in the full and proper sense of the word – and thus it is not, among other things, 'a visible act of the Church' – it might appear that the Church is absent from at least this aspect of my account. This is not so. For a start, even extra-sacramental grace is intimately bound up with the Church. Quoting Schillebeeckx:

> This may indeed be called an extra-sacramental bestowal of grace, but nevertheless the Church will always be involved in it even if only through the daily sacrifice of the Eucharist for the good of all men. When we too receive grace apart from the sacraments it comes through Christ the Mediator in and through his Church the primordial sacrament. ([1960] 1963: 140)

This also relates, obviously, to D'Costa's liturgical point above (see also *Dominus Iesus* 20).

Although this consideration is alone sufficient, the ecclesial nature of my account can be further secured with reference to Teresa. As we have seen, she drew a particular correlation between Mt 25 and Mary's presence at the foot of the Cross. This rests on her conviction that 'When we touch the sick and needy, we touch the suffering body of Christ' (1980: 26), and that this 'suffering body' is the very same one that hung from the Cross. Note, first of all, that the Church is *itself* also the (mystical) 'body of Christ'. Christ's presence in his *minimi* cannot, therefore, be understood as something separate from the Church. Furthermore, Vatican II recognizes that, even prior to Pentecost, the Church was inaugurated on Good Friday. According to LG 3:

> The Church, as the kingdom of Christ already present in mystery, visibly increases through the power of God in the world. This beginning and increase are signified by the blood and water issuing from the open side of Christ crucified (cf. Jn 19.34), and are foretold in the Lord's words concerning his death on the Cross: 'And I, if I am to be lifted up from the earth, will draw all things to myself' (Jn 12.32). (AS III/viii: 785)

And in the words of *Sacrosanctum Concilium* 5: 'from the side of Christ sleeping on the Cross has arisen the marvellous sacrament of the whole Church' (AS II/vi: 411). Through imitating Mary at the foot of the Cross, there is then arguably a sense in which, by being present with those who suffer or are in need, one is analogically present at the inception of the Church. My account is, therefore, thoroughly ecclesial in all its main dimensions. Justified atheists are indeed 'related to the People of God in various ways' (LG 16), not only after death in limbo, but at every stage 'on the road to salvation'.

In the course of this chapter, great stress has been lain on *Christ's presence in those in need*. This was necessary in attempting to give an orthodox, and thus non-Pelagian, account of how atheists may be saved. This chapter is a contribution to the Catholic theology of *salvation*. It is not a treatise of Christian moral theology; still less does it advance any generic meta-ethical theory. I am well aware, however, that this is how it might be construed. In affirming the Teresan interpretation of Mt 25, am I not implying that the hungry are to be fed, not because they are suffering human beings, but because Christ happens to be present in them? And by extension, does this not also entail that those in need are simply *means* for procuring one's own salvation?

Yet this is not the view presented here. Nor is it implied in the account of salvation that I have developed. If Christ were *not* present in the hungry, thirsty, naked, alien, sick, and imprisoned, then one ought still to feed, give drink to, clothe, welcome, comfort, and visit them. The fact that Christ *is* present in them does not change this; they are still, *qua* human beings in need, the proper objects of moral concern. (Although that is not to deny that, for Christians, Christ's presence provides, or *ought to* provide, an additional motivation.) But here is the interesting part. The assumption of an atheistic meta-ethics explains *why* God incarnate's allying himself with those who suffer is not the result of some arbitrary decision. Christ's preferential option for the poor, exemplified in Mt 25, results from the fact that the poor, *qua* poor, are intrinsically and objectively worthy of his opting.[11] This preferential option is, furthermore, incumbent on both God and man. It is for this reason that I speak of God as a *Deus Humanistissimus*, 'the most humanist God'. According to Mt 25, Christ has expressed his solidarity with the poor and oppressed in a radical manner. It is therefore fitting that for those who do not (yet) believe in him, by expressing their own solidarity with the poor and oppressed, they come to encounter him. And in limbo, perhaps, they may come to realize that he and they have more in common than they had previously thought. Seen in this light, then coming to have a post-mortem 'epistemological relationship' with the *Deus Humanistissimus*

---

[11] In a somewhat similar fashion, see Thomas' arguments for the non-arbitrariness of bread and wine being the Eucharistic species (*Summa theologiae*, III, q. 74, a. 1; Thomas Aquinas [1265–74] 1965: 26).

would indeed be 'a fulfillment of what was already present [...] coming to its full maturation' (D'Costa 2009: 172).

CONCLUSION

This chapter has built upon the foundations established in chapter four, in order to develop a new understanding of how, in light of LG 16, atheists can attain salvation. Unlike what I have termed the 'standard view', expounded and critiqued in chapters two and three, this does not rely on any problematic imputation of 'unconscious', 'implicit', 'hidden', 'secret', or 'anonymous' beliefs or faith. Instead, at the core of my account is the scriptural text of Mt 25, and its interpretation in a specific strand of the tradition. In focusing on Mt 25, I am fully cognizant of the naïve and dogmatically unsatisfactory applications to which this pericope has been put in addressing the salvation of non-Christians. But that does not mean that the passage is not, in fact, of fundamental significance in this regard – despite its conspicuous neglect in the dogmatic tradition. Interpretations of Mt 25 as (i) being non-restrictive in scope, and (ii) demanding a strong sense of Christ's presence in, or identity with, his 'least ones' have been cited from the Fathers (Chrysostom, Benedict), hagiographical accounts (Martyrius, Martin of Tours, Christopher, Francis, Elizabeth of Hungary), and the lives and words of saints, blesseds, and servants of God (Hugh of Lincoln, Dorothy Day, Mother Teresa). These testimonies, their resonance in the *sensus fidelium*, and several recent papal and conciliar statements secure the orthodoxy of this interpretation, while at the same time acknowledging both exegetical difficulties in the text itself, and the existence of other ways of reading it in the Catholic and wider Christian tradition. Mother Teresa was singled out both as a pre-eminent representative of this strand, and for having developed certain key ideas that were, however, already present in earlier writers.

The cardinal elements of my full, integrated account have already been summarized above. They will also be presented in fuller detail in the general conclusion to this study, and hence need not be repeated here. What is worth noting, though, is that despite the addition of numerous dogmatic qualifications and caveats, my account nevertheless preserves, and in some cases enhances, much of the plain and literal sense of Mt 25. Three aspects, in particular, are essential to my reading: the ignorance of both the 'blessed' and the 'accursed' as to when they had previously encountered 'the Son of Man' ('Lord, when was it that we...?' – vv. 37, 44); Christ's literal identification with, and presence in, his *minimi* ('you did [not do] it to me' – vv. 40, 45); and the means according to which these unbelievers are consigned either to 'the kingdom prepared for you' or 'the eternal fire prepared for the devil and his angels' ('just as you did [not do] it to one of the least of these' – vv. 40, 45). This latter point is not, however, to be understood in any naïve, salvation-by-works manner. On the contrary, it is in, through, and by Christ (and *ipso facto* in, through, and by his Church) that atheists can be saved. It is just that for unbelievers, it is pre-eminently in *works* (of mercy) that Christ is – in this life, at least – encountered and served.

Conclusion

The singular purpose of this study has been, in effect, to explicate two sentences of LG 16:

> Those indeed who are, without fault, ignorant of the Gospel of Christ and his Church, yet who seek God with a sincere heart, and who knowing his will through the command of conscience, strive under the influence of grace to accomplish works, are able to obtain eternal salvation. Nor does divine Providence deny the assistances necessary for salvation to those who, without fault, have not yet arrived at an express recognition of God and who, not without divine grace, endeavour to attain to an upright life. (AS III/viii: 796–7)

To do this satisfactorily, it has been necessary to consider them in light of three primary contexts: their position within LG, the conciliar literature (especially GS 19–21 and *Ad Gentes* 7), and the wider dogmatic tradition; the theological currents leading up to, and in evidence at, the Council itself; and the realities, social and intellectual, of the potentially millions of human beings to whom these sentences might apply.

My approach has, therefore, been necessarily wide-ranging. Chapter one attempted to engage with atheism in its own right, prior to theologizing about it. It began by noting its status as a vast, global phenomenon (and hence the importance of a serious theological engagement with it). It then dealt with a number of conceptual issues, clarifying and justifying my use of the word 'atheist', exploring the notion of 'practical atheism', and tackling two oft-encountered suggestions: (i) that atheism, or some specific manifestation of it, is itself a 'religion'; and (ii) that it is impossible, or at least very difficult, even to be an atheist.

Chapter two explored the genesis and interpretation of LG 16, at both Vatican II itself, and in the undertakings of major Catholic theologians in the decades surrounding it. In particular, it focused on how and why Catholic understandings of atheism and salvation developed so rapidly in the decades preceding the Council. Based on extensive analysis of primary sources, I explained the nature of these changes, and their crucial importance for comprehending the foundational texts of this enquiry: LG 16 and GS 19–21. Chapter three concentrated on Rahner as being, contrary to popular scholarly belief, representative of a broad trend in Catholic theology. I gave a detailed exposition of his theory of 'anonymous Christians', situating this particularly within the dynamic context of his general theology of atheism. This was then subjected to three main criticisms: the problematic conceptual nature of implicit, or rather unconscious, mental states; the difficulties in stretching the traditional concept of *fides implicita* to encompass those identified in LG 16; and the inadequacy of Rahner's arguments for imputing an implicit faith (allegedly demonstrated by moral seriousness and a sense of life's meaningfulness) to atheists. This last point, in particular, built upon a number of points raised in chapter one. Rahner's arguments for an anonymous or implicit faith in God on the part of self-professed atheists, and by extension the arguments of many other major theologians of his generation, were shown to be problematic – at least, on the magnitude envisioned by Rahner. (The hypothetical possibility of an atheist qualifying as a Rahnerian 'anonymous Christian' was nonetheless conceded, with reference to Dostoevsky's plausible portrayals.)

The fruits produced by these three chapters vindicate my wide-ranging approach to this *quaestio*. Each chapter, while addressing a significant topic in its own right, yielded evidence and insights that were crucial to the developed understanding of how, in light of LG 16, atheists may be saved, advanced and defended in the remaining chapters. Thus chapter four elucidated and elaborated Gavin D'Costa's account of how Jane, a non-theistic Buddhist, might attain salvation within the confines of an orthodoxly Catholic dogmatic framework. This revives the *limbus patrum*, analogically understood, as the after-death location for a righteous, unevangelized non-Christian's coming to the epistemological relationship with Christ necessary for the *visio beatifica*. This is indeed, as he puts it, a case of 'Old Doctrines for New Jobs' (2009: 161).

While fundamentally agreeing with D'Costa, and adopting his schema in constructing my own account, I identified three main difficulties with it. These were: (i) the lack of a sustained discussion

Conclusion 183

of 'unevangelized', especially in light of Vatican II's repeated emphasis on an *ignorantia sine culpa*; (ii) the disparities between Jane's opportunities for receiving and cooperating with grace, and those of a non-religious atheist (a difficulty for me, rather than for D'Costa himself); and (iii) the lingering problems raised by the Catholic tradition's Augustine-inspired prohibition of 'new decisions after death', which D'Costa also accepts. The first of these was broached, at length, in the remainder of chapter four. I offered a 'friendly amendment' to fill this *lacuna* in D'Costa's (and others') theory – drawing on Aquinas, Las Casas, Vitoria, Pius IX, Vatican II, evidence presented in chapter two, and Luckmann and Berger's 'sociology of knowledge' – that offered good grounds for *hoping* that, in modern secularized societies at least, a great many non-believers are in fact *sine culpa*. The second and third difficulties were addressed in the course of chapter five. For the most part, this comprised a detailed theological interpretation of Mt 25.31–46, inspired by a specific, non-restrictive strand of its reception in the Catholic hagiographical and (since Leo XIII's *Rerum Novarum*) magisterial traditions. Particular attention was paid to the witness and writings of Mother Teresa of Calcutta, and the resources which these contain for a (quasi-) sacramental understanding of the atheist's graced encounter with Christ in his *minimi*. Finally, two further objections (one ecclesiological, one meta-ethical) were prevened.

The ultimate outcome of these final two chapters – an answer to the question *how, in light of LG 16 and the Catholic tradition, may an atheist attain eternal life?* – can now be summarized. Obviously, a great many caveats and qualifications, to be found in the foregoing chapters, need to be added to this schematic presentation. Nevertheless, the following may be taken as a reasonably accurate distillation of my conclusions:

1. According to LG 16, someone who is 'without fault, ignorant' of the gospel and the Church, *and* who has 'without fault, [. . .] not yet arrived at an express recognition of [God]' – i.e. is an inculpably ignorant atheist – can attain salvation.

2. But according to LG 14 (and the numerous *de fide* definitions it echoes), *nobody* can be saved without faith, baptism, and the mediation of the (Catholic) Church.

3. **Hence there must be a way of reconciling – even if only 'in ways known to God'** (*Ad Gentes* 7) **– 1 and 2.**

4. One possible solution is to impute an 'implicit' faith to the atheist. This would also include an implicit desire for baptism. Since it is Christ who baptizes, and the Church is his mystical body, then even without sacramental baptism (*in re*), an implicit baptism of desire (*flaminis*) would involve the Church's mediation. Hence 1's trifold requirements are met.

5. 4 gains further credence from the fact that many unbelievers lead moral and meaningful lives. Since (it is argued) the atheist, *qua* atheist, can have no cogent justifications for living like this, then this implies that she holds a belief (and indeed faith) in God of which she is not consciously aware.

6. But 5 is unconvincing. There are indeed plausible, properly atheistic reasons for leading a moral and meaningful life. (Although these are not, be it noted, antithetical to the *actual* existence and workings of the Christian God.)

7. Furthermore, the general notion of 'implicit' (or rather, 'unconscious') mental states is somewhat problematic.

8. **Taken together, 6 and 7 advise against the acceptance of 4.**

9. LG 16 speaks of those who have 'not yet' (*nondum*) accepted the gospel, and have 'not yet' (*nondum*) expressly recognized God. Nevertheless, God is *presently* assisting them on the way to salvation.

10. Since 'not yet' cannot reasonably refer to those who will, later in their earthly lives, become Christians, LG 16 seems to point towards some future, post-mortem resolution of 3.

11. According to the Apostles' Creed, Christ descended into hell on Holy Saturday. The established tradition holds that there, in the *limbus patrum*, he proclaimed the accomplishment of his saving work to the 'holy dead' (i.e. the righteous who had died prior to his advent), before leading them into heaven.

12. The holy dead were, in their earthly lives, (necessarily) inculpably ignorant of Christ and the gospel.

13. The holy dead included both Jews and gentiles. Elsewhere in the patristic tradition may be found the contention that although Christ himself preached only to the Jews in limbo, the apostles (i.e. 'the Church'), after their own deaths, extended this mission to the gentiles also, both preaching and baptizing.

14. Given 11, 12, and 13, the Catholic tradition possesses the resources for explaining how an inculpably ignorant, righteous gentile, who during her earthly life had 'not yet' heard of Christ, can, through the mediation of the Church, receive faith and baptism in the *limbus patrum*.

15. Today, over two millennia after Christ's coming and when the gospel has been preached 'to all nations', it is still possible to be inculpably ignorant of Christ, the gospel, and even the existence of God (1). There are, moreover, strong reasons for thinking that such inculpable ignorance may be very widespread indeed, even in (formerly) Christian countries.

16. Taking 14 and 15 together, it seems reasonable to hypothesize that the *limbus patrum* (or an analogical reality, continuing its function) exists to this day. **As such, then, a preliminary solution to 3 has been found.**

17. However, the tradition also implies that the unbeliever's coming to faith in limbo cannot constitute a genuine *conversion*, since no genuinely new decisions may be made after death. Furthermore, an atheist seems to suffer from a deficiency of opportunities for encountering, and participating with, grace – at least when compared to a Christian, or an observant member of one of the world religions.

18. At Mt 25.40, Christ declares that whatever has been done to 'the least' has been done to him. Sources from both the tradition and magisterium can be cited to support a literal and unrestricted interpretation of these words, entailing that Christ is genuinely present in all those in need. This presence may be understood on analogy with the sacraments, and with the Eucharist in particular.

19. Taking 17 and 18 together, it can be argued that, through performing the works of mercy, the inculpably ignorant atheist encounters Christ himself. Unbeknownst to her, this brings her into a graced (objective) relationship with Christ – a Christ who, like herself, has made a preferential option for the poor. This is the beginning of a relationship which may later, in the *limbus patrum*, come to a full and express maturation.

20. **By qualifying 16 with 19, a possible answer to 3 has been found.**

Two clarifications ought perhaps to be made. In the first place, when mentioning my research topic to various people over the past few years, it has been relatively common for them to assume that I must therefore be researching *universal salvation*. The assumption, I suppose, is that if *even* atheists may be saved, then surely everyone will be. Certainly, it is permissible to 'hope that all men be saved' (see Balthasar 1988). Supports for such a *hope* can be found in both scripture and tradition. It is, for instance, specifically petitioned in the (Holy See-approved) Fátima prayer: 'O my Jesus, forgive us our sins, save us from the fires of hell, and *lead all souls to heaven*, especially those who have most need of your mercy.' Nevertheless, universal salvation has formed no part of my argument here. In fact, LG 14–16, in line with the overwhelming (if not quite unanimous) testimony of scripture, tradition, and magisterium, proceeds from the assumption that some, at the very least, can and will be lost. *Which* or *how many* atheists may be saved is, as I remarked in chapter four, not a subject with which I am, or should be, concerned. I have, of course, offered grounds for presuming a very high incidence of inculpable ignorance, especially in modern secularized societies, including (post-)Christian ones. But even if this presumption is basically correct, it by no means follows that no contemporary unbeliever has *culpably* rejected the gospel. Pius IX's prudence cuts both ways: 'who would arrogate so much to himself, as to be able to designate the limits of this kind of ignorance [. . .]?' ([1854] 1864: 626). Further, as pointed out in chapter five, I make no claims as to *who* or *how many* will fulfil Mt 25's criteria for inheriting 'the kingdom prepared [. . .] from the foundation of this world' (v. 34). Hopefully all will. But then again, while it has made perfect sense for me, in a work entitled *The Salvation of Atheists*, to focus on verse 40's 'you did it to me', equal consideration must also be given to verses 45–6's admonition to 'the goats':

> 'Truly I tell you, just as you did not do it to one of the least of these, you did not do it to me.' And these will go away into eternal punishment [. . .].

This brings me to my second point. My referring to the situation of atheists as 'salvifically problematic', and devoting of an entire book to the '*problemata*' arising from LG 16's assurances that they can indeed be saved, must not be interpreted as implying that I regard the salvation of *anyone*, especially Catholic Christians, to be in any sense *un*-'problematic'. I am particularly cognizant of the fact that it is so often the saints themselves – those of us with *least* to worry about! – who are most acutely aware of their undeservingness, and how gravely imperilled is their own ultimate salvation (see Keenan 2005: 94). Hence, as St Gemma Galgani once told her confessor: 'Think of all that the greatest sinners have committed, I have committed as many' (quoted in Germanus of St Stanislaus [1914] 2000: 157). And elsewhere:

> But can it be true that Jesus is content with my soul? Oh, how often I blush and tremble at seeing myself so unclean in His presence! I have turned away when he called me. Oh, Father, do ask Jesus often to have mercy on my soul! Implore him to pardon my sins. (Ibid.: 152–3)

Furthermore, chapter four's arguments in favour of (inculpable) ignorance *excusing* sin would imply, vice versa, that knowledge *compounds* it. This is why, in chapter one, I drew a sharp distinction between 'practical atheists' and atheists proper, affirming that 'in the context of the Catholic theology of salvation, these two groups cannot in any useful sense be treated together.' There is thus great wisdom in the words of the Lutheran theologian George Lindbeck:

> One can say that the situation of the Christian is in some respects more, not less, perilous than that of the non-Christian. Judgment begins in the house of the Lord (1 Peter 4:17), and many of the first shall be last, and the last first (Matt. 19:30). (1984: 59; see also Hauerwas 2006: 211)

A similar idea, more strongly expressed, is contained in a passage from LG 14 not quoted previously:

> Someone who, although incorporated into the Church, does not persevere in charity, is not saved [. . .]. All the children of the Church ought to remember that their exalted status is to be ascribed not to their own merits, but to the particular grace of Christ. If they do not respond to this in thought, word and deed, not only shall they not be saved, but they shall be more severely judged (Lk 12.48). (AS III/viii: 795)

I mentioned in my introduction, as the ideal to which I was aspiring, Francis Sullivan's notion of 'creative fidelity'. The extent to which my account is either *creative* or (more importantly) *faithful* is for others to judge. I must finally stress, however, that what I have presented is only *one* possible explication of Vatican II's optimism regarding the salvation of atheists. Certainly I believe, and have argued, that it is compatible with LG 16. But so too, for example, and as I have also argued, is the Rahnerian appeal to an implicit or anonymous faith (despite its other problems). No doubt other solutions, more or less satisfactory, remain to be devised by Catholic theologians. According to *Ad Gentes* 7, the ways by which God can lead non-Christians to 'that faith without which it is impossible to please him' are 'known to himself (*sibi notis*)'. Note, though, that it does not state that these either are, or must be, known *only* to himself. Indeed, as *Dominus Iesus* 21 observed: 'Theological expertise is now turned to this subject, in order to understand it more deeply. This contemporary theological study is to be encouraged, since it is undoubtedly useful for better understanding God's plan for salvation, and the ways in which it is accomplished' (AAS 92 [2000]: 762). In a single (long) sentence, my own contribution to this task is as follows:

> *The standard Catholic understanding of how, in light of LG 16, atheists may be saved – imputing implicit or unconscious beliefs (and indeed faith) to righteous unbelievers – is untenable, and a better account – drawing principally on Christ's Descent, a renewed understanding of invincible/inculpable ignorance, and a specific interpretation of Mt 25.31–46 already present in the Catholic tradition – may tentatively be advanced.*

In the words of *Donum Veritatis* quoted in the introduction, it is these 'new opinions' – to which, doubtlessly, 'Many corrections and broadening of perspectives within the context of fraternal dialogue may be needed' – that are my 'offerings made to the whole Church' (AAS 82 [1990]: 1554–5).

Bibliography

Quotations from scripture, except where quoted from others, have been taken from the *New Revised Standard Version: Catholic Edition, Anglicized Text* (Ottawa: Harper Catholic Bibles, 1991) – albeit, on occasion, with my own slight amendments.

1. Archival Sources

Archivio Segretariato per i Non-Credenti [Archive of the Secretariat for Nonbelievers], Pontifical Council for Culture, Vatican City:

Box 1/000. [Loose] Elisabeth Peter, 'Breve Storia del Segretariato per i Non Credenti' (undated, 1972?), 15 pp.

Box 1/000. File 'Relazioni', fol. 6: 'Relaziones della Riunione di alcuni esperti del Segretariato per i Non Credenti', 14 April 1966, 3 pp.

Box 1/000. File 'Rivista del dialogo'

Box 6/000. File 'Documentazione varia', fol. 6: 'Contemporary Atheism', *DO-C [Documentatie Centrum Concilie/Documentazione Olandese Concilio]*, no. 201 (undated), 5 pp.

Box 6/000. File 'Documentazione varia', fol. 7: 'Marx-Leninist Atheism', *DO-C*, no. 202 (undated), 12 pp.

Box 6. File 'R. Padre KARL RAHNER S.J.'

Box 6. File 'R. Padre KARL RAHNER S.J.', fol. 6: 'Letter from Vincentius [Vincenzo] Miano to Carolus [Karl] Rahner, 15 February 1966', 1 p.

Box 6. File 'VORGRIMLER', fol. 15: 'Letter from Cardinal Cicognani (Segreteria di Stato) to Cardinal König, 16 January 1968', 1 p.

Box 13/20. File 'VORGRIMLER'

Stichting Edward Schillebeeckx, Nijmegen, Netherlands:
53/6: 'Herbronning van het priesterlijk apostolaat en activering van het laïcaat' (1953), 43 pp. ['159–202']

2. Other Printed Sources

Abbot, Walter M. and Joseph Gallagher (eds.). 1967. *The Documents of Vatican II: All Sixteen Official Texts Promulgated by the Ecumenical Council 1963–1965* (London: Geoffrey Chapman)

Adam, Karl. [1924] 1969. *The Spirit of Catholicism*, tr. Justin McCann (London: Sheed and Ward)

Alberigo, Giuseppe. 2006. *A Brief History of Vatican II*, tr. Matthew Sherry (Maryknoll, NY: Orbis Books)

Alberigo, Giuseppe and Franca Magistretti. 1975. *Constitutionis Dogmaticae Lumen Gentium: Synopsis Historica* (Bologna: Istituto per le Scienze Religiose)

Alvares, Santiago. 1965. 'Towards an Alliance of Communists and Catholics', *World Marxist Review* 8/6 (June), 27–34

Anonymous. 1954. 'Looking Back', in *The Worker Priests: A Collective Documentation*, tr. John Petrie (London: Routledge & Kegan Paul), 99–108

Arnal, Oscar L. 1984a. *Priests in Working-Class Blue: The History of the Worker-Priests (1943–1954)* (Mahwah, NJ: Paulist Press)

—— 1984b. 'A Missionary "Main Tendue" toward French Communists: The "Temoignages" of the Worker-Priests, 1943–1954', *French Historical Studies* 13/4 (Autumn), 529–56

Ayer, A. J. [1936] 1990. *Language, Truth and Logic* (London: Penguin)

Bagg, Samuel and David Voas. 2010. 'The Triumph of Indifference: Irreligion in British Society', in Phil Zuckerman (ed.), *Atheism and Secularity*, Volume II: *Global Expressions* (Santa Barbara, CA: Praeger), 91–111

Baggini, Julian. 2003. *Atheism: A Very Short Introduction* (Oxford: Oxford University Press)

Bailey, Edward I. 1998. *Implicit Religion: An Introduction* (Middlesex: Middlesex University Press)

Bainbridge, William S. 2008. 'Atheism', in Peter B. Clarke (ed.), *The Oxford Handbook of the Sociology of Religion* (Oxford: Oxford University Press), 319–35

Bainvel, Jean. 1917. *Is There Salvation Outside the Catholic Church?*, tr. J. L. Weidenhan (London: Herder)

Balthasar, Hans Urs Von. 1988. *Dare We Hope 'That All Men Be Saved'? With a Short Discourse on Hell*, tr. Lother Krauth and David Kipp (San Francisco, CA: Ignatius Press)

—— [1966] 1994. *The Moment of Christian Witness*, tr. Richard Beckley (San Francisco, CA: Ignatius Press)

Barrett, David B., George Kurian, and Todd Johnson (eds.). 2001. *World Christian Encyclopedia: A comparative survey of churches and religions in the modern world*, Volume 1, 2nd edn (New York: Oxford University Press)

Barth, Karl. [1963] 1971a. 'The Rationality of Discipleship', in Karl Barth, *Fragments Grave and Gay*, tr. Eric Mosbacher (London: Collins), 40–7

—— [1963] 1971b. 'Christianity or Religion?', in Karl Barth, *Fragments Grave and Gay*, tr. Eric Mosbacher (London: Collins), 27–31

Béguerie, Philippe and Claude Duchesneau. [1989] 1991. *How to Understand the Sacraments*, tr. John Bowden and Margaret Lydamore (London: SCM Press)

Beit-Hallahmi, Benjamin. 2010. 'Morality and Immorality among the Irreligious', in Phil Zuckerman (ed.), *Atheism and Secularity*, Volume 1: *Issues, Concepts, Definitions* (Santa Barbara, CA: Praeger), 113–48

Bent, A. J. Van der. 1971. 'A Decade of Christian-Marxist Dialogue', *Ateismo e Dialogo* 6/2 (June), 23–34

Bercken, William Van Den. 1989. *Ideology and Atheism in the Soviet Union*, tr. H. Th. Wake (Berlin: Mouton de Gruyter)

Berdyaev, Nicholas. [1923] 1934. *Dostoievsky: An Interpretation*, tr. Donald Attwater (London: Sheed and Ward)

Berger, Peter L. [1967] 1990. *The Sacred Canopy: Elements of a Sociological Theory of Religion* (New York: Doubleday)

Berger, Peter L. and Thomas Luckmann. [1966] 1971. *The Social Construction of Reality* (Harmondsworth: Penguin)

Berrigan, Daniel. 1981. 'Introduction', in Dorothy Day, *The Long Loneliness* (New York: Harper & Row)

Blondel, Maurice. [1893] 1984. *Action (1893): Essay on a Critique of Life and a Science of Practice*, tr. Oliva Blanchette (Notre Dame, IN: University of Notre Dame Press)

—— 1934. *La Pensée*, Volume I: *La genèse de la pensée et les paliers de son ascension spontanée* (Paris: Félix Alcan)

Boff, Leonardo. [1972] 1980. *Jesus Christ Liberator: A Critical Christology of Our Time*, tr. Patrick Hughes (London: SPCK)

Borne, Étienne. [1957] 1961. *Modern Atheism*, tr. S. J. Testier (London: Burns and Oates)

Bortnowska, Halina. 1965. 'The Church and the World', *Slant* 1/5 (Spring), 31–3

Bradstock, Andrew and Christopher Rowland (eds.). 2002. *Radical Christian Writings: A Reader* (Oxford: Blackwell)

Brechter, Suso. 1969. 'Decree on the Church's Missionary Activity: Doctrinal Principles', in Herbert Vorgrimler (ed.), *Commentary on the Documents of Vatican II*, Volume IV, tr. W. J. O'Hara (London: Burns and Oates), 112–24

Brierley, Peter. 2006. *Pulling out of the Nosedive: A Contemporary Picture of Churchgoing; What the 2005 English Church Census Reveals* (London: Christian Research)

Brooks, A. C. 2006. *Who Really Cares; The Surprising Truth About Compassionate Conservatism: America's Charity Divide – Who Gives, Who Doesn't, and Why it Matters* (New York: Basic Books)

Bruce, Steve. 1996. *Religion in the Modern World: From Cathedrals to Cults* (Oxford and New York: Oxford University Press)

—— 2002. *God is Dead: Secularization in the West* (Oxford and Malden, MA: Oxford University Press)

Buckley, Michael J. 1987. *At the Origins of Modern Atheism* (London and New Haven, CT: Yale University Press)

Buckley, Michael J. 2004. *Denying and Disclosing God: The Ambiguous Progress of Modern Atheism* (New Haven, CT: Yale University Press)
Bujanda, J. M. DE. 2002. *Index Librorum Prohibitorum 1600–1966* (Montréal: Médiaspaul)
Bullivant, Stephen. 2008a. 'Research Note: Sociology and the Study of Atheism', *Journal of Contemporary Religion* 23/3 (October), 363–8
—— 2008b. 'A House Divided Against Itself: Dostoevsky and the Psychology of Unbelief', *Literature and Theology* 22/1 (March), 16–31
—— 2010. 'The New Atheism and Sociology: Why Here? Why Now? What Next?', in Amarnath Amarasingam (ed.), *Religion and the New Atheism: A Critical Appraisal* (Leiden and Boston, MA: Brill), 109–24
Burigana, Ricardo and Giovanni Turbanti. 2003. 'The Intersession: Preparing the Conclusion of the Council', tr. Matthew J. O'Connell, in Giuseppe Alberigo and Joseph A. Komonchak (eds.), *History of Vatican II*, Volume IV: *Church as Communion. Third Period and Intersession. September 1964–September 1965* (Maryknoll, NY: Orbis Books), 453–615
Calvez, Jean-Yves. 1976. 'Mailing List of this Issue', *Letters on the Service of Faith and New Cultures* 5 (June), 29–32
—— 1980. 'Note', *Letters on the Service of Faith and New Cultures* 12 (February), 1
—— 1981. 'Mailing List (June 1981)', *Letters on the Service of Faith and New Cultures* 15 (June), 29–32
Campbell, Colin. 1971. *Toward a Sociology of Irreligion* (London: Macmillan)
Camus, Albert. [1947] 1960. *The Plague*, tr. Stuart Gilbert (London: Penguin)
—— [1948] 1964. 'The Unbeliever and Christians', in Albert Camus, *Resistance, Rebellion and Death*, tr. Justin O'Brien (London: Hamilton), 47–53
Carey, Patrick. 2007. 'St Benedict Center and No Salvation Outside the Church, 1940–53', *Catholic Historical Review* 93/3 (July), 553–75
Chenu, Marie-Dominique. 1975. 'Jacques Duquesne interviews Father Chenu on the Secretariat for Non-believers', *Ateismo e Dialogo* 10/3 (September), 141
Churchland, Paul M. 1995. *The Engine of Reason, the Seat of the Soul: A Philosophical Journey into the Brain* (London and Cambridge, MA: MIT Press)
Clarke, Peter B. and Peter Byrne. 1993. *Religion Defined and Explained* (Basingstoke: Macmillan)
Clement Of Alexandria. [c. 200] 1983. 'The *Stromata*, or Miscellanies', in Alexander Roberts and James Donaldson (eds. and trs.), *The Ante-Nicene Fathers*, Volume II: *Fathers of the Second Century: Hermas, Tatian, Athenagoras, Theophilus, and Clement of Alexandria (Entire)* (Grand Rapids, MI: Eerdmans), 299–568

Cliteur, Paul. 2009. 'The Definition of Atheism', *Journal of Religion & Society* 11, 1–23

Congar, Yves. [1935] 1938a. 'The Reasons for the Unbelief of Our Times, Pt. 1', *Integration: A Students' Catholic Review* 2/1 (August/September), 13–21

—— [1935] 1938b. 'The Reasons for the Unbelief of Our Times, Pt. 2', *Integration: A Students' Catholic Review* 2/3 (Dececember 1938/January 1939), 10–26

—— 1957. 'Salvation and the Non-Catholic', *Blackfriars* 38/448–9 (July/August), 290–300

—— [1959] 1961. *The Wide World My Parish*, tr. Donald Attwater (London: Darton, Longman and Todd)

—— [1961] 1962. 'The Council in an Age of Dialogue', tr. Barry N. Rigney, *Cross Currents* 12, 144–51

—— 1965. 'The Church: The People of God', tr. Kathryn Sullivan, *Concilium* 1/1 (January), 7–19

—— 1974. 'Talking to Yves Congar: Interview by Tony Sheerin', *Africa: St. Patrick's Missions* (1974), 6–8

—— 1979. 'Archbishop Lefebvre, Champion of "Tradition"? Some Necessary Clarifications', tr. Sarah Fawcett, *Concilium* 119, 95–105

—— [1976] 1982a. 'A Semantic History of the Term "Magisterium"', in Charles E. Curran and Richard A. McCormick (eds.), *Readings in Moral Theology 3: The Magisterium and Morality* (New York: Paulist Press), 297–313

—— [1976] 1982b. 'A Brief History of the Forms of the Magisterium and Its Relations with Scholars', in Charles E. Curran and Richard A. McCormick (eds.), *Readings in Moral Theology 3: The Magisterium and Morality* (New York: Paulist Press), 314–31

—— 1988. *Fifty Years of Catholic Theology: Conversations with Yves Congar*, ed. Bernard Lauret, tr. John Bowden (London: SCM Press)

Conway, Eamonn. 1993. *The Anonymous Christian – A Relativised Christianity?* (Frankfurt Am Main: Peter Lang)

—— 2004. '"So as not to Despise God's Grace": Re-assessing Rahner's Idea of the "Anonymous Christian"', *Louvain Studies* 29/1–2 (Spring-Summer), 107–30

Cope, Lamar. 1969. 'Matthew XXV: 31–46: "The Sheep and the Goats" Reinterpreted', *Novum Testamentum* 11/1 + 2 (January–April), 32–44

Copleston, Frederick C. 1973. 'Contemporary Atheism', *Ateismo e Dialogo* 8/1 (March), 25–32

Craigo-Snell, Shannon. 2008. *Silence, Love and Death: Saying 'Yes' to God in the Theology of Karl Rahner* (Milwaukee, WI: Marquette University Press)

Curtis, D. E. 1997. *The French Popular Front and the Catholic Discovery of Marx* (Hull: University of Hull Press)

D'Costa, Gavin. 1990. '"Extra ecclesiam nulla salus" revisited', in Ian Hamnett (ed.), *Religious Pluralism and Unbelief: Studies Critical and Comparative* (London and New York: Routledge), 130–47
—— 2007. 'Christian Orthodoxy and Religious Pluralism: A Response to Terence W. Tilley', *Modern Theology* 23/3 (July), 435–46
—— 2009. *Christianity and World Religions: Disputed Questions in the Theology of Religions* (Oxford: Blackwell)
Dalton, William Joseph. 1989. *Christ's Proclamation to the Spirits: A Study of 1 Peter 3:18–4:6*, 2nd rev. edn (Rome: Editrice Pontificio Istituto Biblico)
Daniélou, Jean. 1949. *The Salvation of the Nations*, tr. Angeline Bouchard (London: Sheed and Ward)
—— [1956] 1957. *Holy Pagans in the Old Testament*, tr. Felix Faber (London: Longmans, Green and Co.)
Davenport, Thomas H. [1980] 1991. *Virtuous Pagans: Unreligious People in America* (New York: Garland Publishing)
Davie, Grace. 1994. *Religion in Britain since 1945: Believing without Belonging* (Oxford and Cambridge, MA: Blackwell)
Dawkins, Richard. [1993] 2003. 'Viruses of the Mind', in Richard Dawkins, *A Devil's Chaplain: Selected Essays*, ed. Latha Menon (London: Weidenfeld & Nicolson), 128–45
—— 2006. *The God Delusion* (London: Bantam Press)
Day, Dorothy. [1945] 2005. 'Room for Christ', in Dorothy Day, *Selected Writings: By Little and By Little*, ed. Robert Elsberg (London: Darton, Longman and Todd), 94–7
—— [1946] 2005. 'The Mystery of the Poor', in Dorothy Day, *Selected Writings: By Little and By Little*, ed. Robert Elsberg (London: Darton, Longman and Todd), 329–30
—— [1949] 2005. 'Here and Now', in Dorothy Day, *Selected Writings: By Little and By Little*, ed. Robert Elsberg (London: Darton, Longman and Todd), 100–4
Dennett, Daniel C. 1991. *Consciousness Explained* (London: Allen Lane)
—— 2006. *Breaking the Spell: Religion as a Natural Phenomenon* (London: Viking)
Denzinger, Heinrich and Peter Hünermann (eds.). 1991. *Enchiridion symbolorum definitionum et declarationum de rebus fidei et morum*, 37th rev. edn (Freiburg im Breisgau: Herder)
Dinoia, J. A. 1983. 'Implicit Faith, General Revelation and the State of Non-Christians', *Thomist* 47/2 (April), 209–41
—— 1989. 'Karl Rahner', in David F. Ford (ed.), *The Modern Theologians*, Volume I (Oxford: Blackwell), 183–204
—— 1992. *The Diversity of Religions: A Christian Perspective* (Washington, DC: Catholic University of America Press)

Bibliography 195

Dostoevsky, Fyodor. [1872] 2000. *Demons*, tr. Richard Pevear and Larissa Volokhonsky (New York: Everyman)
—— [1868] 2001. *The Idiot*, tr. Richard Pevear and Larissa Volokhonsky (London: Granta)
—— [1880] 2004. *The Brothers Karamazov*, tr. Richard Pevear and Larissa Volokhonsky (London: Vintage)
Duffy, Eamon. 2005. *The Stripping of the Altars: Traditional Religion in England 1400–1580*, 2nd edn (London: Yale University Press)
Dupuis, Jacques. 1997. *Toward a Christian Theology of Religious Pluralism* (Maryknoll, NY: Orbis)
—— 2002. *Christianity and the Religions: From Confrontation to Dialogue*, tr. Phillip Berryman (Maryknoll, NY: Orbis)
Durkheim, Émile. [1912] 1976. *The Elementary Forms of the Religious Life*, tr. Joseph W. Swain (London: Routledge)
Dych, William V. 1992. *Karl Rahner* (London: Geoffrey Chapman)
Edgell, Penny, Joseph Gerteis and Douglas Hartmann. 2006. 'Atheists as "Other": Moral Boundaries and Cultural Membership in American Society', *American Sociological Review* 71/2 (April), 211–34
Edwards, Denis. 1986. *What Are They Saying About Salvation?* (Mahwah, NJ: Paulist Press)
Egan, Eileen. 1985. *Such a Vision of the Street: Mother Teresa – The Spirit and the Work* (London: Sidgwick and Jackson)
Eminyan, Maurice. 1960. *The Theology of Salvation* (Boston, MA: St Paul Editions)
Endean, Philip. 1998. 'Von Balthasar, Rahner, and the Commissar', *New Blackfriars*, 79/923 (April), 33–8
—— 2001. *Karl Rahner and Ignatian Spirituality* (Oxford: Oxford University Press)
Epstein, Mikhail. 1999. 'Post-Atheism: From Apophatic Theology to "Minimal Religion"', in Mikhail Epstein, Alexander Genis, and Slobodanka Vladiv-Glover, *Russian Postmodernism: New Perspectives on Post-Soviet Culture*, tr. Slobodanka Vladiv-Glover (Oxford and New York: Berghahn Books), 345–93
Escrivá, Josemariá. [1939] 1985. *The Way* (Dublin: Four Courts)
Fairhurst, Alan M. 1981. 'Death and Destiny', *Churchman* 98/4, 313–25
Farias, Miguel and Mansur Lalljee. 2008. 'Holistic Individualism in the Age of Aquarius: Measuring Individualism/Collectivism in New Age, Catholic, and Atheist/Agnostic Groups', *Journal for the Scientific Study of Religion* 47/2 (June), 277–89
Fiddes, Paul S. 1989. *Past Event and Present Salvation: The Christian Idea of Atonement* (London: Darton, Longman and Todd)
Finn, Richard. 2006. *Almsgiving in the Later Roman Empire: Christian Promotion and Practice (313–450)* (Oxford: Oxford University Press)

Flannery, Austin (ed.). 1975. *Vatican II: The Conciliar and Post Conciliar Documents* (Dublin: Pillar Books)
Flew, Antony. 1976. 'The Presumption of Atheism', in Antony Flew, *The Presumption of Atheism & Other Philosophical Essays on God, Freedom and Immortality* (London: Elek/Pemberton), 13–30
Flynn, Gabriel. 2004a. 'The Role of Unbelief in the Theology of Yves Congar', *New Blackfriars* 85/998 (July), 426–43
—— 2004b. *Yves Congar's Vision of the Church in a World of Unbelief* (London: Ashgate)
Fouilloux, Étienne. 1995. 'The Antepreparatory Phase: The Slow Emergence from Inertia (January, 1959–October, 1962)', tr. Matthew J. O'Connell, in Giuseppe Alberigo and Joseph A. Komonchak (eds.), *History of Vatican II, Volume I: Announcing and Preparing Vatican Council II* (Maryknoll, NY: Orbis Books), 55–166
Fowler, Jeaneane. 1999. *Humanism: Beliefs and Practices* (Brighton: Sussex Academic Press)
Frank, Joseph. 1995. *Dostoevsky: The Miraculous Years 1865–1871* (London: Robson Books)
Gallagher, Michael Paul. 1980. *Approaches to Unbelief: A comparative study of various developments in contemporary pastoral theology, including some accounts of the religious question in modern literature* (Queen's University, Belfast, unpublished doctoral thesis)
—— 1995. *What Are They Saying About Unbelief?* (Mahwah, NJ: Paulist Press)
Garaudy, Roger. 1967. *From Anathema to Dialogue: The Challenge of Marxist-Christian Cooperation*, tr. Luke O'Neill and Edward Quinn (London: Collins)
Garrigou-Lagrange, Reginald. [1914] 1939. *God: His Existence and His Nature*, Volume II (St Louis, MO: Herder)
Gerald of Wales. [c. 1213] 1877. *Vita S. Remigii, et Vita S. Hugonis*, ed. James F. Dimock (London: Longman)
Germanus of St Stanislaus. [1914] 2000. *The Life of St. Gemma Galgani*, tr. A. M. O'Sullivan (Rockford, IL: Tan Books)
Gill, Robin. 1992. *Moral Communities: The Prideaux Lectures for 1992* (Exeter: University of Exeter Press)
Gilson, Étienne. [1941] 2002. *God and Philosophy* (London and New Haven, CT: Yale University Press)
Godin, Henri and Yvan Daniel. [1943] 1949. 'France A Missionary Land?', ed. and tr. Maisie Ward, in Maisie Ward, *France Pagan?* (London: Sheed and Ward), 65–191
Gräb, Wilhelm. 2007. 'Säkularisierung – das Ende der Religion oder der Verfall der Kirchen?', in Christina von Braun, Wilhelm Gräb, and Johannes Zachhuber (eds.), *Säkularisierung: Bilanz und Perspektiven einer umstrittenen These* (Münster: Lit-Verlag), 75–95

Gray, John. [2002] 2003. *Straw Dogs: Thoughts on Humans and Other Animals* (London: Granta)
—— [2002] 2004. 'Sex, atheism and piano legs', in John Gray, *Heresies: Against Progress and Other Illusions* (London: Granta), 41–8
Gray, Sherman W. 1989. *The Least of My Brothers: Matthew 25:31–46: A History of Interpretation* (Atlanta, GA: Scholars Press)
Grillmeier, Aloys. 1967. 'Dogmatic Constitution on the Church: The People of God', in Herbert Vorgrimler (ed.), *Commentary on the Documents of Vatican II*, Volume I, tr. Kevin Smyth (London: Burns and Oates), 153–85
Gutiérrez, Gustavo. 1993. *Las Casas: In Search of the Poor of Jesus Christ*, tr. Robert R. Barr (Maryknoll, NY: Orbis Books)
Hagner, Daniel A. 1995. *Matthew 14–28* (Dallas, TX: Word)
Hanke, Lewis. 2002. *The Spanish Struggle for Justice in the Conquest of America* (Dallas, TX: Southern Methodist University Press)
Harrington, Daniel J. 1991. *The Gospel of Matthew* (Collegeville, MN: Liturgical Press)
Harris, Sam. [2004] 2006. *The End of Faith: Religion, Terror and the Future of Reason* (London: Simon & Schuster)
—— [2006] 2007. *Letter to a Christian Nation* (London: Bantam Press)
Hauerwas, Stanley. 2006. *Matthew* (London: SCM Press)
Hebblethwaite, Peter. 1967. *The Council Fathers and Atheism: The Interventions at the Fourth Session of Vatican Council II* (New York: Paulist Press)
—— 1975. *The Runaway Church* (London: Collins)
—— 1977. *The Christian–Marxist Dialogue: Beginnings, Present Status and Beyond* (London: Darton, Longman and Todd)
Heidegger, Martin. [1927] 2000. *Being and Time*, tr. John Macquarrie and Edward Robinson (Oxford: Blackwell)
Hill, Edmund. 1988. *Ministry and Authority in the Catholic Church* (London: Geoffrey Chapman)
Hill Fletcher, Jeannine. 2006. 'Responding to Religious Difference: Conciliar Perspectives', in Raymond F. Bulman and Frederick J. Parrella (eds.), *From Trent to Vatican II: Historical and Theological Investigation* (New York: Oxford University Press), 267–81
Hillman, Eugene. 1966. '"Anonymous Christianity" and the Missions', *Downside Review* 85/277 (October), 361–79
Hiorth, Finngeir. 2003. *Atheism in the World* (Oslo: Human-Etisk Forbund)
Holy See. 1909–. *Acta Apostolicae Sedis* (Rome: Typis Vaticanis)
—— [1865–1908] 1968–9. *Acta Sanctae Sedis* (New York: Johnson Reprint)
—— 1997. *Catechismus Catholicae Ecclesiae* (Vatican City: Libreria Editrice Vaticana)
Hünermann, Peter. 2006. 'The Final Weeks of the Council', tr. Matthew J. O'Connell, in Giuseppe Alberigo and Joseph A. Komonchak (eds.), *History of Vatican II*, Volume V: *The Council and the Transition. The*

Fourth Period and the End of the Council. September 1965–December 1965 (Maryknoll, NY: Orbis Books), 363–483

Hunt, Stephen J. 2002. *Religion in Western Society* (Basingstoke: Palgrave)

Hyman, Gavin. 2010. *A Short History of Atheism* (London: I. B. Tauris)

Iacopo Da Varazze. [c. 1260] 1998. *Legenda Aurea*, Volume II, ed. Giovanni Paolo Maggioni (Florence: Sismel)

International Theological Commission. 2007. *The Hope of Salvation for Infants who Die Without Being Baptised* (London: Catholic Truth Society)

Ivanov, Vyacheslav. 1959. *Freedom and the Tragic Life: A Study in Dostoevsky*, ed. S. Konovalov, tr. Norman Cameron (New York: Noonday Press)

Jackson, Julian. 1988. *The Popular Front in France: Defending Democracy 1934–1938* (Cambridge: Cambridge University Press)

Jeffner, Anders. 1988. 'Atheism and Agnosticism', in Stewart Sutherland, Leslie Houlden, Peter Clarke, and Friedhelm Hardy (eds.), *The World's Religions* (London: Routledge), 52–60

Jüngel, Eberhard. 1975. 'Extra Christum nulla salus – als Grundsatz natürlicher Theologie? Evangelische Erwägungen zur "Anonymität" des Christenmenschen', in Elmar Klinger (ed.), *Christentum innerhalb und außerhalb der Kirche* (Freiburg: Herder), 122–38

Justin Martyr. [c. 150] 1948. 'First Apology', in Thomas B. Falls (ed. and trans.), *Writings of Saint Justin Martyr* (Washington, DC: Catholic University of America Press), 33–111

Kahl, Joachim. 1971. *The Misery of Christianity: A Plea for Humanity without God*, tr. N. D. Smith (London: Pelican)

Kasper, Walter. [1982] 1984. *The God of Jesus Christ*, tr. Matthew J. O'Connell (London: SCM Press)

—— [1987] 1989. *Theology and Church*, tr. Margaret Kohl (London: SCM Press)

—— 2006. 'The Pastoral Constitution *Gaudium et Spes*', in James Hanvey (ed.), *Reasons for Living and Hoping:* Gaudium et Spes *40 Years On* (London: Heythrop Institute for Religion, Ethics & Public Life), 7–28

Keenan, James F. 2005. *The Works of Mercy: The Heart of Catholicism* (Lanham, MD: Sheed and Ward)

Kennedy, Philip. 1993. *Deus Humanissimus: The Knowability of God in the Theology of Edward Schillebeeckx* (Fribourg: Fribourg University Press)

—— 2006. *A Modern Introduction to Theology: New Questions for Old Beliefs* (London and New York: I. B. Tauris)

Kerr, Fergus. [1986] 1997. *Theology after Wittgenstein*, 2nd edn (London: SPCK)

—— 1997. *Immortal Longings: Versions of Transcending Humanity* (London: SPCK)

—— 2007. *Twentieth-Century Catholic Theologians* (Oxford: Blackwell)

Kilby, Karen. 2004. *Karl Rahner: Theology and Philosophy* (London: Routledge)
Knitter, Paul F. 1985. *No Other Name? A Critical Survey of Christian Attitudes Toward the World Religions* (London: SCM Press)
König, Franz. 1968. 'Das II. Vatikanische Konzil und das Sekretariat für Nightglaubenden', *Internationale Dialog Zeitschrift* 1/1, 79–88
—— 1986. *Where is the Church Heading?*, tr. Thomas Kala (Slough: St Paul Publications)
—— 2005. *Open to God, Open to the World*, ed. Christa Pongratz-Lippitt (London: Burns and Oates)
Kolodiejchuk, Brian (ed.). 2008. *Mother Teresa: Come Be My Light* (London: Rider)
Krieg, Robert A. 1997. *Romano Guardini: A Precursor of Vatican II* (Notre Dame, IN: University of Notre Dame Press)
Krier Mich, Marvin L. 1998. *Catholic Social Teaching and Movements* (Mystic, CT: Twenty-Third Publications)
Küng, Hans. [1962] 1963. *That the World May Believe: Letters to Young People*, tr. Cecily Hastings (London: Sheed and Ward)
—— 1967. *The Church*, tr. Ray and Rosaleen Ockenden (London: Burns and Oates)
—— [1974] 1978. *On Being a Christian*, tr. Edward Quinn (London: Fount)
—— 1991. *Theology for the Third Millennium: An Ecumenical View*, tr. Peter Heinegg (London: Collins)
Kurtz, Paul. 2007. '"Yes" to Naturalism, Secularism, and Humanism', *Free Inquiry* 27/3 (April/May), 4–7
Landucci, Pier Carlo. 1976. 'La salvezza degli atei secondo il Concilio Vaticano II', *Divinitas* 20/1 (February), 97–100
Las Casas, Bartolomé De. [1552] 1971. *History of the Indies*, ed. and tr. Andrée M. Collard (New York: Harper Torchbooks)
—— [c. 1550] 1974. *In Defense of the Indians*, ed. and tr. Stafford Poole (DeKalb, IL: Northern Illinois University Press)
—— [1542] 1992. *A Short Account of the Destruction of the Indies*, tr. Nigel Griffin (London: Penguin)
—— [1552] 1992. *The Only Way*, ed. Helen Rand Parish, tr. Francis Patrick Sullivan (Mahwah, NJ: Paulist Press)
Lash, Nicholas. [1992] 2002. *Believing Three Ways in One God: A Reading of the Apostles' Creed* (London: SCM Press)
—— 2007. 'Where does *The God Delusion* come from?', *New Blackfriars* 88/1017 (September), 507–21
Lee, Lois. 2011. 'From "neutrality" to dialogue: Constructing the religious other in British non-religious discourse', in Maren Behrensen, Lois Lee, and Ahmet Selim Tekelioglu (eds.), *Modernities Revisited: IWM Junior Visiting Fellows' Conferences*, Volume XXIX. Text published online at:

\<http://www.iwm.at/index.php?option = com_ content&task = view&id = 426&Itemid = 125>. Accessed on 14 February 2011.

Lepp, Ignace. [1961] 1963. *Atheism in Our Time*, tr. Bernard Murchland (New York: Macmillan)

Leprieur, François. 2001. 'Do the Baptised Have Rights? The French Worker-Priest Crisis, 1953-4', in John Orme Mills (ed.), *Justice, Peace, and Dominicans 1216-2001* (Dublin: Dominican Publications), 161-80

Levi, Primo. [1986] 1989. *The Drowned and the Saved*, tr. Raymond Rosenthal (London: Abacus)

Levitt, Mairi. 1996. *'Nice when they are young': Contemporary Christianity in Families and Schools* (Aldershot: Avebury)

Liddell, George Henry and Robert Scott. 1869. *A Greek-English Lexicon*, 6th rev. edn (Oxford: Clarendon Press)

Lindbeck, George A. 1984. *The Nature of Doctrine: Religion and Theology in a Postliberal Age* (Philadelphia, PA: Westminster)

Loew, Jacques. [1946] 1950. *Mission to the Poorest*, tr. Pamela Carswell (London: Sheed and Ward)

Lombardi, Riccardo. [1942] 1956. *The Salvation of the Unbeliever*, tr. Dorothy M. White (London: Burns and Oates)

Lubac, Henri De. [1953] 1956. *The Splendour of the Church*, tr. Michael Mason (London and New York: Sheed and Ward)

—— [1956] 1960. *The Discovery of God*, tr. Alexander Dru (London: Darton, Longman and Todd)

—— [1938] 1964. *Catholicism: A Study of Dogma in Relation to the Corporate Destiny of Mankind*, tr. Lancelot C. Sheppard (New York: Mentor-Omega Books)

—— [1967] 1969. *The Church: Paradox and Mystery*, tr. James R. Dunne (Shannon: Ecclesia Press)

—— [1944] 1995. *The Drama of Atheist Humanism*, tr. Edith M. Riley, Anne Englund Nash, and Mark Sebanc (San Francisco, CA: Ignatius Press)

Luther, Martin. [1522] 1961. 'Preface to the Epistles of St James and St Jude', tr. Bertram Lee Woolf, in John Dillenberger (ed.), *Martin Luther: Selections from His Writings* (Garden City, NY: Anchor), 35-7

Luz, Ulrich. [1989] 2005. *Matthew 21-28: A Commentary*, tr. James E. Crouch (Minneapolis, MN: Fortress Press)

Macintyre, Alasdair. [1958] 2004. *The Unconscious: A Conceptual Analysis*, 2nd rev. edn (Oxford and New York: Routledge)

Macneil, James L. 1997. *A Study of Gaudium et Spes 19-22: The Second Vatican Council Response to Contemporary Atheism* (Lewiston, NY: Edwin Mellen)

Magrath, Oswin. 1968. 'The Wider Ecumenism', *New Blackfriars* 49/580 (September), 624-8

Maritain, Jacques. 1949. 'On the Meaning of Contemporary Atheism', *Review of Politics* 2, 267–80
—— [1947] 1953. 'A New Approach to God', tr. anon., in Jacques Maritain, *The Range of Reason* (London: Geoffrey Bles), 86–102
—— [1953] 1955. *Approaches to God*, tr. Peter O'Reilly (London: Allen & Unwin)
Markham, Ian S. (ed.). 2000. *A World Religions Reader*, 2nd edn (Oxford: Blackwell)
Martin, Michael. 1990. *Atheism: A Philosophical Justification* (Philadelphia, PA: Temple University Press)
—— 2002. *Atheism, Morality and Meaning* (Amherst, NY: Prometheus Books)
—— 2007a. 'General introduction', in Michael Martin (ed.), *The Cambridge Companion to Atheism* (Cambridge: Cambridge University Press), 1–7
—— 2007b. 'Atheism and Religion', in Michael Martin (ed.), *The Cambridge Companion to Atheism* (Cambridge: Cambridge University Press), 217–32
Matteo, Anthony M. 1992. *Quest for the Absolute: The Philosophical Vision of Joseph Maréchal* (DeKalb, IL: Northern Illinois University Press)
Mawson, T. J. 2005. *Belief in God: An Introduction to the Philosophy of Religion* (Oxford: Clarendon Press)
McCabe, Herbert. 2005. *The Good Life: Ethics and the Pursuit of Happiness* (London: Continuum)
McCool, Gerald. 1994. *The Neo-Thomists* (Milwaukee, WI: Marquette University Press)
McGrath, Alister. 2004. *The Twilight of Atheism: The Rise and Fall of Disbelief in the Modern World* (London: Rider)
McNamara, Kevin. 1968. 'The People of God', in Kevin McNamara (ed.), *Vatican II: The Constitution on the Church: A Theological and Pastoral Commentary* (London: Geoffrey Chapman), 103–62
McNicholl, Ambrose. 1968. 'God, Man and World', in Denys Turner (ed.), *The Church in the World* (Dublin: Scepter Books), 9–24
Melloni, Alberto. 2000. 'The Beginning of the Second Period: The Great Debate on the Church', tr. Matthew J. O'Connell, in Giuseppe Alberigo and Joseph A. Komonchak (eds.), *History of Vatican II*, Volume III: *The Mature Council. Second Period and Intersession. September 1963–September 1964* (Maryknoll, NY: Orbis Books), 1–115
Metz, Johann Baptist. 1965. 'Unbelief as a Theological Problem', tr. Tarcisius Rattler, *Concilium* 6/1 (June), 32–42
Miano, Vincenzo. 1967. 'The Tasks Facing the Secretariat for Non-Believers', *Concilium* 3/3 (March), 62–5
Migne, Jacques Paul. 1844–64. *Patrologia Graeca*, 161 volumes (Paris: Migne)
—— 1857–66. *Patrologia Latina*, 221 volumes (Paris: Migne)

Moeller, Charles. 1966. 'Man, the Church and Society', in John H. Miller (ed.), *Vatican II: An Interfaith Appraisal* (London and Notre Dame, IN: University of Notre Dame Press), 413–21
—— 1969. 'Pastoral Constitution on the Church in the Modern World: History of the Constitution', in Herbert Vorgrimler (ed.), *Commentary on the Documents of Vatican II*, Volume V, tr. W. J. O'Hara (London: Burns and Oates), 1–76
Moltmann, Jürgen. [1973] 2001. *The Crucified God: The Cross of Christ as the Foundation and Criticism of Christian Theology*, tr. R. A. Wilson and John Bowden (London: SCM Press)
Morali, Ilaria. 2004. '*Fides* e *influxus gratiae* nell'uomo che ignora il vangelo. Lettura di LG 16, 20–22 nel quadro della Storia del Dogma', in Carmen Aparicio Valls, Carmelo Dotolo, and Gianluigi Pasquale (eds.), *Sapere teologico e unità della fede: Studi in onore del Prof. Jared Wicks* (Rome: Editrice Pontificia Università Gregoriana), 172–206
Moser, Mary Theresa. 1985. *The Evolution of the Option for the Poor in France 1880–1965* (Lanham, MD: University Press of America)
Mother Teresa. 1975. *A Gift for God*, ed. Malcolm Muggeridge (London: Fount)
—— 1980. *Mother Teresa: In My Own Words*, ed. José Luis González-Balado (London: Hodder & Stoughton)
—— 1991. *Loving Jesus*, ed. José Luis González-Balado, tr. Susana Labastida (London: Fount)
Muggeridge, Malcolm. 1971. *Something Beautiful for God: Mother Teresa of Calcutta* (London: Collins)
Nielsen, Kai. 1970. 'Humanism and Atheism', *Ateismo e Dialogo* 5/3 (October), 30–3
—— 2001. 'Atheism', in Lawrence C. Becker and Charlotte B. Becker (eds.), *Encyclopedia of Ethics*, Volume I, 2nd edn (New York and London: Routledge), 98–102
Norman, Richard. 2004. *On Humanism* (London and New York: Routledge)
Nys, Hendrik. [1966] 1968. *La salvezza senza Vangelo: Studio historico e critico del problema della <<salvezza degli infedeli>> nella recente letteratura teologico (1912–1964)*, tr. Vincenzo Calvo and Fabio Fabbri [from French] (Rome: Editrice A.V.E.)
O'Callaghan, Michael Finbar. 1986. *Jacques Maritain, Karl Rahner and the Implicit Knowledge of God: A Comparative Study* (University of Lancaster, unpublished doctoral thesis)
O'Collins, Gerald. 2007. *Jesus Our Redeemer: A Christian Approach to Salvation* (Oxford: Oxford University Press)
—— 2008. *Salvation for All: God's Other Peoples* (Oxford: Oxford University Press)

O'Dea, Thomas F. 1961. 'Catholic Sectarianism: A Sociological Analysis of the So-Called Boston Heresy Case', *Review of Religious Research* 3/2 (Autumn), 49–63

O'Sullivan, Noel. 2007. 'Henri de Lubac's *Surnaturel*: An Emerging Christology', *Irish Theological Quarterly* 72/1 (February), 3–31

Onfray, Michel. [2005] 2007. *Atheist Manifesto: The Case Against Christianity, Judaism, and Islam*, tr. Jeremy Leggatt (New York: Arcade Publishing)

Oppy, Graham. 2006. *Arguing about Gods* (Cambridge: Cambridge University Press)

Ott, Ludwig. [1957] 1963. *Fundamentals of Catholic Dogma*, 6th edn, ed. James Bastible, tr. Patrick Lynch (Cork: Mercier)

Pals, Daniel L. 2006. *Eight Theories of Religion*, 2nd edn (New York: Oxford University Press)

Pasquale, Frank L. 2007. 'Unbelief and Irreligion, Empirical Study and Neglect of', in Tom Flynn (ed.), *The New Encyclopedia of Unbelief* (Amherst, NY: Prometheus), 760–6

Pérez-Esclarín, Antonio. 1980. *Atheism and Liberation*, tr. John Drury (London: SCM Press)

Perrin, Henri. [1945] 1947. *Priest-Workman in Germany*, tr. Rosemary Sheed (London: Sheed and Ward)

―― [1958] 1965. *Priest and Worker: The Autobiography of Henri Perrin*, tr. Bernard Wall (London: Macmillan)

Pitstick, Alyssa Lyra. 2007. *Light in Darkness: Hans Urs von Balthasar and the Catholic Doctrine of Christ's Descent into Hell* (Grand Rapids, MI and Cambridge: Eerdmans)

Pius IX. [1854] 1864. 'Singulari Quadem', in Pius IX, *Pii IX Pontificis Maximi Acta: Pars Prima*, Volume I (Rome: Typographia Bonarum Artium), 620–31

―― [1863] 1867. 'Quanto Conficiamur Moerere', in Pius IX, *Pii IX Pontificis Maximi Acta: Pars Prima*, Volume III (Rome: Typographia Bonarum Artium), 609–21

―― [1864] 1867. 'Syllabus', in Pius IX, *Pii IX Pontificis Maximi Acta: Pars Prima*, Volume III (Rome: Typographia Bonarum Artium), 701–17

Poole, Stafford. 1992. '"Are They Not Men?"', in Charles H. Lippy, Robert Choquetter, and Stafford Poole, *Christianity Comes to the Americas 1492–1776* (New York: Giniger), 79–90

Preston, Geoffrey. 1966. 'The Church and the World', *Slant* 2/1 (February/March), 10–13

Rahner, Karl. 1957. 'Atheismus II. Philosophisch – III. Theologisch', in Michael Buchberger, Josef Höfer, and Karl Rahner (eds.), *Lexikon für Theologie und Kirche*, Volume I: *A – Baronius* (Freiburg: Verlag Herder), 983–9

―― [1950] 1961. 'Concerning the Relationship between Nature and Grace', in Karl Rahner, *Theological Investigations*, Volume I, tr. Cornelius Ernst (London: Darton, Longman and Todd), 297–317

Rahner, Karl. [1954] 1961. 'The Prospects for Dogmatic Theology', in Karl Rahner, *Theological Investigations*, Volume I, tr. Cornelius Ernst (London: Darton, Longman and Todd), 1–18

—— [1947] 1963. 'Membership of the Church according to the Teaching of Pius XII's Encyclical "Mystici Corporis Christi"', in Karl Rahner, *Theological Investigations*, Volume II, tr. Karl-H. Kruger (London: Darton, Longman and Todd), 1–88

—— [1956] 1964. 'The Logic of Concrete Individual Knowledge in Ignatius of Loyola', in Karl Rahner, *The Dynamic Element in the Church*, tr. W. J. O'Hara (London: Burns and Oates), 84–170

—— [1959] 1966. 'The Theology of the Symbol', in Karl Rahner, *Theological Investigations*, Volume IV, tr. Kevin Smyth (London: Darton, Longman and Todd), 221–52

—— [1960] 1966a. 'What is Heresy?', in Karl Rahner, *Theological Investigations*, Volume V, tr. Karl-H. Kruger (London: Darton, Longman and Todd), 468–512

—— [1960] 1966b. 'Nature and Grace', in Karl Rahner, *Theological Investigations*, Volume IV, tr. Kevin Smyth (London: Darton, Longman and Todd), 165–88

—— [1960] 1966c. 'Poetry and the Christian', in Karl Rahner, *Theological Investigations*, Volume IV, tr. Kevin Smyth (London: Darton, Longman and Todd), 357–67

—— [1961] 1966. 'Christianity and the Non-Christian Religions', in Karl Rahner, *Theological Investigations*, Volume V, tr. Karl-H. Kruger (London: Darton, Longman and Todd), 115–34

—— [1962] 1966a. 'Thoughts on the Possibility of Belief Today', in Karl Rahner, *Theological Investigations*, Volume V, tr. Karl-H. Kruger (London: Darton, Longman and Todd), 3–22

—— [1962] 1966b. 'Latin as a Church Language', in Karl Rahner, *Theological Investigations*, Volume V, tr. Karl-H. Kruger (London: Darton, Longman and Todd), 366–416

—— [1954] 1967a. 'The Christian among Unbelieving Relations', in Karl Rahner, *Theological Investigations*, Volume III, tr. Karl-H. and Boniface Kruger (London: Darton, Longman and Todd), 355–72

—— [1954] 1967b. 'Reflections on the Experience of Grace', in Karl Rahner, *Theological Investigations*, Volume III, tr. Karl-H. and Boniface Kruger (London: Darton, Longman and Todd), 86–91

—— 1968. 'Atheism', tr. W. J. O'Hara, in Karl Rahner, Adolf Darlap et al. (eds.), *Sacramentum Mundi: An Encyclopedia of Theology*, Volume I (London: Burns and Oates), 116–22

—— [1964] 1969. 'Anonymous Christians', in Karl Rahner, *Theological Investigations*, Volume VI, tr. Karl-H. and Boniface Kruger (London: Darton, Longman and Todd), 390–8

——— [1966] 1972a. 'The Historicity of Theology', in Karl Rahner, *Theological Investigations*, Volume IX, tr. Graham Harrison (London: Darton, Longman and Todd), 64–82

——— [1966] 1972b. 'Christian Humanism', in Karl Rahner, *Theological Investigations*, Volume IX, tr. Graham Harrison (London: Darton, Longman and Todd), 187–204

——— [1967] 1972. 'Atheism and Implicit Christianity', in Karl Rahner, *Theological Investigations*, Volume IX, tr. Graham Harrison (London: Darton, Longman and Todd), 145–64

——— [1964–5] 1973. *Belief Today*, tr. M. M. Heelan, Ray and Rosemary Ockenden, and William Whitman (London: Sheed and Ward)

——— [1968] 1974. 'Theological Considerations on Secularization and Atheism', in Karl Rahner, *Theological Investigations*, Volume XI, tr. David Bourke (London: Darton, Longman and Todd), 166–84

——— [1969] 1974. 'The Experience of God Today', in Karl Rahner, *Theological Investigations*, Volume XI, tr. David Bourke (London: Darton, Longman and Todd), 149–65

——— 1974. 'Christology in the Setting of Modern Man's Understanding of Himself and of his World, in Karl Rahner, *Theological Investigations*, Volume XI, tr. David Bourke (London: Darton, Longman and Todd), 215–29

——— 1975a. 'Atheism', in Karl Rahner (ed.), *Encyclopedia of Theology: A Concise Sacramentum Mundi*, tr. anon. (London: Burns and Oates), 47–54

——— 1975b. 'Grace. II. Theological', in Karl Rahner (ed.), *Encyclopedia of Theology: A Concise Sacramentum Mundi*, tr. anon. (London: Burns and Oates), 587–94

——— [1971] 1976. 'Observations on the Problem of the "Anonymous Christian"', in Karl Rahner, *Theological Investigations*, Volume XIV, tr. David Bourke (London: Darton, Longman and Todd), 280–94

——— [1976] 1977. *Meditations on Freedom & the Spirit*, tr. Rosaleen Ockenden, David Smith, and Cecily Bennett (London: Burns and Oates)

——— [1976] 1978. *Foundations of Christian Faith: An Introduction to the Idea of Christianity*, tr. William V. Dych (London: Darton, Longman and Todd)

——— [1978] 1979. 'Ignatius of Loyola Speaks to a Modern Jesuit', in Karl Rahner and Paul Imhof, *Ignatius of Loyola*, tr. Rosaleen Ockenden (London: Collins), 9–38

——— 1979. 'The One Christ and the Universality of Salvation', in Karl Rahner, *Theological Investigations*, Volume XVI, tr. David Morland (London: Darton, Longman and Todd), 199–224

——— [1977] 1983. 'Yesterday's History of Dogma and Tomorrow's Theology', in Karl Rahner, *Theological Investigations*, Volume XVII, tr. Margaret Kohl (London: Darton, Longman and Todd), 3–34

Rahner, Karl [1979] 1985. *I Remember: An Autobiographical Interview with Meinhold Krauss*, tr. Harvey D. Egan (London: SCM Press)

—— [1979] 1986. 'A Theologian's Lot', tr. Thomas F. O'Meara, in Karl Rahner, *Karl Rahner in Dialogue*, ed. Paul Imhof, Hubert Biallowons, and Harvey D. Egan (New York: Crossroad), 210–15

—— [1982] 1988. 'The Act of Faith and the Content of Faith', in Karl Rahner, *Theological Investigations*, Volume XXI, tr. Hugh M. Riley (London: Darton, Longman and Todd), 151–61

—— [1982] 1990. 'The Future of the World and of the Church', tr. Daniel Donovan, in Karl Rahner, *Faith in a Wintry Season*, ed. Paul Imhof, Hubert Biallowons, and Harvey D. Egan (New York: Crossroad)

—— [1983] 1990. 'In Dialogue with Atheists', tr. Robert J. Braunreuther, in Karl Rahner, *Faith in a Wintry Season*, ed. Paul Imhof, Hubert Biallowons, and Harvey D. Egan (New York: Crossroad), 125–7

—— [1984] 1990. 'Atheists and Believers', tr. Robert J. Braunreuther, in Karl Rahner, *Faith in a Wintry Season*, ed. Paul Imhof, Hubert Biallowons, and Harvey D. Egan (New York: Crossroad), 129–37

—— [1946] 1993. *On Prayer*, tr. anon. (Collegeville, MN: Liturgical Press)

—— and Herbert Vorgrimler. [1976] 1983. 'Opus Operatum', in Karl Rahner and Herbert Vorgrimler (eds.), *Concise Theological Dictionary*, 2nd English edn, ed. Cornelius Ernst, tr. Richard Strachan et al. (London: Burns and Oates), 350–1

Ratzinger, Joseph. 1958. 'Die Neuen Heiden und die Kirche', *Hochland* 5, 1–11

—— 1969. 'Pastoral Constitution on the Church in the Modern World: The Dignity of the Human Person', in Herbert Vorgrimler (ed.), *Commentary on the Documents of Vatican II*, Volume V, tr. W. J. O'Hara (London: Burns and Oates), 115–63

—— [1965] 1970. 'The Church's Mission in the World', in Mario Cuminetti and Fernando Vittorino Joannes (eds.), *Rethinking the Church*, tr. Edmund Burke (Dublin: Gill and Macmillan), 45–54

—— 1972. *Das neue Volk Gottes: Entwürfe zur Ekklesiologie* (Düsseldorf: Patmos-Verlag)

—— 1985. *The Ratzinger Report: An Exclusive Interview on the State of the Church*, ed. Vittorio Messori, tr. Salvator Attanasio and Graham Harrison (London: Fowler Wright Books)

—— [1977] 1988. *Eschatology: Death and Eternal Life*, ed. Aidan Nichols, tr. Michael Waldstein (Washington, DC: Catholic University of America Press)

—— 2000. 'L'ecclesiologia della costituzione <<Lumen Gentium>>', in Rino Fisichella (ed.), *Il Concilio Vaticano II: Recezione e attualità alla luce del Giubileo* (Milan: Edizioni San Paolo), 66–81

Rees, B. R. 1988. *Pelagius: A Reluctant Heretic* (Woodbridge: Boydell Press)

Bibliography

Robertson, Roland. 1970. *The Sociological Interpretation of Religion* (Oxford: Blackwell)

Röper, Anita. [1963] 1966. *The Anonymous Christian*, tr. Joseph Donceel (New York: Sheed and Ward)

Röper, Friedrich and Harald Röper. 2009. 'The Woman of the Anonymous Christian', in Andreas R. Batlogg, Melvin E. Michalski, and Barbara G. Turner (eds. & trs.), *Encounters with Karl Rahner: Remembrances of Rahner by those who knew him* (Marquette, WI: Marquette University Press), 273–80

Routhier, Gilles. 2006. 'Finishing the Work Begun: The Trying Experience of the Fourth Period', tr. Matthew J. O'Connell, in Giuseppe Alberigo and Joseph A. Komonchak (eds.), *History of Vatican II, Volume V: The Council and the Transition. The Fourth Period and the End of the Council. September 1965–December 1965* (Maryknoll, NY: Orbis Books), 49–184

Ruane, Janet M. 2005. *Essentials of Research Methods: A Guide to Social Science Research* (Malden, MA: Blackwell)

Ruse, Michael. 2005. *The Evolution–Creation Struggle* (London and Cambridge, MA: Harvard University Press)

Saint-Arnaud, Jean-Guy. 2010. '"I'm an Atheist, Thank God!" On the Spiritual Life of Atheists', *Way* 49/2 (April), 97–109

Salkeld, Brett. 2011. *Can Catholics and Evangelicals Agree about Purgatory and the Last Judgement?* (Mahwah, NJ: Paulist Press)

Sanders, John. 1994. *No Other Name: Can Only Christians Be Saved?* (London: SPCK)

Saward, John. 2005. *Sweet and Blessed Country: The Christian Hope for Heaven* (Oxford: Oxford University Press)

Schillebeeckx, Edward. [1960] 1963. *Christ the Sacrament of Encounter with God*, rev. edn, tr. various (London: Sheed and Ward)

—— 1965. 'The Church and Mankind', tr. James Byrne and Theodore Westow, *Concilium* 1/1 (January), 34–50

—— [1957] 1966. *Christus sacrament van de Godsontmoeting* (Bilthoven: Nelisson)

—— [1953] 1971. 'Priest and Layman in a Secular World', in Edward Schillebeeckx, *World and Church*, tr. N. D. Smith (London and Sydney: Sheed and Ward), 32–76

—— [1961] 1979. 'Non-Religious Humanism and Belief in God', in Edward Schillebeeckx, *God and Man*, tr. Edward Fitzgerald and Peter Tomlinson (London: Sheed and Ward), 41–84

—— [1971] 1981. *The Understanding of Faith: Interpretation and Criticism*, tr. anon. (London: Sheed and Ward)

—— 1983. *God is New Each Moment*, tr. David Smith (Edinburgh: T. & T. Clark)

Schweizer, Eduard. 1976. *The Good News According to Matthew*, tr. David E. Green (London: SPCK)
Schwerdtfeger, Nikolaus. 1994. 'Der "anonyme Christ" in der Theologie Karl Rahners', in Mariano Delgado and Matthias Lutz-Bachmann (eds.), *Theologie aus Erfahrung der Gnade: Annäherungen an Karl Rahner* (Berlin: Morus), 72–94
Scola, Angelo and Paolo Flores D'Arcais. 2008. *Dio? Ateismo della ragione e ragioni della fede* (Venice: Marsilio)
Searle, John R. 1992. *The Rediscovery of the Mind* (London and Cambridge, MA: MIT Press)
—— 1994. *Mind: A Brief Introduction* (New York: Oxford University Press)
—— 1997. *The Mystery of Consciousness* (London: Granta)
Secretariat For Non-Believers. 1966. 'Elenco degli Ecc. Vescovi Membri e dei Signori Consultori', *Bollettino di Informazione [del Segretariato per i Non Credenti]* 1/3 (September), 68–73
—— 1968. *Dialogue with Non-Believers* (Rome: Typis Polyglottis Vaticanis)
Segundo, Juan Luis. [1968] 1980. *Grace and the Human Condition*, tr. John Drury (Dublin: Gill and Macmillan)
Sheehan, Thomas. 2005. 'Rahner's transcendental project', in Declan Marmion and Mary E. Hines (eds.), *The Cambridge Companion to Karl Rahner* (Cambridge: Cambridge University Press), 29–42
Smart, Ninian. 1996. *The Religious Experience*, 5th edn (London: Prentice-Hall)
Smith, George H. [1979] 1989. *Atheism: The Case Against God* (Buffalo, NY: Prometheus Books)
Sobrino, Jon. 2008. '*Extra Pauperes Nulla Salus*: A Short Utopian-Prophetic Essay', in Jon Sobrino, *No Salvation Outside the Poor: Prophetic-Utopian Essays*, tr. Joseph Owens (Maryknoll, NY: Orbis), 35–76
Strange, Daniel. 2002. *The Possibility of Salvation Among the Unevangelised: An Analysis of Inclusivism in Recent Evangelical Theology* (Carlisle: Paternoster Press)
Strohm, Paul. 2000. *Theory and the Premodern Text* (Minneapolis, MN: University of Minnesota Press)
Sullivan, Francis A. 1983. *Magisterium: Teaching Authority in the Catholic Church* (Dublin: Gill and Macmillan)
—— 1992. *Salvation Outside the Church?: Tracing the History of the Catholic Response* (London: Geoffrey Chapman)
—— 1996. *Creative Fidelity: Weighing and Interpreting Documents of the Magisterium* (Mahwah, NJ: Paulist Press)
Swinburne, Richard. 1993. *The Coherence of Theism*, rev. edn (Oxford: Oxford University Press)
Tanner, Norman P. (ed.). 1990a. *Decrees of the Ecumenical Councils*, Volume I: *Nicaea I to Lateran IV* (London: Sheed and Ward)

—— 1990b. *Decrees of the Ecumenical Councils*, Volume II: *Trent to Vatican II* (London: Sheed and Ward)
Taylor, Charles. 1998. 'Modes of Secularism', in Rajeev Bhargava (ed.), *Secularism and Its Critics* (New Delhi: Oxford University Press), 31–53
—— 2007. *A Secular Age* (London and Cambridge, MA: Harvard University Press)
Thomas Aquinas. [c. 1259] 1925. *S. Thomae Aquinatis: Quaestiones Disputatae. Tomus Primus: De Veritate*, ed. Pierre Mandonnet (Paris: Lethielleux)
—— [c. 1262–7] 1953. *S. Thomae Aquinatis Doctoris Angelici: Catena Aurea in Quatuor Evangelia, I: Expositio in Matthaeum et Marcum*, ed. Angelico Guarienti (Turin: Marietti)
—— [1265–74] 1965. *St Thomas Aquinas: Summa Theologiae*, Volume LVIII: *The Eucharistic Presence (3a. 73–8)*, ed. William Barden (London: Blackfriars)
—— [1265–74] 1969. *St Thomas Aquinas: Summa Theologiae*, Volume XXV: *Sin (1a2ae. 71–80)*, ed. John Fearon (London: Blackfriars)
—— [1265–74] 1974. *St Thomas Aquinas: Summa Theologiae*, Volume XXXI: *Faith (2a2ae. 1–7)*, ed. John O'Brien (London: Blackfriars)
—— [1265–74] 1975. *St Thomas Aquinas: Summa Theologiae*, Volume LVI: *The Sacraments (3a. 60–5)*, ed. David Bourke (London: Blackfriars)
Thomas of Celano. [1229] 1926. *Vita Prima S. Francisci Assisiensis et eiusdem Legenda ad Usum Chori*, ed. Fathers of the College of St Bonaventure (Florence: Quaracchi)
—— [1247] 1927. *Vita Secunda S. Francisci Assisiensis*, ed. Fathers of the College of St Bonaventure (Florence: Quaracchi)
Thrower, James. 1971. *A Short History of Western Atheism* (London: Pemberton Books)
—— 1992. *Marxism-Leninism as the Civil Religion of Soviet Society* (Lampeter: Edwin Mellen)
Tiessen, Terrance L. 2004. *Who Can Be Saved? Reassessing Salvation in Christ and World Religions* (Leicester and Downers Grove, IL: InterVarsity Press)
Torres, Camilo. [1964] 1973. 'Revolution: Christian Imperative', in Camilo Torres, *Revolutionary Priest: His Complete Writings and Messages*, ed. John Gerassi, tr. various (Harmondsworth: Pelican), 270–301
Trumbower, Jeffrey A. 2001. *Rescue for the Dead: The Posthumous Salvation of Non-Christians in Early Christianity* (Oxford: Oxford University Press)
Turner, Denys. 2002a. 'How to be an Atheist', in Denys Turner, *Faith Seeking* (London: SCM Press), 3–22
—— 2002b. 'Apophaticism, idolatry and the claims of reason', in Oliver Davies and Denys Turner (eds.), *Silence and the Word: Negative Theology and Incarnation* (Cambridge: Cambridge University Press), 11–34
Tylor, E. B. [1871] 1903. *Primitive Culture*, 4th edn (London: Murray)

Uleman, James S. 2005. 'Introduction: Becoming Aware of the New Unconscious', in Ran R. Hassin, James S. Uleman, and John A. Bargh (eds.), *The New Unconscious* (New York: Oxford University Press), 3–15

Vass, George. 1985. *A Theologian in Search of a Philosophy. Understanding Karl Rahner*, Volume I (London: Sheed and Ward)

―― 1998. *A Pattern of Doctrines 2: The Atonement and Mankind's Salvation. Understanding Karl Rahner*, Volume IV (London: Sheed and Ward)

Vatican II. [1962–5] 1970–80. *Acta Synodalia Sacrosancti Concilii Oecumenici Vaticani II*, multiple volumes/parts (Rome: Typis Polyglottis Vaticanis)

Vitoria, Francisco de. [1539] 1952. *De Indis recenter inventis, et De jure belli Hispanorum in barbaros*, ed. Walter Schötzel (Tübingen: Verlag Mohr)

Voas, David and Alasdair Crockett. 2005. 'Religion in Britain: Neither Believing nor Belonging', *Sociology* 39/1 (February), 11–28

Wachtel, Nathan. 1984. 'The Indian and the Spanish Conquest', tr. Julian Jackson, in Leslie Bethell (ed.), *The Cambridge History of Latin America*, Volume I: *Colonial Latin America* (Cambridge: Cambridge University Press), 207–48

Weger, Karl-Heinz. 1980. *Karl Rahner: An Introduction to His Theology*, tr. David Smith (London: Burns and Oates)

Wernick, Andrew. 2001. *Auguste Comte and the Religion of Humanity: The Post-Theistic Program of French Social Theory* (Cambridge: Cambridge University Press)

Wielenberg, Erik J. 2005. *Value and Virtue in a Godless World* (Cambridge: Cambridge University Press)

Williams, Rowan. 2008. 'Secularism, Faith and Freedom', in Graham Ward and Michael Hoelzl (eds.), *The New Visibility of Religion: Studies in Religion and Cultural Hermeneutics* (London: Continuum), 45–56

Wilson, Wynne. 1995. *New Arrivals: A Practical Guide to Non-religious Naming Ceremonies*, 4th rev. edn (London: British Humanist Association)

Wolf, Kenneth Baxter. 2003. *The Poverty of Riches: St. Francis of Assisi Reconsidered* (Oxford: Oxford University Press)

Wolf-Meyer, Matthew. 2005. 'The Feeling of Atheism, Contempt, and the Constitution of American Moral Citizenship', Working Paper, American Mosaic Project, Department of Sociology, University of Minnesota, Minneapolis, MN

Zuckerman, Phil. 2007. 'Atheism: Contemporary Numbers and Patterns', in Michael Martin (ed.), *The Cambridge Companion to Atheism* (New York: Cambridge University Press), 47–65

―― 2010. 'Introduction: The Social Scientific Study of Atheism and Secularity', in Phil Zuckerman (ed.), *Atheism and Secularity*, Volume I: *Issues, Concepts, Definitions* (Santa Barbara, CA: Praeger), vi–xii

Index

absolute atheism 63–4
Adam, Karl 46, 80
Ad Gentes 73–4, 128, 139, 188
agnosticism 16, 139 n. 16
Alexander VI, Pope 47, 135
anonymous Christs 172
anonymous Christianity
  explication of 78–80, 85–96
  critique of 82–3, 96–112
  and implicit faith 85–96, 101–12
  development of theory 85–7
  and epistemology 93–4, 96
  and psychology 95–6, 111
  precursors 58, 65
  reception of 80–3
  and theology of grace 87–92
  terminology 81–3, 85–6, 91
  and Vatican II 97–9
  see also Rahner, Karl
anthropology, Christian 9–10, 64, 75
Apostolicam Actuositatem 152, 158
Ardigo, Roberto 38–9
atheism *passim*
  causes of 53–5, 64, 68, 71, 139–40, 142, 145; *see also* Christian misconduct
  impossibility of 60, 64–6
  possibility of 36–41
  see also absolute atheism; agnosticism; New Atheism; practical atheism; pseudo-atheism
atheist, definition of 14–18
atheists, numbers of 13–14
Augustine, St 19, 85, 94–5, 164–5
  and baptism 125 n. 8
  and Christ's descent 119–22
  on post-mortem conversion 120–2, 127, 129, 171
Ayer, A. J. 16

Bailey, Edward 29
Bainvel, Jean 45, 80
Balthasar, Hans Urs von 81–3, 110
baptism
  of blood (*sanguinis*)125
  of desire (*flaminis/in voto*) 46–7, 73, 125, 184
  necessity of 124–5
  sacramental (*in re*) 125
  see also salvation, criteria for; Christopher, St; sacramental theology
Barth, Karl 19–20, 34
beatific vision 11, 174
Bede, St 151
belief
  propositional 18–20
  unconscious 92–6, 99–101, 106–12;
  see also implicit faith
  see also faith
Bellarmine, St Robert 121, 171
Benedict, St 155
Benedict XII, Pope 11
Benedict XVI, Pope 8 n. 6, 25, 144, 152–3, 158; *see also* Ratzinger, Joseph
Berger, Peter 143–5
Blondel, Maurice 20, 60–4, 80, 100
Bonaventure, St 157–8
'Boston Heresy Case', *see* Feeney, Leonard
Brechter, Suso 74
Brierley, Peter 40 n. 8
Buckley, Michael 142
Buddhism 27–9, 31, 116, 130–1
Byrne, Peter 29–31, 35

Câmara, Hélder 68 n. 13
Camus, Albert 23, 109, 167; *see also* Rieux, Dr
Chenu, Marie-Dominique 37, 53, 59, 70
Christian misconduct 64, 68, 71, 139
Christopher, St 156–8, 162
Chrysostom, St John 154–5, 158, 162, 164
Church, necessity of 45–50, 66–7, 72–6, 78, 175–6
Churchland, Paul 99–101, 111
Clarke, Peter 29–31, 35
Clement of Alexandria, St 119–22, 125

Clement XI, Pope 47, 165
Colombini, St John 155
Columbus, Christopher 135
communism 64–5, 68, 71, 142
Comte, Auguste 31, 36, 53 n. 4
Congar, Yves 46, 48, 59
  anonymous Christianity 80–1
  implicit faith 80
  salvation of non-Christians 50–1, 66–7, 78 n. 2, 113
  reasons for unbelief 54–5, 70–1
  and Vatican II 70–1, 73–4
conscience 47, 62, 73, 93–5, 131, 164
conversion 120–2, 127, 129, 153, 174, 185
Copleston, Frederick 39, 53
creative fidelity 8, 79, 187
Crockett, Alasdair 30
Cross 171, 176; *see also* paschal mystery
Cyprian, St 47, 151

D'Costa, Gavin 115–31, 153, 172
  baptism 124–5
  critique 126–31
  and Dismas 124
  and 'Jane' 116–31
  limbo of the Fathers/just 117–25, 168
  post-mortem 'maturation' 124, 127, 129–30, 171–4, 177–8
  and the 'unevangelized' 128–9
Daniel, Yvan 55
Daniélou, Jean 53, 59, 80
  salvation of non-Christians 49, 65–6
  at Vatican II 70–1
Davie, Grace 30
Dawkins, Richard 38–9, 145 n. 21
Day, Dorothy 154, 158–9
Dei Verbum 6
Dennett, Daniel 12
'Denzinger-theology' 7–8
descent into hell, *see* hell, Christ's descent into
dialogue 51–4, 68–70, 72, 77, 140
DiNoia, Joseph 101–6, 111, 115
Dismas 124–5
Dives and Lazarus, parable of (Lk 16.19–31) 169
Dominus Iesus 75–6, 130, 188
Donum Veritatis 4, 188
Dostoevsky, Fyodor 36–7, 64–5, 109–12, 142, 169 n. 7
Dupuis, Jacques 128
Durkheim, Émile 30

Elizabeth of Hungary, St 157
Emmaus road (Lk 24.13–32) 172
Epstein, Mikhail 142
Escrivá, St Josemaría 4–5
Eucharist 154, 158, 165–8, 174, 176 n. 11
evangelization 55–9, 69, 72, 136–8
existentialism 71
Extra Ecclesiam nulla salus 45–50, 66–7, 72–6; *see also* Church, necessity of
extrinsicism, *see* grace, theology of

faith
  nature of 18–21, 94–5
  necessity of 79, 133; *see also* salvation, criteria for
  see also implicit faith
Feeney, Leonard 47–8
Fernández de Oviedo, Gonzalo 136
Fessard, Gaston 52–3
Florence, Council of 152
Flynn, Gabriel 55
Fowler, Jeaneane 33–4
Francis, St 157
Freud, Sigmund 95

Galgani, St Gemma 187
Garaudy, Roger 51
Garrone, Gabriel-Marie 69
Gaudium et Spes 67–72
  definition of atheism 17–18
  inculpable ignorance 139–42, 145–6
  salvation 75–6
Gilson, Étienne 60 n. 9, 96
Girardi, Giulio 69, 70
Godin, Henri 55
Gómez, José 25 n. 3
grace 50, 73–6
  experience of 91–2
  opportunities for receiving 130–1, 153, 166–7, 171–4, 185
  theology of 87–92
  and works 73–6, 164–5
Gray, John 27–9, 34, 36
Gray, Sherman 151, 154
Gregory the Great, Pope St 155, 158, 166 n. 6
Gregory of Nyssa, St 9–10
Guardini, Romano 53

hagiography 154–8
Harrington, Daniel 151
Harris, Sam 12, 29

heaven 10–11
hell
  Christ's descent into 117
  Gehenna/Sheol 117
  and scripture 118
  see also limbo of the Fathers/just
Heidegger, Martin 89
Hick, John 128
Hiorth, Finngeir 41
Hilary of Poitiers, St 151
holy dead, see limbo of the Fathers/just
Holy Innocents 170
Hugh of Lincoln, St 156, 158, 162
humanism 27–36, 68

implicit faith
  critique of concept 101–9
  and morality 22, 58, 106–9, 172–3
  plausible model 109–112
  and Rahner 80–1, 83, 85–96
  and salvation of atheists 60, 63–7, 76
  traditional understanding 101–3
  and philosophy of mind 99–101
inculpable ignorance 24, 44–6, 131–46
  D'Costa 128–9
  and invincible ignorance 132–9
  New World 135–9
  Pius IX 44–5, 73–4, 85, 132, 135, 141
  scriptural roots 133
  Thomas Aquinas 134–5, 141
  Vatican II 131–2, 139–42
  see also Las Casas, Bartolomé de;
    Vitoria, Francisco de
Innocent X, Pope 47
International Theological
  Commission 125
intrinsicism, see grace, theology of
invincible ignorance, see inculpable
  ignorance

James, Letter of 20–1, 24
Jerome, St 151
John XXIII, Pope 67
John Paul II, Pope 24–5, 153, 160, 166
Jordan of Saxony, Bl. 155
Justin Martyr, St 37

Kahl, Joachim 39
Kasper, Walter 81
Kenny, Anthony 38–9
Kerr, Fergus 54, 89, 100–1
Khrushchev, Nikita 32

Kilby, Karen 92
Kirillov (Demons) 64, 109–12
König, Franz 69, 97, 140
Küng, Hans 53, 74, 80–1
Kurtz, Paul 27

Las Casas, Bartolomé de 132, 135–9, 141
Lash, Nicholas 19
last judgement see Matthew 25
Lee, Lois 15
Lenin, Vladimir 32
Leo the Great, Pope St 155
Leo IX, Pope St 155, 158
Leo XIII, Pope 43, 152–3
Lepp, Ignace 111
Levi, Primo 169 n. 7
limbo of the just/Fathers (limbus patrum)
  117–25, 168, 171–4, 177–8
  Patristic tradition 118–22
Lindbeck, George 115, 187
Loew, Jacques 58, 70
Lubac, Henri de 37
  anonymous Christianity 80–2
  causes of atheism 54, 64
  French unbelief 53–4, 59
  implicit faith 96, 100–1
  salvation of non-Christians 49–50,
    74, 78 n. 2
  theology of grace 87–9
  at Vatican II 70–1
Luckmann, Thomas 143–5
Lumen Gentium
  and ecclesiology 1 n. 1, 176
  and D'Costa 117, 126–31
  inculpable ignorance 131–3, 145–6
  postmortem 'solution' 126–7
  salvation of atheists 72–6, 172–3,
    passim
Luther, Martin 21
Luz, Ulrich 151

McCool, Gerald 60
McGrath, Alister 14
Macintyre, Alasdair 106
magisterium 5–6, 73
Maréchal, Joseph 60 n. 8, 63, 96
Maritain, Jacques 20–4, 53, 62–4, 65,
  71, 96–7
Mariology 170–1, 176
Markham, Ian 34
Martin, Michael 16–17
Martin of Tours, St 156–7

214 Index

Martyrius, St 155–6
Marxism-Leninism 28–36, 72; see also communism
Marxist-Christian engagement 51–9, 77, 108
Matthew 25 113, 149–79
  and dogmatic tradition 150–3
  and the Eucharist 154–5, 158, 162–3
  exegesis 150–1, 153, 169–70
  and hagiography 154–8
  minimi/ae ('least ones') 150, 169–70
  non-parabolic nature 149
  (quasi-) sacramental interpretation 158, 162, 165–8, 174
  reception history 151–9
  see also Teresa of Calcutta, Bl.
meta-ethics 22–4, 106–9, 164–5, 172–3, 177–8, 184
methodology 4–9, 145, 153, 157–8, 163
Metz, Johann Baptist 67, 70
Miano, Vincenzo 70
minimi/ae ('least ones'), see Matthew 25
Missionaries of Charity 159, 162–3
Moltmann, Jürgen 37
morality 22–4, 58, 62–6, 172
  and implicit faith 93–5, 106–9
  see also meta-ethics
Mother Teresa, see Teresa of Calcutta, Bl.
Myshkin, Prince (*The Idiot*) 36–7, 142

nature, see grace
negative theology 36, 142
New Atheism 11–12, 40
Nielsen, Kai 23, 109
nihilism 64, 142
non-Christian saints 49, 124
non-theistic religions 27–36
  and salvation 27–8, 35, 116, 130–1

O'Collins, Gerald 115, 128
Onfray, Michel 40–1
Origen 118–19, 151

paschal mystery 9–10, 75–6
Paul VI, Pope 68–70
Pelagius, see Pelagianism
Pelagianism 21, 75–6, 164–5, 175
Pérez-Esclarín, Antonio 37
Perrin, Henri 57–8
Pitstick, Alyssa 118
Pius IX, Pope 44, 73–4, 85, 132, 135, 186
Pius XI, Pope 43

Pius XII, Pope 43–4, 47, 67, 88
plausibility structures, see sociology of knowledge
practical atheism 20–6, 61, 94–5
preparatio evangelica 130
presumption of innocence, see inculpable ignorance
priest-workers 56–9
pseudo-atheism 63–5
purgatory 10, 124

Rahner, Karl 37, 77–114, 169 n. 8, 174
  inculpable ignorance 128, 145
  pastoral emphasis 59, 83–5
  practical atheism 19
  as representative 80–3
  'supernatural existential' 87–91
  theological method 7–8, 88–9
  theology of grace 87–92
  transcendental experience 92
  and Vatican II 70, 97–9
  see also anonymous Christianity
Ratzinger, Joseph 51, 67, 74, 78 n. 2, 80–1; see also Benedict XVI, Pope
religion, definition of 29–36
'Religion of Humanity', see Comte, Auguste
religious pluralism 144–5
Requerimiento 137–8
Rieux, Dr (*The Plague*) 23, 109, 164–5, 167–8, 172
Röper, Anita 86

sacramental theology 165–8, 176, 177 n. 11; see also baptism; Eucharist
Sacrosanctum Concilium 167, 176
Saigh, Maximos IV 140
saints, as source for theology 153–4, 157–8
salvation
  criteria for 1, 9–10, 79, 104, 116–18, 152
  hope for 85, 147, 186
  nature of 9–11, 75–6, 116–17, 127
  of Christians 187
  of non-Christians 44–51, 72–6, 115–16, *passim*
  optimism 73–4, 139
  post-mortem solutions 118–22, 126–7, 173
  see also baptism; Church, necessity of; Matthew 25; universal salvation

Sanders, John 118
Sartre, Jean-Paul 57
Schillebeeckx, Edward 65, 81–3, 86, 113, 173
Schwerdtfeger, Nikolaus 85–6
Scola, Angelo 36
Searle, John 99–100, 106, 111
Secretariat for Non-Believers 69–71, 77
secular humanism, *see* humanism
secularism 25
sensus fidelium 157–8
Šeper, Franjo 140
Severus, Sulpicius 156
Shepherd of Hermas 119
Silva Henríquez, Raúl 68
sin 9–10, 187
Smart, Ninian 32
Smith, George H. 21–2, 24
Society of Jesus 69–70, 77 n. 1
sociology of atheism
  numbers 13–14
  French working classes 54–6
  morality 22
sociology of knowledge 139, 143–5
Stephen I, Pope 47
Suenens, Leo 140
Sullivan, Francis 8, 74, 187
Swinburne, Richard 23

Taylor, Charles 26, 39
Teresa of Calcutta, Bl. 154, 158–79
  and Eucharist 162–3, 165–7
  life 159–60
  and Matthew 25: 161–3, 169
  and salvation of non-Christians 161
  spiritual crisis 160
  see also Missionaries of Charity

theology of religions 115–16
Thomas Aquinas, St 64, 168
  and Eucharist 166, 177 n. 11
  implicit faith 102
  invincible ignorance 134–5, 141
  Matthew 25 151
Thomas of Celano 157
Thrower, James 34
Tikhon, Bishop (*Demons*) 37
Trent, Council of 9, 164–5
Turner, Denys 36
Tylor, E. B. 30

unconscious 63–6
  mental states 92–6, 99–101, 106–12
  blindsight 106
  and psychology 95–6
  see also implicit faith
universal salvation 186

Varazze, Bl. Iacopo da 156
Vatican II 67–76, 97–9, *passim*;
  see also Ad Gentes; *Apostolicam Actuositatem*; *Gaudium et Spes*; *Lumen Gentium*; *Sacrosanctum Concilium*
Vitoria, Francisco de 132, 136–9, 141
Voas, David 30
Vorgrimler, Herbert 77

worker-priests, *see* priest-workers
works 20–1, 75, 164, 179; *see also* works of mercy
works of mercy 168–70, 174, 179;
  see also Matthew 25

Zuckerman, Phil 13–14

Lightning Source UK Ltd.
Milton Keynes UK
UKHW011120280719
346893UK00001B/4/P